The Chef's Companion

THE
Chef's
COMPANION

A Concise Dictionary of Culinary Terms

Elizabeth Riely

ILLUSTRATIONS BY
DAVID MILLER

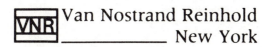
Van Nostrand Reinhold
New York

For my Mother and Father

Printed in the United States of America
Designed by Beth Tondreau

Van Nostrand Reinhold
115 Fifth Avenue
New York, New York 10003

Chapman & Hall
2-6 Boundary Row
London SE1 8HN, England

Thomas Nelson Australia
102 Dodds Street
South Melbourne, Victoria 3205, Australia

Nelson Canada
1120 Birchmount Road
Scarborough, Ontario M1K 5G4, Canada

16 15 14 13 12 11 10 9 8

LIBRARY OF CONGRESS CATALOGING-IN-PUBLICATION DATA
Riely, Elizabeth Gawthrop
  The chef's companion.

  "A CBI book."
  1. Food—Dictionaries.   2. Cookery—Dictionaries.
3. Wine and wine making—Dictionaries. I. Title.
TX349.R48 1986   641'.03'21   85-27142
ISBN 0-442-27846-2

Preface

The culinary boom of the last fifteen years in this country has brought great changes in the way we think about food. Many foreign cuisines and ethnic styles of cooking, once known to few, have gained considerable popularity. More and more people have become involved in food preparation either as a profession or as a pastime. This increased interest in food has led, in turn, to a greater appreciation of our own regional American cooking.

The Chef's Companion reflects these developments in the culinary world by bringing together information from a wide range of sources. The scope of the book is broad, and I have had in mind the needs of home cooks as well as professional chefs, culinary students, restaurateurs, and foodservice managers. The definitions are brief, to the point, and intended for quick reference in the kitchen.

The book includes many entries not only for classic French and other European cuisines, but also for Chinese, Japanese, Indian, Middle Eastern, and Latin American foods. In addition, it contains entries for dishes and styles of preparation; cooking techniques and equipment; pastries and cheeses; foreign-language words for common foodstuffs (translated into English); and edible plants, animals, and fish not widely known. Notable figures in the history of food and gastronomy are briefly identified. Since wine is an integral part of gastronomy, many names and terms—major wine regions and vineyards, grape varieties, and wine-making techniques— will be found here. There are also numerous entries for beers and liqueurs.

Entries for sauces, styles, and garnishes are listed by the particular name of each. For example, the entry for *sauce béchamel* will be found under *béchamel*, not under *sauce*; the entry for *poulet à la Marengo* (chicken Marengo) will be found under Marengo, not under *poulet* or chicken. This unusual feature of the dictionary enables the user to find information quickly and easily. Generous use has been made of cross references. These are indicated by **boldface** type. In the entries for foreign dishes, the country, culture, or language of origin is given in parentheses. Culinary dictionaries often perpetuate the same errors and misinformation. In an effort to correct such errors, I have called attention to common misspellings as well as basic misunderstandings.

This dictionary makes no pretense of being all-inclusive. From the beginning it was intended to be concise; words in English for very familiar foods or kitchen techniques (apple, beef, chop, pare, etc.) have therefore been omitted. Some users will doubtless wish I had included more entries or more detailed definitions; they may refer to the specialized works listed in the bibliography. Fortunately, there is a growing number of excellent culinary books to serve the requirements of both the professional and the amateur chef.

Countries, Cultures, and Languages Abbreviated

Aus.	Austria
Bel.	Belgium
Braz.	Brazil
Brit.	Britain
Carib.	Caribbean
Chin.	China
Den.	Denmark
Fr.	France, French
Ger.	Germany, German
Gr.	Greece
Hung.	Hungary
Ind.	India
Indon.	Indonesia
Ir.	Ireland
It.	Italy, Italian
Jap.	Japan
Jew.	Jewish
Kor.	Korea
Leb.	Lebanon
Mex.	Mexico
Mid. E.	Middle East
Mor.	Morocco
Neth.	Netherlands
Nor.	Norway
Phil.	Philippines
Pol.	Poland
Port.	Portugal
Russ.	Russia
Scand.	Scandinavia
Scot.	Scotland
Sp.	Spain, Spanish
Swed.	Sweden
Switz.	Switzerland
Thai.	Thailand
Tun.	Tunisia
Turk.	Turkey

Acknowledgments

I am very grateful to many colleagues and friends for generously sharing their knowledge of food and culinary traditions around the world. For help with various entries in the dictionary I would like to thank Eli Alperowicz, Bonnie Brown, Susanna Harwell-Tolini, Sheryl Julian, Margaret Leibenstein, Patricia Miller, Sally Pian, Nina Simonds, Edward Tolini, Joyce Toomre, and Barbara Ketcham Wheaton.

Phyllis Hanes, food editor of the *Christian Science Monitor,* allowed me to use her extensive culinary library on numerous occasions and gave freely of her knowledge. To Marianne Gateson Riely I owe a special debt: in our conversations she listened patiently and offered many helpful suggestions. At Van Nostrand Reinhold my editor, Jeanette Mall, supported the book from the beginning with enthusiasm and understanding; my copy editor, Emily Pearl, made valuable contributions to the manuscript and her keen eye saved me from a variety of errors. David Miller has my particular thanks for the imagination and care he gave to the illustrations.

Finally, I would like to thank my husband, John Riely, who always gave me help and encouragement when I needed it.

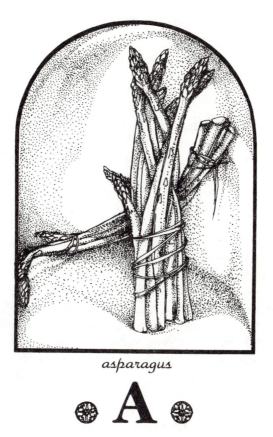

asparagus

❋ A ❋

Aal (Ger.) Eel.

abaissage (Fr.) Rolling out pastry dough.

abalone A **mollusk** whose single large adductor muscle connecting its single shell is edible; used widely in Japanese and Chinese cooking, either fresh, dried, or canned; found throughout the Pacific Ocean, off the coast of California, and in the English Channel, where it is called ormer.

abatis (Fr.) External poultry trimmings, such as wing tips, necks, and feet; sometimes used interchangeably with **abats** for giblets.

abats (Fr.) Poultry giblets and meat offal; internal organs or variety meats, such as hearts, liver, sweetbreads, and gizzards; sometimes used interchangeably with **abatis.**

abbacchio (It.) A very young suckling lamb.

abricot (Fr.) Apricot.

absinthe A green liqueur flavored with **wormwood** leaves and **anise;** highly intoxicating and therefore outlawed in many countries.

abura (Jap.) Oil.

aburage (Jap.) Deep-fried **tōfu.**

acciuga (It.) Anchovy.

aceite (Sp.) Oil.

aceituna (Sp.) Olive.

acetic acid The acid in vinegar that comes from a second fermentation of wine, beer, or cider.

aceto (It.) Vinegar; *aceto balsamico* is a very fine vinegar, made in Modena, Italy, aged in special casks for a dark, mellow, subtle flavor.

aceto-dolce (It.) A sweet-and-sour mixture of vegetables and fruits used in Italy as an **antipasto.**

achiote (Sp.) **Annatto.**

acidophilus milk Milk slightly soured with the *lactobacillus acidophilus* bacteria, which converts the lactose in milk to lactic acid, making it both easy to digest and healthful.

acidulated water Water to which a small amount of lemon juice or vinegar has been added; used to prevent fruits and vegetables from discoloring and to blanch certain foods, such as **sweetbreads.**

Acton, Eliza (1799–1859) A poet *manqué,* whose best-selling cookbook, *Modern Cookery for Private Families* (1845), is notable for its clear and well-organized directions to the middle-class housewife in pre-industrial England.

adega (Port.) A wine cellar or storage space, usually above ground.

adobo (Phil.) A stew, usually made with pork or other meat, or sometimes with chicken or seafood, with a thick spicy sauce made piquant with vinegar; the Mexican version of the dish is made more pungent still by a spicy marinade of red chili peppers.

adrak (Ind.) Fresh ginger root.

adzuki (Jap.) See **azuki.**

aemono (Jap.) Salad.

agar-agar (Malay) An Oriental seaweed used by commercial food processors as a gelatin substitute in soups, sauces, jellies, and ice cream; it has a remarkable capacity for absorbing liquids—far greater than that of **gelatin** or **isinglass.**

age (Jap.) Deep-fried.

aging A method of improving and maturing the flavor of a food, such as game, cheese, or wine, by allowing controlled chemical changes to take place over time.

agiter (Fr.) To stir.

aglio (It.) Garlic.

agneau (Fr.) Lamb.

agnello (It.) Lamb.

agnolotti (It.) Stuffed squares of pasta, such as ravioli, with a meat filling.

agrio (Sp.) Sour.

aguacate (Sp.) Avocado.

aguardiente (Sp.) A very strong Spanish liqueur, similar to Italian **grappa** or French **marc.**

aiglefin (Fr.) Haddock.

aigre (Fr.) Sour, tart, bitter.

aiguillette (Fr.) A thin strip of poultry cut lengthwise from the breast; also a strip of meat cut lengthwise with the grain.

ail (Fr.) Garlic.

aïoli (Fr.) A garlic mayonnaise from Provence, thick and strongly flavored, usually served with seafood; also spelled *ailloli.*

airelle rouge (Fr.) Cranberry.

aji (Jap.) Horse mackerel; flavor.

ajo (Sp.) Garlic; *ajo e ojo* is an Italian dialect name for a spaghetti sauce of garlic sautéed in olive oil. See **aglio** and **olio.**

ajouter (Fr.) To add an ingredient.

akvavit (Swed.) A strong, colorless liquor distilled from grain or potatoes and flavored variously, often with **caraway;** served very cold and drunk neat, often with beer, before or after the meal.

à la (Fr.) In the style of, the full phrase being *à la mode de;* this term designates a specific garnish; often the *à la* is assumed rather than stated, so that a dish such as *Sole à la bonne femme,* for instance, is usually contracted to *Sole bonne femme.*

albóndigas (Sp.) Spicy Spanish or Mexican meatballs made of pork, beef, etc.; also a dumpling.

Albuféra (Fr.) A suprême sauce with meat glaze and pimento butter; the garnish à l'Albuféra consists of poultry stuffed with risotto, truffles, and **foie gras** with elaborate tartlets; also a small cake topped with chopped almonds.

albumen The protein portion of egg white, comprising its greater part, which coagulates with heat; also found in milk, animal blood, plants, and seeds.

alcachofa (Sp.) Artichoke.

alcohol See **fermentation.**

al dente See **dente, al.**

ale English beer made from unroasted barley malt and hops, quickly fermented, and drunk fresh; usually stronger and more bitter than beer; varies in color from light to dark.

algérienne, à l' (Fr.) Garnished with tomatoes braised in oil and sweet-potato croquettes.

Ali-Bab The pseudonym of Henry Babinski, a French gourmand who, as an engineer on location and desperate for good food, taught himself to cook. His mammoth *Gastronome Pratique* (1928), which has since become a classic, shows that he learned very well.

aliolo (Sp.) **Aïoli.**

allemande (Fr.) Veal **velouté** reduced with white wine and mushroom essence, flavored with lemon juice, and bound with egg yolks; *sauce allemande,* which means "German sauce," is a basic classical sauce.

all-i-oli (Sp.) **Aïoli.**

allspice A spice made from the berries of the Jamaica pepper tree, dried and ground, which tastes like a combination of cloves, nutmeg, and cinnamon (hence its name); used in sweet and savory cooking.

allumette (Fr.) A strip of puff pastry with either a sweet or savory filling or garnish; also potatoes, peeled and cut into matchstick-sized strips.

almeja (Sp.) Clam.

almendra (Sp.) Almond.

alose (Fr.) Shad.

Aloxe-Corton A village in Burgundy that produces excellent red and white wines and has some of the most celebrated **Côte d'Or** and **Côte de Beaune** vineyards.

aloyau (Fr.) Sirloin.

Alsace A province in northeastern France along the Rhine, whose German and French cuisine reflects its political history; famous for its **foie gras, charcuterie,** ducks, wine, and many other specialties.

alsacienne, à l' (Fr.) Garnished with sauerkraut and ham or sausages, or with other Alsatian specialties.

Altenburger (Ger.) A soft, uncooked cheese made from goats' milk or goats' and cows' milk mixed; has a delicate white mold on the exterior and a creamy, smooth, flavorful interior.

Alto Adige A valley in northeastern Tirolean Italy around Bolzano, which exports a large quantity of good wines, both red and white, across the border to Austria.

amai (Jap.) Sweet.

amalgamer (Fr.) To mix, blend, or combine ingredients.

amandine (Fr.) Garnished with almonds; often misspelled *almondine.*

amaretto (It.) See **macaroon.**

ambrosia Food of the gods which, in Greek mythology, they ate with nectar; a fruit dessert, often citrus, topped with grated coconut.

américaine, à l' (Fr.) Garnished with sliced lobster tail and truffles; also, a dish of lobster sautéed with olive oil and tomato in the style of Provence; often confused with **armoricaine.**

amiral, à l' (Fr.) A classic fish garnish of mussels, oysters, crayfish, and mushrooms in **sauce normande,** enriched with crayfish butter.

amontillado A Spanish **sherry,** literally in the **Montilla** style, usually somewhat darker and older than a **fino;** the term is sometimes loosely used to mean a medium sherry.

amoroso A kind of **oloroso** sherry, sweetened and darkened.

amuse-gueule (Fr.) Slang for cocktail appetizer, "taste tickler."

anadama An American yeast bread made from white flour with cornmeal and molasses.

anago (Jap.) Conger eel.

Anaheim chili See **güero.**

ananas (Fr. and Ger.) Pineapple.

ancho (Mex.) A deep-red chili pepper, fairly mild in flavor and dried rather than fresh, about five inches long and three inches wide.

anchois (Fr.) Anchovy.

anchovy A small silvery fish, sometimes broiled or fried fresh like a **sardine,** but most often salted and canned; sometimes used in **whitebait.**

ancienne, à l' (Fr.) Various preparations, often fricasseed and garnished in the old-fashioned style; usually a mixture such as cockscombs and truffles; there are classic recipes for braised beef rump and chicken *à l'ancienne.*

andalouse, à l' (Fr.) Garnished with tomatoes, sweet red peppers, eggplant, and sometimes rice **pilaf** and **chipolata** sausages or ham.

andouille (Fr.) A sausage made from pork **chitterlings** and **tripe,** sliced and served cold as an hors d'oeuvre.

andouillette (Fr.) A sausage similar to **andouille** but made from the small intestine rather than the large; the many varieties are sold poached, then grilled before serving hot with strong mustard.

angel food cake A sponge cake made with stiffly beaten egg whites but no yolks, producing a light and airy texture and white color.

angel hair See **capelli d'angelo.**

angelica An herb of the parsley family used for medicinal and culinary purposes; it flavors several liqueurs and confections and often imparts a green color.

angels on horseback Oysters wrapped in bacon, skewered, grilled, and served on buttered toast fingers; a favorite hors d'oeuvre or **savory** in England.

anglaise, à l' (Fr.) English style—that is, plainly boiled or roasted, or coated with an egg-and-breadcrumb batter and deep-fried.

angler See **monkfish.**

angostura bitters See **bitters.**

anguille (Fr.) Eel; *anguila* in Spanish; *anguilla* in Italian.

animelles (Fr.) The culinary term for testicles of animals, especially rams; *animelles* are less popular in Europe today than formerly but still common in the Middle East; in Italy, *animelle* means sweetbreads.

anise An herb of Mediterranean origin, highly regarded by the ancient Greeks and Romans, that tastes like licorice and is used in many parts of the world; its potent seeds flavor several liqueurs, as well as cheeses, pastries, and confections; not to be confused with **fennel.**

anitra (It.) Duck.

Anjou   A northwest central region of France, around Angers and Saumur, known for its wines, both still and sparkling, and for excellent poultry, fish from the Loire, and produce, especially pears; **Curnonsky,** the great gastronome, came from Anjou and praised its cuisine and wine in his writings.

Anna, pommes   See **pommes Anna.**

annatto   A red dye from the fruit of a South American tree, used to color cheese, butter, and confectionery.

antipasto   (It.)   Literally "before the pasta," an *antipasto* is an appetizer or starter; *antipasti,* like *hors d'oeuvres variés,* exist in great variety and profusion.

aonegi   (Jap.)   Japanese green onion.

apéritif   A drink, usually alcoholic, taken before the meal to stimulate the appetite.

Apfel   (Ger.)   Apple; *Apfelstrudel* is thin **strudel** dough filled with apples, white raisins, and spices—a very popular dessert in Germany and Austria.

aphrodisiac   A food or drink that arouses the sexual appetite.

Apicius   The name of three ancient Romans celebrated for their gluttony, with which their name has become synonymous; a cookbook written by one of them survives in two manuscripts, both ninth-century translations.

appareil   (Fr.)   A mixture of ingredients ready for use in a preparation, such as an *appareil à biscuit.*

appellation contrôlée   (Fr.)   Two words found on French wine labels, designating a particular wine by its place of origin, grape variety, or district tradition; this control, used for the best French wines, was established in 1935 to guarantee that the wine is what its label claims it to be, and it is strictly enforced by French law. Similar attempts have been made to certify cheese, both by type and by origin. Sometimes abbreviated to AC or AOC.

appellation d'origine   (Fr.)   The name of a wine, giving its geographic location, be it a château, vineyard, town, river valley, or general region.

Appenzell   (Switz.)   A whole-milk cows' cheese made in large wheels, cured, and washed in a brine with white wine and spices, which impart their flavor; the cheese is pale straw-colored with some holes and a yellow brown rind; similar to **Emmental,** it is firm, buttery, yet piquant.

apple butter   A preserve made of apples that have been peeled, cored, and sliced; it is cooked slowly for a long time, usually with sugar, cider, and spices, until it is reduced to a thick, dark spread.

applejack   Brandy distilled from fermented cider; **Calvados** is one type.

apple pandowdy   See **pandowdy.**

apple schnitz   Dried apple slices, much used in Pennsylvania German cooking for such dishes as apple pie and *Schnitz un Gnepp* (apple and smoked ham stew with dumplings).

aquavit   See **akvavit.**

Arabian coffee   Coffee ground to a powder, spiced with cardamom, cloves, or even saffron, and drunk without sugar or milk; in Arab countries, the ceremony of its preparation and service is symbolic of hospitality.

arabic   See **gum arabic.**

arabica   A type of coffee tree grown at high altitudes, low yielding but producing the best quality of coffee; see also **robusta.**

arachide   (Fr.)   Peanut.

aragosta   (It.)   Lobster.

arak   (Mid. E.)   A liqueur made from various plants; strong and anise-flavored.

arància   (It.)   Orange.

Arborio rice   (It.)   Short, fat-grained Italian rice that is perfect for **risotto** and similar moist rice dishes.

Arbroath smokies   (Scot.)   Small haddock that are gutted, salted, and smoked but not split until broiling before serving.

archiduc, à l'   (Fr.)   Seasoned with paprika and blended with cream.

arenque   (Sp.)   Herring.

Argenteuil   (Fr.)   Garnished with asparagus; named for a region in northern France where the best asparagus is grown.

arhar dal   (Ind.)   Lentils.

aringa   (It.)   Herring.

arista   (It.)   Roast loin of pork.

arlésienne, à l'   (Fr.)   Garnished with eggplant and tomato, cooked in oil with fried onion rings; there are other garnishes by this name, but all contain tomatoes.

Armagnac   A famous brandy from Gascony, in southwestern France, which can be compared to **Cognac;** it is dry, smooth, dark, and aromatic.

armoricaine, à l'   (Fr.)   Lobster in the Breton style, after the ancient Roman name for Brittany and often confused with **à l'américaine;** the sliced lobster is sautéed in olive oil with tomato.

aromatic   A plant, such as an herb or spice, that gives off a pleasing scent and is used to flavor food or drink.

arrack   See **arak.**

arroser   (Fr.)   To baste or moisten.

arrowroot   A powdered flour from the root of a tropical plant, used as a flour or thickener; in cooking it remains clear when mixed with other foods, rather than turning cloudy, and is easily digested.

arroz (Sp.)   Rice; when cooked and combined with other foods it makes dishes such as *arroz con pollo,* rice with chicken.

arsella (It.)   Mussel.

artichaut (Fr.)   Artichoke—a favorite French vegetable.

arugula (It.)   **Rocket.**

asado (Sp.)   Roasted or broiled.

asciutta   See **pasta asciutta.**

Asiago d'Allevo (It.)   A scalded-curd cheese usually made from skimmed evening and whole morning cows' milk and aged up to two years; the large wheels have a thin brownish rind and a smooth pale paste with holes; other Asiago cheeses from Vicenza, Italy, are used mainly as table cheeses.

aspartame   A new artificial sweetener, much sweeter than sugar; not suitable for cooking or use with acids.

asperge (Fr.)   Asparagus.

aspic   A clear jelly made from meat or vegetable stock and gelatin, strained, cleared, and chilled; used to dress savory foods of all kinds by covering them in a mold or surrounding them, chopped into cubes, as a garnish; also used for sweet dishes, based on a fruit juice and gelatin aspic.

assaisonner (Fr.)   To season; *assaisonnement* means seasoning, condiment, or dressing.

Assam   A tea, from the province in northern India of the same name, which is strong and pungent in character and often blended with milder teas.

Asti Spumanti   A sweet sparkling white wine from the town of Asti in the Piedmont region of northern Italy.

Asturias (Sp.)   A strong, sharp-flavored cheese from northern Spain.

athénienne à l' (Fr.)   Garnished with onion, eggplant, tomato, and sweet red pepper fried in olive oil.

atole (Mex.)   A thin gruel drink varying widely but usually made from cornmeal; it can be flavored with sugar and fruit or chocolate or with chili.

attereau (Fr.)   A metal skewer on which sweet or savory food is threaded, breadcrumbed, and deep-fried.

aubergine (Fr.)   Eggplant.

Auflauf (Ger.)   **Soufflé.**

Aufschnitt (Ger.)   A variety of thinly sliced cold meats and sausages sold in German delicatessens; cold cuts.

aurore, à l' (Fr.)   **Béchamel** sauce colored pink with a small amount of tomato puree.

Auslese (Ger.)   A superior German wine made from particularly ripe and fine grapes specially picked at harvest and pressed separately from the other grapes, making a sweeter and more expensive wine. See also **Trockenbeerenauslese.**

Ausone, Château   A famous and very fine Bordeaux wine from St.-Émilion, a first-growth vineyard.

Auster   (Ger.)   Oyster.

Auvergne   A mountainous region in central France known for its relatively simple, straightforward, robust cooking; the Auvergne is renowned for its fine cheeses, charcuterie, vegetables and fruits, nuts, wild mushrooms, lamb, and freshwater fish.

aveline   (Fr.)   Hazelnut, **filbert.**

avgolemono   (Gr.)   A soup made from egg yolks and lemon juice, combined with chicken stock and rice, that is very popular in the Balkans; also a sauce made from egg yolks and lemon juice.

azafrán   (Sp.)   Saffron.

azúcar   (Sp.)   Sugar.

azuki   (Jap.)   A dried bean, russet with a white line at the eye, used widely in Japan and prized for its sweet flavor; *azuki* flour is used in confections and puddings in Japan and China.

Bacchus

• B •

---

baba A yeast cake with raisins that is baked in a special cylindrical mold and soaked with syrup and rum or sometimes **Kirsch;** supposedly named by Stanislaus I. Lesczyinski, King of Poland, when he steeped a **Kugelhopf** in rum and named it after Ali Baba.

baba ghanoush (Mid. E.) Puree of eggplant flavored with **tahini,** lemon juice, olive oil, and garlic; spelled variously.

Babinski, Henry See **Ali-Bab.**

babka See **baba.**

bacalhau (Port.) Salt cod; the Spanish spelling is *bacalao.*

Bacchus The Roman god of wine; Dionysus in Greek mythology.

backen (Ger.) To bake.

Backhühn, Backhändl (Ger.) Chicken rolled in breadcrumbs, then fried.

Backobst (Ger.) Dried fruit.

Backpflaume (Ger.) Prune.

badaam (Ind.) Almond.

Baden A province in southwest Germany containing the Black Forest and many vineyards, producing mostly white wines.

bagel An unsweetened yeast bread, traditionally eggless, shaped like a doughnut, cooked first in boiling water, and then baked; often eaten with **lox** and cream cheese.

bagna caôda (It.) "Hot sauce"; Piedmont dialect term for **bagna cauda.**

bagna cauda (It.) A sauce of garlic and anchovies in oil and butter, served warm with raw vegetables; from Piedmont.

baguette (Fr.) A long cylindrical loaf of French bread.

bai cai (Chin.) Bok choy, literally "white cabbage," a vegetable with thick white stems and long, narrow, chardlike leaves, often used in stir-fried dishes.

baigan (Ind.) Eggplant.

bain-marie (Fr.) A container of warm water in which a smaller pot or pots rest, to provide slow even heat and protect the contents from overheating; a hot-water bath used on the stove or in the oven; a double boiler is a type of *bain-marie.*

ba jiao (Chin.) Chinese star anise (literally, "eight points"); this seed from the magnolia family flavors marinades and slowly cooked dishes; although anise flavored, it is no relation to **fennel.**

bake To cook food by surrounding it with hot dry air in an oven or on hot stones or metal.

bake blind To bake a pastry shell unfilled; the dough is pricked with the tines of a fork, fitted with grease-proof paper, filled with dried beans or rice as a weight, and partially baked.

baked Alaska Ice cream set on sponge cake, the whole masked with meringue and quickly browned in a hot oven; the air bubbles insulate the ice cream from the heat.

bakers' cheese Pasteurized skimmed-milk cows' cheese used by bakers in the U.S.; it is similar to cottage cheese but smoother, softer, and sourer.

baking powder A leavening agent for bread and pastry; when moistened, it produces carbon dioxide to aerate and lighten dough. There are many types, each combining alkaline and acidic material. In double-acting baking powder, the chemical action occurs twice, first when moistened and second when heated.

baking soda Bicarbonate of soda; a leavening agent similar to **baking powder** but used with an acid such as sour milk.

baklava (Turk.) A Middle Eastern sweet pastry made of extremely thin sheets of **phyllo** dough layered with chopped nuts and honey syrup, baked with butter and oil, and cut into diamonds.

balachan, blachan A Malaysian condiment of fermented shrimp or other seafood with chilies; salty and pungent, it is an acquired taste; spelled variously.

ballotine, ballottine (Fr.) A large piece of meat, often poultry or occasionally fish, which is boned, possibly stuffed, rolled or shaped, braised or roasted, and served hot or cold; *ballottine* is often confused with **galantine,** which is poached and served cold with its own jelly; also known as *dodine.*

baloney   See **mortadella.**

balsamella   (It.)   **Béchamel** sauce.

balsam pear   See **bitter melon.**

balut   (Phil.)   A fertilized duck egg nearly ready to hatch; considered a great delicacy to Filipinos and some Malaysians but an acquired taste to others.

bamboo   A tropical treelike grass whose young shoots are eaten raw, freshly boiled, or canned in the Orient.

bami goreng   (Indon.)   See **nasi goreng.**

banane   (Fr.)   Banana.

Banbury cake   (Brit.)   A cake from Oxfordshire, England, of oval flaky pastry filled with currants, lemon peel, and spices.

banger   (Brit.)   Slang for sausage that is filled with ground pork and breadcrumbs.

bannock   (Scot.)   A traditional Scottish cake of barley, wheat, or oatmeal; large and round, varying widely according to region.

Banyuls   A sweet fortified dessert wine, usually red but also rosé or white; primarily made from the **Grenache** grape, in the town of the same name in the eastern French Pyrenees.

bào   (Chin.)   Abalone.

baobab   A central African tree with a very thick trunk; its fruit, called monkey bread, is eaten fresh and made into a refreshing, healthful drink, while its edible leaves are dried and powdered.

bap   (Brit.)   A small round loaf of soft white bread, eaten in Scotland and parts of England for breakfast.

bar   (Fr.)   Sea bass.

baraquille   (Fr.)   A triangular stuffed pastry hors d'oeuvre.

barbabiètola   (It.)   Beet root; the tops are **biètola.**

barbacoa   (Mex.)   Meat cooked in a barbecue pit; also, by extension, the word often means breakfast.

Barbaresco   A renowned red wine from the Italian Piedmont; produced from the **Nebbiolo** grape.

barbecue, barbeque   A method of cooking marinated food on a grill or spit over a hardwood, charcoal, or briquette fire; the name also extends to marinades and social gatherings at such cookouts.

barberry   A shrub whose berries are pickled or ripened and made into various preserves, syrup, and wine; red in color, high in acid; also called Oregon grapes.

barbue   (Fr.)   **Brill.**

bard   To tie extra fat, usually bacon, around fish, poultry, or meat to baste it while cooking. The barding fat is usually removed before serving.

Bardolino A popular red wine made in northern Italy; fruity, light, best drunk young.

barigoule, à la (Fr.) Artichokes blanched, trimmed, stuffed with **dux-elles,** wrapped in bacon, braised in white wine, and served with a reduction of the cooking broth.

Bar-le-Duc A red currant preserve whose name comes from the town in the French Lorraine where it is made.

barley An ancient and hardy grain grown in most climates, but today a staple only in the Middle East. In the modern world barley is used mostly for animal feed and for malt for brewing and distilling; only a small proportion is used for soup, cereal, and bread.

Barolo An Italian red wine from the Piedmont, south of Turin, made from the **Nebbiolo** grape; deep, full-bodied, and slow-maturing, it is an exceptional wine.

baron In England, a double sirloin of beef roasted for ceremonial occasions; in France, the saddle and two legs of lamb or mutton.

barquette (Fr.) A boat-shaped pastry shell filled and baked as an hors d'oeuvre or sweet; the name sometimes applies to vegetable cases for stuffing, such as zucchini.

Barsac An area within the Sauternes district of Bordeaux that produces a white dessert wine that is fairly sweet and fruity.

basil A pungent herb from the mint family used extensively in Mediterranean cooking; the basis of **pesto** sauce.

basilico (It.) **Basil.**

bass A name for many fish, not necessarily related, some of which are separately entered under their individual names.

baste To moisten during cooking by spooning liquid over food, in order to prevent drying out and toughness.

bâtarde (Fr.) A sauce of white **roux** with water, bound with egg yolks, with butter and lemon juice added; the name means "bastard," so called for its indirect relationship to other classic sauces.

Bâtard-Montrachet A vineyard in Burgundy producing an excellent white wine; small in volume but dry, flavorful, and possessing a fine bouquet, it is made entirely from **Chardonnay** grapes.

batata (Sp. and Port.) Sweet potato.

bâton, bâtonnet (Fr.) Shaped like a little stick; vegetables such as potatoes cut in this manner are generally larger than **allumettes** or **julienne.**

batter A liquid mixture of flour and milk or water before it is spooned, poured, or dipped for cooking; it can be thick or thin but when no longer liquid it becomes **dough.**

batter bread See **spoon bread.**

batterie de cuisine (Fr.) Kitchen utensils.

battuto (It.) A base for soups and stews consisting of diced onion, garlic, celery, and herbs, cooked in oil or pork fat, to which the rest is added; after the *battuto* is cooked it becomes a **soffrito.**

baudroie (Fr.) Monkfish.

Bauernsuppe (Ger.) A peasant soup of vegetables, legumes, and bacon; the adjective *bauern* means peasant or country-style.

Baumkuchen (Ger.) A traditional tall Christmas cake, baked in many layers to resemble the rings of a tree trunk, and iced with barklike chocolate.

Bavarian cream A cold custard pudding, often molded into peaks, made from gelatin, eggs, whipped cream, and various sweet flavorings.

bavarois (Fr.) **Bavarian cream,** but not to be confused with the *bavaroise* drink of sweetened tea enriched with egg yolks and milk and perhaps flavored with citrus.

bavette (Fr.) Tip of sirloin; flank steak.

bay An herb from the laurel family whose dried leaves are an ingredient of the **bouquet garni** and whose leaves and berries have many medicinal uses; symbolic of intellectual achievement or victory.

bayerisch (Ger.) Bavarian, of the southern region of West Germany around Munich.

Bayonne A town in the French Pyrenees famous for its fine cured hams.

bean curd See **tōfu.**

bean sprout The germinated seed pod of a leguminous plant whose nutritional value is between that of a seed and a vegetable; bean sprouts are eaten fresh or lightly cooked and are appreciated for their crisp texture.

bean threads (Chin.) See **fěn sī.**

béarnaise (Fr.) A sauce of the warm emulsion type in classical French cuisine; wine vinegar is reduced with shallots and tarragon, then cooled; egg yolks and butter are beaten in and the mixture is strained and finished with chopped tarragon and perhaps chervil; served primarily with grilled meat, fowl, and eggs; one of the classic sauces.

Beaufort (Fr.) A whole-milk cows' cheese from the French Savoy; similar to **Gruyère** and available year-round.

Beauharnais, à la (Fr.) A classical garnish for **tournedos** made of stuffed mushrooms, artichoke hearts, **château potatoes,** and *Beauharnais* sauce (**béarnaise** with puréed tarragon).

Beaujolais A region in southern Burgundy producing a popular red wine from the **Gamay** grape; pleasant, fruity, and light, best served cool and drunk young; *Beaujolais Nouveau* is new **Beaujolais** wine bottled immediately after fermentation; very light, fruity, and pleasant.

Beaulieu A vineyard in the Napa Valley producing some of the best California wines, especially their **Cabernet Sauvignon.**

Beaune A city in Burgundy and the center of its wine trade; see **Côte d'Or.**

bécasse (Fr.) Woodcock; the Italian word is *beccaccia.*

bec fin (Fr.) A slang term for a connoisseur of fine food.

béchamel (Fr.) A basic white sauce of milk stirred into a **roux,** thickened, and flavored with onion.

bêche de mer See **sea cucumber.**

beef Stroganoff Strips of beef sautéed with chopped onions and mushrooms, thickened with sour cream; an American dish.

beef Wellington Fillet topped with **duxelles,** wrapped in puff pastry, and baked.

beer Any beverage made by the action of yeast on an infusion of malted cereal, brewed, flavored with hops, and fermented.

Beerenauslese (Ger.) A celebrated German wine made from overripe berries selected individually from specially chosen bunches of grapes; a sweet, fruity, intense wine of extraordinary flavor and expense.

Beetensuppe (Ger.) **Borsch.**

Beeton, Isabella (1836–1865) An English journalist and author of *The Book of Household Management,* which appeared in England in a women's magazine published by her husband (1859–61) and then in book form (1861), with a tremendous and lasting influence; the large scope of Mrs. Beeton's book on domestic economy included estimates of cost, quantities, and preparation times.

beignet (Fr.) Food dipped in batter and fried in deep fat.

Bei jīng kǎo yā (Chin.) Peking duck: an elaborate and famous dish made from specially reared ducks; the bird is inflated with air to dry the skin, then smeared with a honey mixture and hung for a long time to dry again; it is then roasted until crisp, the skin removed to be served separately, and the meat shredded; skin and meat are served together with sliced scallions and cucumbers all rolled up in pancakes spread with a soybean sauce and eaten with the fingers.

Beilagen (Ger.) Accompanying dishes, such as vegetables or salad.

belegtes Brot (Ger.) Sandwich, usually open-faced.

Belgian endive A specially cultivated chicory whose leaves are cut off and shielded from the light, so that new pale yellow leaves grow back in their characteristic cigar shape; used fresh in salads or braised in various preparations; this curious new vegetable was discovered in the last century near Brussels, where it is mostly grown today during fall and winter; also called witloof.

bell pepper See **pepper (sweet bell).**

Belon oysters Choice oysters from the river of the same name in Brittany.

Bel Paese (It.)   A semisoft, mild, uncooked Italian cheese made from whole cows' milk; it is produced on a large scale and is very popular.

beluga caviar   Choicest caviar from the white sturgeon.

Bénédictine   A liqueur originally made by the monks of that order in Fécamp, Normandy, based on **Cognac** and flavored with many herbs and plants; B & B is a drier combination of Bénédictine and brandy.

benne seeds   Sesame seeds, brought from Africa with the slave trade and used especially in the Black cooking of South Carolina, often to symbolize happiness.

Bercy (Fr.)   A classic fish sauce of white wine and fish **fumet** reduced with shallots and finished with butter and parsley; also made with meat glaze and beef marrow for grilled meat.

bergamot   A bitter, pear-shaped orange whose skin is used for its essential oil in perfume-making; also the name of a pear and a type of mint.

Bergkäse (Ger.)   A hard yellow cheese from the Bavarian Alps; this is really a generic name for various cooked pressed cheeses from the region.

Berliner Weisse (Ger.)   A pale, tart ale made from wheat and low in alcohol; often drunk with a dash of raspberry syrup for refreshment.

Bernkastel   A town in the Moselle region of West Germany with some of the region's best vineyards, all estate-bottled wines.

betterave (Fr.)   Beetroot.

beurre blanc (Fr.)   A sauce of white wine and shallots reduced, thickened with butter, and served warm with seafood, poultry, or vegetables.

beurre Chivry (Fr.)   A compound butter flavored with parsley, tarragon, chives, and shallots.

beurre manié (Fr.)   Flour and butter, usually in equal proportion, kneaded together into a paste to thicken sauces and gravies; the flour can be browned or not.

beurre noir (Fr.)   A sauce of butter cooked until brown, often flavored with chopped parsley, capers, and vinegar; served with fish or brains.

bhara, bharva (Ind.)   Stuffed.

bhojia (Ind.)   Vegetables stir-fried and highly spiced.

bhona (Ind.)   Fried.

bicarbonate of soda   See **baking soda.**

bicchiere (It.)   A measuring glass roughly equivalent to one cup.

bien cuit (Fr.)   Well done, as for steak.

Bierwurst (Ger.)   A fat sausage of pork, pork fat, and beef, dark reddish brown in color.

bietola (It.)   Swiss chard.

bigarade (Fr.)   A classic brown sauce for roast duck made of caramelized sugar, lemon and orange juice, stock, and **demi-glace,** with blanched zest.

bigos (Pol.) A hunter's stew of sauerkraut with sausages, bacon, mushrooms, red wine, and meat (usually venison).

bilberry A small berry similar to the blueberry but usually smaller and tarter, with the same silvery cast; used for pies, jams, etc.; native to Europe, especially Northern Europe.

Billy Bi (Fr.) Mussel soup with cream and white wine, originally created for a customer at Maxim's without the mussels themselves, but now usually served with them.

bind To hold together by means of a **liaison.**

Bingen A wine town of Hessia, West Germany, overlooking the Rhine and Nahe Rivers, producing excellent white wines.

bird's nest See **yàn cài.**

bird's nest fryer A hinged double wire basket for deep-frying straw-potato nests to be filled with other food, such as peas.

Birne (Ger.) Pear.

biryani (Ind.) A substantial rice dish, variously prepared, similar to **pilaf.**

Bischofsbrot (Ger.) An Austrian cake containing dried fruit and chocolate drops.

biscuit A small flat cake, usually round and unsweetened, originally double-baked (see **zwieback**), hence its name; the term now covers a wide variety of small cakes and breads.

biscuit de Savoie (Fr.) A sponge cake from Savoy, often baked in a **brioche parisienne** mold and served with fruit.

biscuits à la cuillère (Fr.) Ladyfingers; so named because before the invention of the pastry bag they were shaped by dropping the dough from a spoon.

biscuit tortoni See **tortoni.**

bishop A mulled wine drink, often made with port or champagne, flavored with orange and lemon, cinnamon, clove, and other spices; a traditional drink in England and northern Europe.

Biskote (Ger.) Ladyfinger.

Bismarck herring Herring that are marinated in vinegar, filleted and split, seasoned with onion, and eaten with sour cream.

bisque A thick soup puree, often made from shellfish to which the pulverized shells are added. Originally a poultry or game soup, *bisque* has gradually come to mean a puree, thickened perhaps with cream.

bitter melon A gourd vegetable, quite sour in flavor, with a ridged rind resembling a furrowed cucumber, used in Malaysian and Oriental cooking. Also called balsam pear.

bitters A liquid, usually alcoholic, steeped with aromatic herbs and roots and used as a tonic or as a flavoring for alcoholic drinks.

Bitto A cows' milk cheese from Sondrio in Italy which is aged from two months to three years and used as a table or grating cheese; it is popular in Italy grated or sprinkled on top of **polenta** with butter.

bivalve   A **mollusk** with two hinged shells, such as a clam, mussel, or oyster.

bizcochos borrachos   (Sp.)   Sponge cakes sugared, splashed with wine, and sprinkled with cinnamon.

black bass   A freshwater fish of several varieties, both smallmouth and largemouth, with firm, lean meat; suitable for most kinds of cooking.

black bean   A common bean variety, black, shiny, and sweet; this dried bean is a staple food in Central and South America, especially in rice dishes, stews, **frijoles refritos,** and in the southern United States, as in black bean soup.

black butter   See **beurre noir.**

black-eyed pea   A white pea with a black eye, brought to the southern United States from Africa in the seventeenth century with the slave trade; a favorite bean in Black American cooking, either fresh or dried, and an essential ingredient in dishes such as **hopping John.**

Black Forest   A wooded, mountainous region of southwestern West Germany, producing a strongly flavored smoked ham; its name also designates a rich chocolate cake (see **Schwarzwalder Kirschtorte**).

black pepper   See **pepper (black).**

black pudding   See **blood sausage.**

black sea bass   A small midAtlantic warm-weather fish; its lean, delicate white flesh is suitable for most cooking methods and is widely used in Chinese cuisine.

blackstrap   Dark, heavy, strong molasses originally made in the West Indies and considered low-quality but nutritious and flavorful for certain uses.

blakhan   (Indon.)   A salty and pungent shrimp paste, related to the Philippine **balachan** and other Oriental fermented fish condiments.

blanc   (Fr.)   Cooking stock or **court bouillon** in which certain foods, such as artichokes, are cooked to retain their color; it usually includes a little flour mixed with water; lemon juice and butter or oil are sometimes included.

blanc de blancs   (Fr.)   A white Champagne wine made from white grapes.

blanch   To immerse vegetables, fruit, or meat in boiling water briefly, then plunge into cold water to stop cooking; this technique is used to firm or soften flesh, to set color, to peel off skin, or to remove raw flavor.

blancmange   A medieval or older jellied mixture originally made of pulverized almonds and veal stock, spiced and sweetened; *blancmange* has changed over the centuries into a kind of pudding or custard.

blanquette   (Fr.)   A stew of veal, chicken, or lamb braised in stock, thickened with egg yolks and cream, and garnished with mushrooms and small white onions; the sauce is always white.

blé (Fr.) Wheat.

blending Mixing wines of different qualities or origins to produce a better wine or to give consistency; usually an honorable practice but sometimes unscrupulous.

bleu (Fr.) Very rare, as for steak; rarer than **à point.**

bleu, au (Fr.) A method of preparing trout or other fish whereby the fish is killed immediately before being plunged into a boiling **court bouillon** with vinegar, which turns the skin bluish and curls the body of the fish.

Bleu d'Auvergne (Fr.) A whole-milk cows' cheese made in several areas in the French Auvergne; it is a soft, unpressed blue cheese with a distinctive flavor.

blind Huhn (Ger.) A casserole of beans, vegetables, dried apples, and bacon.

blini (Russ.) Pancakes, usually of buckwheat flour, often served with sour cream and caviar.

bloater (Brit.) Inshore herring that are lightly salted and smoked, then gutted only just before serving.

Blockwurst (Ger.) A sausage of beef and pork, similar to salami.

blond de veau (Fr.) White veal stock; *blond de volaille* means clear chicken stock.

blondir (Fr.) To cook lightly in fat.

blood sausage A sausage colored black and flavored with blood and diced pork fat from fresh-killed pigs.

blue cheese Cheese injected with a mold such as *Penicillium roqueforti* (from **Roquefort,** the oldest cheese of the genre), which gives the cheese its characteristic flavor and blue green veining; there are many varieties, some of which are individually noted.

blue crab A variety of **crab** found on the Chesapeake Bay, eastern Atlantic, and Gulf coastlines, best appreciated in the form of **soft-shell crab.**

bluefish A voracious fish found off the North American east coast and in the Mediterranean; its oily and flavorful flesh takes well to assertive seasonings and accompaniments; best for baking, broiling, and smoking.

Blue Point A species of oyster found off the coast of Long Island, usually served raw.

Blumenkohl (Ger.) Cauliflower.

Blutwurst (Ger.) **Blood sausage.**

Bock (Ger.) A strong Bavarian beer, usually dark.

bodega (Sp.) A wine cellar or store.

boeuf à la bourguignonne (Fr.) See **bourguignonne, à la.**

bogavante (Sp.) Large-clawed lobster.

Bohne (Ger.) Bean.

boil To cook in liquid at or above the boiling point (100° Celsius, 212° Fahrenheit), when liquid bubbles and evaporates into steam; a rolling boil is a vigorous boil.

boiled dinner See **New England boiled dinner.**

bok choy See **bai cai.**

boletus A genus of wild mushroom of which the bolete, *cèpe,* or *porcino,* as it is variously known, is best known and most prized; with a thick fleshy cap and stem, the *cèpe* grows in chestnut and oak woods from June to November and is eaten fresh and dried; not to be confused with other species.

bollito (It.) Boiled; refers especially to mixed boiled meats.

bologna See **mortadella.**

bolognese, alla (It.) See **ragù bolognese.**

Bombay duck An Indian fish (*bombil*) that is dried and used to flavor curry dishes.

bombe (Fr.) Ice cream that is layered and packed into a special mold, originally shaped like a bomb.

bonbon (Fr.) Candy, sweet.

bonito A small member of the tuna family; often used in Japanese cooking dried, salted, or flaked.

bonne femme, à la (Fr.) Prepared in a simple home style, often accompanied by small onions and mushrooms, in a white wine sauce flavored with lemon juice.

boquerón (Sp.) Anchovy or whitebait.

borage An herb, Mediterranean in origin, used to flavor vegetables and beverages; its flowers are made into fritters, its young leaves are used in salads, and its mature leaves are cooked like spinach and finely chopped.

Bordeaux A seaport city and capital of the Gironde on the Garonne River in southwest France; the Bordeaux region is famous for the large quantity of red and white wine it produces, some of it very fine.

bordelaise, à la (Fr.) Garnished with a reduction sauce of red or white wine with bone marrow and chopped parsley; with *cèpes* added; with **mirepoix;** or a garnish of artichokes and potatoes.

börek (Turk.) A very thin pastry filled with savory stuffing, folded or rolled up, and fried or baked.

borlotto bean A common bean variety, usually dried; this splotched brown bean is especially popular in Italy where it is cooked to a creamy puree or added to soups.

borracha, salsa (Mex.) Literally "drunken sauce"; made with **pasilla** chilies, orange juice, onion, and tequila.

borsch, borscht (Pol. and Russ.) A soup based on fresh beets (which impart their vibrant color), meat broth, and winter vegetables, and often flavored with **kvass;** the soup varies widely but is always served with sour cream; traditional for Christmas Eve, without meat.

Boston baked beans Navy beans flavored with molasses and salt pork and baked in an earthenware pot; originally prepared on Saturday and cooked in a communal oven to allow Puritan housewives to observe the Sabbath—hence Boston's nickname of Bean Town.

Boston brown bread A traditional accompaniment to **Boston baked beans,** this rye bread is flavored with molasses and often contains whole wheat and cornmeal; the dark sweet bread is steamed, usually in baking powder tins.

botifarra (Sp.) **Blood sausage.**

Botrytis cinerea See **noble rot.**

bottom round See **round.**

bouchée (Fr.) A small puff-pastry savory, literally a "mouthful," filled variously.

boucher (Fr.) Butcher.

bouchon (Fr.) Cork.

boudin noir (Fr.) **Blood sausage.**

bouillabaisse (Fr.) This famous specialty from Marseilles, originally a hearty fisherman's stew, is made from a wide variety of native fish and shellfish and flavored with saffron; the exact recipe is hotly disputed.

bouillir (Fr.) To boil.

bouillon (Fr.) Stock or broth that forms the basis of soups and sauces; it can be made from vegetables, poultry, or meat boiled in water, depending on its use, and need not contain gelatin.

boulage (Fr.) Shaping the dough in baking.

boulanger (Fr.) Baker.

boulangère, à la (Fr.) Garnished with braised onion and potato.

boule-de-neige (Fr.) A dessert pastry resembling snowballs (hence the name), of round cakes dipped in whipped cream; made in individual servings.

bouquet (Fr.) The aroma of wine, which gives it much of its character and charm.

bouquet garni (Fr.) A bunch of herbs tied together in a small bundle for flavoring a dish as it cooks and removed before serving; it usually includes parsley, thyme, and bay leaf, among other herbs.

bouquetière, à la (Fr.) Meat garnished with vegetables that are arranged in bouquets.

bourgeoise, à la (Fr.) Braised meat garnished with carrots, onions, and diced bacon.

Bourgogne (Fr.) Burgundy.

bourguignonne, à la   (Fr.) Served with a red wine sauce garnished with mushrooms, small onions, and diced bacon.

bourride   (Fr.) A fish stew from Provence, similar to **bouillabaisse,** served on a **croûte,** and flavored with **aïoli.**

boysenberry   A hybrid cultivar of the blackberry that tastes like a raspberry, developed early in this century and named after an American, Rudolf Boysen.

braciola   (It.) Cutlet or chop.

Brägenwurst   (Ger.) Smoked sausage of pig's brains, oats, flour, and onions; long and thin.

brains   Usually from a calf or lamb, brains should first be blanched in **acidulated water,** then poached in a **court bouillon** or fried in butter; often served with **beurre noir** or **noisette.**

braise   To cook in a small amount of flavored liquid in a tightly covered pan over low heat.

bran   The thin brown outer covering of the wheat grain, which is removed during the refining of white flour; although bran is not absorbed into the body during digestion, its fiber, usually eaten in baked goods and breakfast cereal, is beneficial.

brandade   (Fr.) A salt-cod dish from Provence in which cod is pounded with olive oil, milk, and garlic into a thick, flavorful puree and served with **croûtes;** the name derives from the Provençal word for stirred; see also **morue.**

brandy   A spirit distilled from wine (types of brandy are separately entered).

brasato   (It.) Braised.

Braten   (Ger.) A cut of meat roasted in the oven or braised on the stove.

Brathering   (Ger.) Herring that is grilled or floured and fried, then pickled in a boiled vinegar marinade; usually served cold.

Bratwurst   (Ger.) A sausage of spiced pork, fried or grilled; very popular.

Braunschweiger   (Ger.) Liver sausage.

brawn   See **head cheese.**

Brazil nut   The nut of a tall tree indigenous to the Amazon and growing mostly in the wild. The woody pod, looking something like a coconut, contains up to twenty seeds whose segments fit together in their husks; the nut is white, creamy, and high in fat. The tree grows only in Brazil and, curiously, almost all of the nuts are exported.

breadfruit   The fruit of a tree native to the Pacific; large, round, and starchy, it is eaten boiled or baked; sometimes confused with its blander-tasting relative, jackfruit.

bread sauce   (Brit.) A sauce of milk thickened with bread crumbs; served with poultry and game.

bream   Several different species of fish, including the excellent Mediterranean **gilthead** and the American **porgy.**

bresaola   (It.)   Dried salt beef sliced from the fillet, served as an **antipasto;** a specialty of northern Lombardy.

Bresse   A region in southern Burgundy famous for its excellent chickens and for its blue cheese, *Bleu de Bresse.*

bretonne, à la   (Fr.)   Garnished with fresh white haricot beans.

brewer's yeast   See **yeast.**

brick   A scalded-curd, surface-ripened whole-milk cows' cheese first made in Wisconsin; it is shaped in bricks and also weighted with bricks during pressing, hence its name; the taste and texture is between **Cheddar** and **Liederkranz.**

brider   (Fr.)   To truss.

Brie   A soft uncooked cows' milk cheese from the region of the same name east of Paris; made in large flat discs, this cheese, with its white, surface-ripened rind and smooth buttery interior, is made similarly to **Camembert** and is renowned for its fine aroma and taste.

brill   A member of the **flounder** family.

Brillat-Savarin, Jean Anthelme   (1755–1826)   A French lawyer and magistrate who is remembered today for his great treatise on gastronomy, *The Physiology of Taste,* published in 1825.

brinjal   (Ind.)   Eggplant.

brioche   (Fr.)   A cake or pastry made from a rich yeast dough containing butter and eggs, often baked in a characteristic fluted mold with a smaller knob on top (*brioche parisienne*), as well as in various other shapes and sizes.

brisket   A cut of beef from the lower forequarter, between the foreshanks and short plate; usually braised or cured for **corned beef.**

brisling   The sprat, a small fish similar to the **herring.**

Brittany   A province in northwest France noted for its fresh and saltwater fish and shellfish, **Muscadet** wine, cider, and many other foods.

broa   (Sp.)   Cornbread.

broad bean   See **fava.**

broche, à la   (Fr.)   Spit-roasted.

brochet   (Fr.)   **Pike.**

brochette   (Fr.)   A skewer for grilling pieces of food.

brodo   (It.)   Broth or bouillon; *brodo ristretto* is consommé.

Brolio   A celebrated and ancient vineyard in the Italian Chianti district in Tuscany; the wine is robust and long-lived.

bronzino   (It.)   Sea bass.

Bröschen   (Ger.)   Sweetbreads.

Brot   (Ger.)   Bread.

brou   (Fr.)   A liqueur made from walnut husks.

brouillé (Fr.) Scrambled.

Brouilly A wine-producing district in Beaujolais with one of the best wines of that type.

brown To cook by high heat, causing the surface of the food to turn dark and imparting a richer, cooked flavor; browning affects the outside of food only, leaving the inside moist; it can be achieved by sautéing, frying, grilling, or heating under a broiling unit; see also **caramel.**

brown betty An American pudding made of sliced fruit thickened with breadcrumbs, sweetened, and baked; usually made with apples.

brown sauce See **espagnole.**

brown sugar Refined sugar with a thin coating of **molasses;** not to be confused with raw, unrefined sugar.

brûlé (Fr.) Burned or flamed, as in burnt-brandy or **crème brûlée.**

brunoise (Fr.) A mixture of vegetables cut into small dice and cooked slowly in butter for soups, sauces, etc.; **bâtonnets** cut across into cubes make *brunoise.*

Brunswick stew A Southern American stew originally made with squirrel or whatever game was available, but now mostly made with chicken and a variety of vegetables.

bruschetta (It.) Bread slices toasted, rubbed with garlic, and dribbled with new green olive oil; a specialty of Rome.

brut Very dry Champagne to which virtually no sugar has been added; drier than "extra dry."

bruxelloise, à la (Fr.) Garnished with Brussels sprouts, braised endives, and **château potatoes** and served with a Madeira sauce.

Bual A type of **Madeira,** golden in color and quite sweet, now usually drunk as a dessert wine; the name comes from the particular grape variety.

bubble and squeak (Brit.) Boiled meat, usually beef, fried with cabbage and sometimes potatoes.

bûche de Noël (Fr.) Literally Yule log; the traditional French **gâteau** for Christmas, made of **génoise** and **buttercream** and decorated to look like a log.

buckwheat flour Not a true cereal, buckwheat flour is made from dry fruit seeds of the plant; most popular in Russia (see **blini**), buckwheat is made into pancakes and special breads (sometimes mixed with wheat) but mostly used for fodder; also called saracen wheat or saracen corn.

budín (Sp.) Pudding; the Italian word is *budino.*

bue (It.) Beef; the Spanish word is *buey.*

buffalo fish A freshwater American fish with sweet, white, lean flesh; a type of sucker, the buffalo is similar to **carp** and versatile in cooking.

bulghur (Mid. E.) Cracked wheat, hulled and parboiled, originally Persian; this nutty-textured cereal is ground in different grades for various dishes such as **tabbouleh, kibbeh,** and **pilaf;** also spelled *bulgur* and *burghul.*

bullabesa (Sp.) Fish stew of Catalonia; a cousin of **bouillabaisse.**

Bündnerfleisch (Switz.) Cured, dried beef sliced very thin.

buñuelo (Sp.) Fritter.

burdock A large plant whose leaves, young shoots, and roots are used for food and drink; much favored in Japan, where it is known as *gobo.*

burghul See **bulghur.**

burgoo A thick stew, originally a porridge for sailors, later containing many different meats and vegetables and thickened with okra; associated with the southern United States and Kentucky.

Burgos (Sp.) A fresh ewes' milk cheese, from the Spanish province of the same name; mild, soft, and pleasant, often served for dessert; the rindless discs weigh approximately three pounds.

Burgundy A province southeast of Paris, famous for its red and white wines; **Beaujolais, Chablis, Pouilly-Fuissé,** and those of the **Côte d'Or,** separately entered, are the best known.

burnet An herb whose leaves, which taste like cucumber, are used to flavor salads, cool drinks, vinegar, and sauces.

burrida (It.) A fish stew from Genoa (a cousin of **bourride**).

burrito (Sp.) A **taco** of wheat rather than maize (**tortilla**), folded to enclose a filling.

burro (It.) Butter.

Busserl (Ger.) Small round sweet pastries, literally "kiss."

buta (Jap.) Pork.

butter bean Lima bean.

buttercream A mixture of butter, sugar, and egg yolks or custard, flavored in a wide variety of ways and used to ice or garnish dessert pastries and cakes.

butterfly To cut open and spread the sides apart (as with butterfly wings), especially for a piece of meat or fish.

buttermilk The residue from churned butter, containing the milk casein, which has a slightly sour flavor; buttermilk is easily digested and is often used with baking soda for breads and pastries; nowadays usually made from a culture.

chèvre

• C •

Cabernet (Fr.) A grape variety that partly makes up red Bordeaux wines and many of the world's best clarets; *Cabernet Sauvignon,* higher in tannin, is slower maturing and longer lasting than *Cabernet; Cabernet Franc* is more productive.

Cabernet Rosé d'Anjou (Fr.) A rosé wine, of the *Cabernet Franc* grape, from the Loire Valley.

cabillaud (Fr.) Fresh cod; see also **morue.**

cabinet See **Kabinett.**

cabra (Sp.) Goat.

Cabrales (Sp.) A blue-veined cheese from northern Spain; usually made from goats' milk but sometimes from cows' and sheep's milk; earthy, pungent, yet mellow in flavor; sometimes called *Picón.*

cabrito (Sp.) Kid.

cacao A tree from whose seeds, fermented, roasted, and ground, come chocolate and cocoa; native to South America, it now grows in many tropical countries around the globe.

cacciagione (It.) Game.

26

cacciatora (It.) Hunter's style: in a sauce of mushrooms, onions, tomatoes, and herbs with wine.

Caciocavallo (It.) A whole-milk cows' cheese, spindle-shaped and tied with string, from southern Italy; made by the spun-curd method. Table cheeses are aged for two months, grating cheeses up to twelve, and their flavor ranges from delicate and sweet to more pungent with age; this pale straw-colored cheese is used for eating and cooking and is sometimes smoked.

Caen, à la mode de (Fr.) A classic preparation for **tripe** in which blanched squares of tripe are slowly braised with onions, carrots, leeks, blanched ox feet, herbs, garlic, brandy, and white wine; it is cooked for twelve hours in a **hermetically** sealed **marmite.**

Caerphilly (Brit.) A cows' milk cheese, mild, crumbly, moist, and slightly sour; the traditional lunch of the Welsh coal miners, it is now mostly made in western England rather than Wales.

Caesar salad Romaine lettuce with croutons, coddled eggs, and grated Parmesan cheese in an olive oil vinaigrette flavored with garlic and Worcestershire sauce; anchovies are often added; created in 1924 by Caesar Cardini, an Italian restaurateur in Tijuana.

café au lait (Fr.) Coffee with hot milk; the Italian term is *caffelatte.*

Cahors (Fr.) A fine red wine from the city of the same name in Toulouse, made from the **Malbec** grape; very dark red, slow maturing, long lasting.

cai juan (Chin.) Egg roll; a square crêpelike wrapper made from an egg, flour, and water batter, usually stuffed with pork, cabbage, or other vegetables, rolled up, and deep-fried or steamed, or sometimes shredded for garnishing; the egg roll, very popular in Cantonese-American cooking, is thicker and less elegant than the **spring roll** and should not be confused with it.

caille (Fr.) Quail.

Cajun Originally, this term pertained to the French Canadian settlers in Louisiana, a corruption of Acadia (from the colony of Acadia in southeastern Canada); Cajun cooking combines French methods with rural southern ingredients and is often confused with **Creole; gumbo** and **jambalaya** are typical dishes of this unique cuisine.

calabacita (Sp.) Zucchini.

calabaza (Sp.) Pumpkin.

calabash See **passion fruit.**

calamaro (It.) Squid.

Caldaro A town in the Italian Tirol that produces a number of light and pleasant red and white wines.

calderada (Sp.) A thick Galician fish stew similar to **bouillabaisse.**

caldereta (Sp.) A meat or fish stew, whose name derives from the cauldron or pot in which it is cooked.

caldo (It.) Hot; in Spanish and Portuguese, *caldo* means broth.

caliente (Sp.) Hot.

Californian chili (Mex.) See **guëro.**

callaloo (Carib.) The leafy green tops of the **taro** plant, cooked into a spicy vegetable stew with okra, eggplant, tomatoes, onions, garlic, chilies, herbs, salt pork or other meat, coconut milk, and sometimes crab; a popular and variable native dish related to **Creole** crab **gumbo;** also spelled *calalou* and *callilu.*

calmar (Fr.) Squid.

Calvados Apple brandy from the town of the same name in Normandy.

calzone (It.) A turnover made of pizza dough and stuffed with various savory fillings, usually in individual portions; originally from Naples and now popular in the U.S.

camarón (Sp.) Shrimp.

Cambridge sauce A mayonnaiselike sauce of hard-boiled egg yolks, anchovies, capers, herbs, mustard, vinegar, and oil, finished with chopped parsley.

Camembert (Fr.) A cows' milk cheese, soft and creamy with a white mold rind; from the town of the same name in Normandy; neither cooked nor pressed, this rich cheese in four-inch rounds is very popular and famous and, at its best—farmhouse cheese from unpasteurized milk—superb.

camote (Sp.) Sweet potato.

campagnola (It.) Country style, usually with onions and tomatoes.

canapé (Fr.) A small piece of bread spread or garnished with savory food and served as an hors d'oeuvre.

canard sauvage (Fr.) Wild duck.

caneton (Fr.) Duckling.

cangrejo (Sp.) Crab.

canneberge (Fr.) Cranberry.

cannèlla (It.) Cinnamon; the French word is *cannelle.*

cannellini (It.) White kidney beans.

cannelloni (It.) Pasta squares usually boiled, stuffed, rolled, and baked in a sauce.

cannoli (It.) Pastry tubes or horns filled with ricotta cheese, chocolate, and candied citron.

Cantal (Fr.) A cows' milk cheese from the French **Auvergne,** uncooked, pressed, and cured for three months; similar to **Cheddar,** this ancient cheese, known by the Romans, is cylindrical in shape with a nutty, full flavor.

cantaloupe See **muskmelon.**

Cantenac A town in the **Médoc** region of France that produces several excellent clarets.

capeado (Sp.) Dipped in batter and fried.

capelli d'angelo (It.) Angel hair pasta; the thinnest pasta, almost too fine to cut by hand. This pasta has recently become popular with the health-conscious, putting a new twist on the old riddle: which weighs less, a pound of angel hair or a pound of macaroni?

caper The bud or young fruit of a climbing plant, native to Africa and the Mediterranean, which is pickled to make a condiment; nasturtium buds or seeds are sometimes substituted.

capitolade (Fr.) Cooked chicken or other food, chopped and served in a sauce; a kind of chicken hash.

capitone (It.) Large conger eel.

capon A castrated male chicken, whose flesh is well fattened (it gains up to ten pounds in as many months). Capon is prepared like chicken, although its flesh has a distinctive taste of its own.

caponata (It.) A Sicilian vegetable salad of fried eggplant, onions, olives, anchovies, capers, and tomatoes.

cappelletti (It.) Small squares of pasta stuffed and shaped like little hats, hence their name; very similar to **tortellini.**

cappone (It.) Capon.

cappuccino (It.) **Espresso** coffee with hot frothy milk, often dusted with cocoa powder or cinnamon.

capretto (It.) Kid.

capsicum See **chili.**

carambola A fruit (commonly referred to as star fruit), native to Malaysia and pale yellow green, with five pointed ridges around the central core. It is star-shaped when sliced across.

caramel Sugar dissolved in water and cooked to a rich dark brown color; caramelized sugar is used in candy, desserts, stocks, and sauces.

caraway An herb in the parsley family whose anise-flavored seeds are used in making cheese, bread, and pastry, and whose milder leaves are used in cooking; a staple seasoning in German and Hungarian cuisine.

carbonado (Sp.) A beef stew from Argentina combining apples, pears, tomatoes, onions, and potatoes.

carbonara, alla (It.) A spaghetti sauce with bacon, eggs, Parmesan cheese, and (usually) cream.

carbonnade à la flamande (Bel.) A beef stew from Flanders flavored with bacon, onions, and a little brown sugar, and simmered in beer. The term *carbonnade* originally referred to meat cooked over charcoal.

carciòfo (It.) Artichoke.

cardamom A spice of the ginger family whose pungent seeds are dried and used in Oriental, Indian, and Middle Eastern cooking.

cardinal, à la (Fr.) A fish garnish of **béchamel** sauce flavored with truffle essence, lobster butter and slices, and cayenne pepper; *cardinal* sometimes refers to a brilliant red dessert sauce of pureed raspberries, strained and sweetened.

cardoon A vegetable cultivated for its stalks and tender leaves; closely related to the artichoke, although it looks different.

Carême, Antonin (1784–1833) A French chef who, by organizing the workings of the professional kitchen and thus grand classical cuisine, is regarded as its founder; Carême worked for many great patrons, but his fame rests mostly on his erudite books; see also **pièce montée** and **sauce.**

cari (Fr.) Curry.

carmine A red dye used for food coloring, obtained from the female cochineal insect.

carne (It. and Sp.) Meat.

carob An evergreen tree whose pods are eaten both fresh and dried; high in sugar and protein, carob is used for confectionery (often as a chocolate substitute) and in pharmaceuticals and animal feed; carob may be the biblical locusts—a mistranslation of locust bean—that St. John ate in the desert.

caroline (Fr.) A small savory éclair stuffed and eaten as an hors d'oeuvre.

carp A freshwater fish found in Asian, European, and American waters which, unless farmed, tends to live in muddy water; it is cooked and used in many ways, including **gefilte fish.**

carpaccio (It.) Very thin slices of raw beef fillet served with mustard sauce, mayonnaise, or olive oil and lemon juice.

carrageen, carragheen Commonly known as "Irish moss," really a seaweed that grows wild along the north Atlantic shore; the red plant is eaten fresh or dried, when it is bleached almost white; used in sweet and savory dishes and as an excellent source of gelatin.

carré d'agneau (Fr.) Loin or rack of lamb; *carré,* literally "square," can also mean best end of neck, sometimes of veal or pork as well as lamb or mutton.

carrots à la Vichy (Fr.) Sliced carrots cooked, if possible, in Vichy mineral water, with butter, a little sugar, and salt until glazed, and garnished with chopped parsley.

casaba A large winter melon or muskmelon with yellow ribbed skin and very pale flesh.

casalinga (It.) Homemade.

cascabel (Mex.) A small, round, dried chili pepper with a smooth reddish brown skin, about one inch across and fairly hot; its name (literally, rattlesnake) refers to its rattle.

cashew A kidney-shaped nut of an Amazonian tree much favored in South American, Indian, and Asian cooking; the nut is attached to an applelike false fruit; wine, vinegar, and liqueur are made from the cashew.

casing   The intestinal membrane that is cleaned and stuffed with sausage forcemeat; a synthetic tubing used similarly.

cassata   (It.)   Ice cream molded in contrastingly colored layers with candied fruits soaked in liqueur; also a rich chocolate dessert from Sicily combining layers of sponge cake and ricotta with candied fruits.

cassava   See **tapioca.**

cassia   A type of cinnamon often confused with cinnamon proper when sold in powdered form, as in the U.S.; cassia is reddish brown, cinnamon a lighter tan.

cassis   (Fr.)   Black currant; a liqueur made from black currants is called *crème de cassis* and it is used alone or mixed to make apéritifs such as *Kir*—white wine colored with a few drops of *cassis*—or *Kir royale,* made with Champagne.

cassoulet   (Fr.)   A stew of dried haricot beans baked with various meats (usually pork and mutton), preserved goose or duck, onions, etc., in an earthenware pot; from the **Languedoc** region.

castagna   (It.)   Chestnut.

caster sugar   (Brit.)   Superfine sugar.

catalane, à la   (Fr.)   Garnished with sautéed eggplant and rice pilaf, and sometimes also with tomatoes.

catfish   A fresh- and saltwater fish with a slick, scaleless skin, sharp, poisonous spines, and "whiskers" (hence its name); the catfish is very popular in the southern United States where it is increasingly farmed; cooked in various ways, especially deep-fried, usually pan-dressed, steaked, or filleted.

caudle   (Brit.)   A hot spiced drink, often including wine or ale, with a cereal base; a favorite cold-weather beverage in England and Scotland.

caul   The thin, fatty membrane, like netted lace, from a pig's or sheep's intestines; used to contain and cover **pâtés,** roasts, etc.; the fat melts away during cooking.

cave   (Fr.)   Wine cellar.

caviar   Sturgeon roe, especially beluga, but loosely used for other fish roe.

cavolfiore   (It.)   Cauliflower.

cavolo   (It.)   Cabbage.

cayenne pepper   Red chili pepper, dried and ground fine; in Mexico this pepper, about three inches long, is widely available fresh year-round.

cazuela   (Sp.)   Earthenware casserole.

cebiche   (Sp.)   See **seviche.**

cebolla   (Sp.)   Onion.

Cebreto   (Sp.)   A blue-veined cheese with a creamy texture and yellow rind.

ceci   (It. and Sp.)   Chick-peas, garbanzo beans.

celeriac   Celery root—a variety of celery cultivated for its fat, bulbous root rather than its stalks; best when peeled and shredded for salads and hors d'oeuvre.

cellophane noodles   See **fĕn sī.**

cena   (It. and Sp.)   Supper.

cèpe   (Fr.)   See **boletus.**

cerdo   (Sp.)   Pork.

cerfeuil   (Fr.)   Chervil.

cerise   (Fr.)   Cherry.

cervelas   (Fr.)   A sausage of pork meat and fat (and formerly brains), flavored with garlic; also called *saucisson de Paris;* some nouvelle cuisine seafood sausages are called *cervelas.*

cervelles   (Fr.)   Brains.

cerveza   (Sp.)   Beer.

cèrvo   (It.)   Venison.

cetriòlo   (It.)   Cucumber.

Chabichou   (Fr.)   A goats' milk cheese from Poitou, France, small and conical or cylindrical in shape, soft and mild in flavor; also called *Chabi.*

Chablis   (Fr.)   A small town and its environs in Burgundy, southeast of Paris, producing a well-known white wine of the same name from the **Chardonnay** grape; dry, clean, "flinty," pale-colored, it can vary widely in quality; in other countries, the term *Chablis* has little meaning.

chafing dish   A metal pan or dish heated from below with a flame, hot coals, or electricity, for warming or cooking food; from the French word *chauffer,* to heat.

chah   (Ind.)   Tea.

challah   (Jew.)   Traditional Sabbath bread, made with oil, water, egg yolks, and honey, and baked in a braided loaf; for holidays it is often baked in a braided knot or spiral with raisins.

chalupa   (Mex.)   A boat-shaped **tortilla,** stuffed variously.

Chambertin   A vineyard in the **Côte d'Or** producing exceptional red Burgundy; ancient and celebrated, it is well worth its expense; Alexandre Dumas, who was not a wine drinker, wrote that "nothing makes the future look so rosy as to contemplate it through a glass of Chambertin."

Chambolle-Musigny   A village in the **Côte d'Or** of Burgundy that produces delicate, aromatic, and excellent red wines.

chambrer   (Fr.)   To bring wines up from the cellar to allow them to rise to room temperature before serving.

Champagne   Sparkling white wine from the French region of Champagne, made by a specific process from particular grapes, strictly delineated by law; properly speaking, only these wines should be called *Champagne*, although the term is used loosely, especially in California.

champignon (Fr.) Mushroom.

channa (Ind.) Chick-peas.

chanterelle (Fr.) A wild mushroom, yellow and trumpet-shaped with a ruffled edge; before being used in cooking, *chanterelles* are heated with salt in a covered pan to disgorge their liquid and then drained.

Chantilly (Fr.) Whipped cream, sweetened and sometimes flavored with vanilla or liqueur; also **hollandaise** or **mayonnaise** with whipped cream folded in at the last minute; a kind of **mousseline.**

chǎo (Chin.) To stir-fry.

chap The lower cheek or jaw of a pig.

chapelure (Fr.) Brown breadcrumbs.

chapon (Fr.) A heel of bread rubbed with garlic and olive oil; can be either rubbed along the rim of the salad bowl to impart its flavor or added to the salad itself; not necessarily removed before serving; *chapon* also means **capon.**

chaptalization A method of adding sugar to grape juice before fermentation, especially in bad years in cooler climates, to enable wine to reach minimum alcoholic content; a process not necessarily but often abused. Named for Chaptal, a French chemist (and Napoleon's Minister of Agriculture).

char A member of the **trout** and **salmon** family; the Arctic char is particularly good for eating.

charcuterie (Fr.) The art of preparing meat, especially pork; the meat specialties, such as sausages, ham, **rillettes, galantines,** and **pâtés,** made in a French butcher's shop.

charcutière (Fr.) Sauce **Robert** with julienne of gherkins added just before serving; served primarily with grilled pork chops and other meats.

Chardonnay A grape variety from which many excellent white wines are made.

charentais (Fr.) A sweet and succulent French melon with yellow green ribbed skin and orange flesh.

charlotte (Fr.) A classic dessert, originally an apple compote in a pail-shaped mold lined with buttered bread and served hot. **Carême** elevated this to **Bavarian cream** in a ladyfinger-lined mold to make *charlotte russe.* A *charlotte royale* replaces the ladyfingers with sponge cake cut into many thin layers sandwiched with jam; in a further elaboration, *charlotte royale à l'ancienne,* thin layers of jelly roll line a shallow mold filled with Bavarian cream.

Charolais (Fr.) French cattle fed on grass rather than grain (as in the U.S.), producing the lean but flavorful beef favored in France; also a **chèvre** from the *Charolais* region of Burgundy.

Chartreuse (Fr.) A liqueur made by Carthusian monks, originally in Grenoble but now largely in Voiron, France, and Tarragona, Spain; the liqueur comes in two types, yellow and green, the latter being higher proof.

Chassagne-Montrachet A **commune** in the southern **Côte d'Or** producing outstanding white wines and very good reds.

Chasselas (Fr.) A white grape variety, producing a light and fruity wine; although it does not make the best wines, it is valued for its hardiness and productivity and cultivated extensively, especially in Switzerland.

chasseur (Fr.) A classic sauce of sliced sautéed mushrooms and shallots reduced with white wine, enriched with **demi-glace** and butter, and finished with chopped parsley; *chasseur* is the French word for hunter.

château-bottled Wine bottled where it was produced by the vineyard owner, especially in Bordeaux; this term ensures authenticity, if not quality, from the better vineyards; a statement such as *"Mise en bouteilles au Domaine"* or *" . . . par le Propriétaire"* should be on the main wine label.

chateaubriand (Fr.) Beef cut from the middle of the fillet, grilled and garnished with **château potatoes** and **béarnaise sauce**; *chateaubriand sauce* is a reduction of white wine, shallots, herbs, and mushrooms, with **demi-glace** and butter added.

Châteauneuf-du-Pape A famous red wine from the village of the same name in the Rhône Valley, near Avignon, the site of the French pope's summer home in the fourteenth century.

château potatoes (Fr.) Potatoes cut into small ovals and sautéed in butter.

chatni (Ind.) Chutney; a condiment, originally created to accompany Indian curries, of fruit and spices cooked with vinegar and sugar as a preservative; much loved by the English and anglicized into chutney.

chaud-froid (Fr.) Poultry, game, or meat that is cooked but served cold, usually covered with aspic or a special sauce and highly garnished.

chausson aux pommes (Fr.) Apple turnover.

Chavignol (Fr.) A small, soft French goats' milk cheese from Sancerre.

chayote (Sp.) A vegetable of the melon and gourd family, with a prickly ribbed skin and pear shape; native to Mexico and the Antilles, it is often used in Spanish cooking and is prepared in a wide variety of ways; also called custard marrow and *mirliton*.

Cheddar A whole-milk cows' cheese, originally from Somerset, England, in which the curd is scalded, pressed, and aged; this style is made in factories the world over, while true farmhouse Cheddar, made with unpasteurized milk, wrapped in cloth, and matured for six months to two years, is one of the great cheeses; the technique called *cheddaring* is a combination of milling and turning the curd.

chef de cuisine (Fr.) Executive chef.

chef de partie (Fr.) Section chef, such as *saucier* or **pâtissier.**

chemiser (Fr.) To coat a mold with aspic, ice cream, or some other lining; *en chemise*, literally "in a shirt," means any food in a coating, such as potatoes in their jackets or ice cream covered with a thin brittle layer of chocolate.

Chenin Blanc (Fr.) A grape variety from which excellent white wine is made.

cherimoya A tropical South American tree of the custard apple family with large green-skinned fruit; after peeling the smooth or scaly skin, the interior pulp is eaten raw and unsweetened; its taste is somewhere between that of the pineapple and the strawberry.

Cherry Heering (Den.) Brandy distilled from cherries, including a high proportion of stones.

chervil An herb of the parsley family, originating in Russia and the Middle East and known from ancient times; its delicate flavor, slightly aniselike, is lost in stewing and drying, so it is best used fresh.

Cheshire An English cows' milk cheese, cooked, hard-pressed, and aged, made in red (with **annatto**), white (uncolored), and blue; a venerable cheese that cannot be made elsewhere because of the special salty Cheshire pastureland; called *Chester* on the continent.

Chester See **Cheshire.**

cheveux d'ange (Fr.) Angel hair pasta, the thinnest **vermicelli.** See also **capelli d'angelo.**

chèvre (Fr.) Goat; by extension, goats' milk cheese that, properly speaking, is soft and fresh, uncooked and unpressed; specific *chèvre* cheeses are individually entered.

chevreuil (Fr.) Venison; roebuck.

Chevrotin (Fr.) A cheese of goats' milk, or occasionally a mixture of goats' and cows' milk, from Savoy; the cheese is uncooked, pressed, and shaped in a small disc.

Chianti (It.) A red Italian table wine, ranging from pleasant to exceptional; very popular abroad as well as in its native Tuscany; *Chianti Classico* is particularly distinguished; Chianti bottles, or *fiaschi,* are shipped in their familiar woven-straw coverings.

Chiaretto (It.) An Italian rosé wine produced near Lake Garda; light, fresh, and agreeable; *Chiarello* is virtually the same wine.

chicken-fried steak Steak dipped in batter and fried crisp like chicken; a Black American specialty.

chicken à la Kiev Boned chicken breast rolled up to enclose an herb-flavored butter, egg-and-breadcrumbed, and deep-fried; the delicious butter has been known to squirt out on the unwary diner.

chicken paprikash   See **paprikás csirke.**

chicken steak   A cut of beef from the **chuck,** in small individual portions with a characteristic white streak down the center.

chicken Tetrazzini   Strips of cooked chicken and spaghetti in a cream sauce flavored with sherry and Parmesan, *gratiné;* named for the Italian coloratura soprano Luisa Tetrazzini.

chick-pea   A round legume, often dried, used extensively in Mediterranean, Middle Eastern, Indian, and Mexican cooking; an important ingredient in **couscous, hummus,** and many soups and stews.

chicory   A group of related plants—including **Belgian endive, radicchio, escarole,** wild chicory (the roots of the latter are roasted and used to flavor coffee), and a bitter green often called curly endive, which is cooked or used in salads.

chiffonnade   (Fr.)   Leaf vegetables sliced into very thin strips, particularly lettuce and **sorrel** shredded and sautéed in butter.

chilaquiles   (Mex.)   **Tortillas** layered with beans, ham, chicken, tomato sauce, and cheese.

Child, Lydia Maria (1802–1880)   An American abolitionist and author whose cookbook, *The American Frugal Housewife* (1829), gained wide popularity due to its common sense and directness.

chili   The fruit of the pepper plant, from the *Capsicum* family, ranging in its many varieties from mild to fiery hot; the pungency is concentrated in the white tissue attached to the seeds, which should be handled with care. Originating in South America, chili peppers are used in many cuisines the world over; in common usage the word *chili* implies hot peppers. No relation to **black pepper,** an error first made by Columbus, who thought the chilies in the West Indies were the black pepper of the Indies. The plural of the Spanish word *chile* is *chiles;* the English spelling is either *chili* or *chilli,* with the plural *chilies* or *chillies*—a source of much confusion.

chili con carne   A Mexican-American dish of beef highly seasoned with *chili* peppers and other spices and herbs; there are many variations, the subject of considerable controversy.

chilindrón, a la   (Sp.)   See **pollo a la chilindrón.**

chili powder   Dried crushed chili peppers with other dried spices and herbs, including onion, garlic, cumin, cloves, coriander, and oregano.

Chincoteague   A species of oyster from the Chesapeake Bay region, closely related to the **Blue Point.**

chine   To separate the backbone from the ribs of a roast to make carving easier.

Chinese anise   See **ba jiao.**

Chinese beans   "Yard-long" beans, also called asparagus beans; bright green in color.

Chinese gooseberry   See **kiwi.**

Chinese parsley　Coriander.

Chinese sausages　Sausages usually of pork meat and fat, spiced and dried, and reddish in color; sometimes pork liver or even duck liver sausages are available in Chinese groceries in the U.S.

chinois　(Fr.)　A fine-mesh conical sieve shaped like a coolie hat—hence its name.

chinook　See **salmon.**

chipolata　(Sp.)　A small sausage flavored with chives; in classical French cuisine the term designates a garnish of the sausages with braised chestnuts, diced pork, and glazed onions and carrots.

chipotle　(Mex.)　A brownish red chili pepper with wrinkled skin; dried, smoked, and often canned, this chili is very hot and has a distinctive smoky flavor.

chiqueter　(Fr.)　To flute the edges of pastry with the fingertips.

chitterlings, chitlings　The small intestines of animals, usually pigs, often cleaned and filled with scraps to make sausages which go by the same name; popular in Black and southern American cooking.

chive　An herb of the onion family, whose tall thin leaves delicately flavor savory foods.

chlodnik　(Pol.)　A cold summer soup of beet greens and roots, cucumbers, and onions, flavored with herbs, vinegar, and **kvass,** and garnished with sour cream; a warm-weather variety of **borsch.**

cholent　(Jew.)　**Brisket** with potatoes, lima beans, and pearl barley, slowly cooked overnight to be ready for the Sabbath.

chongos　(Sp.)　A custard pudding with lemon and cinnamon.

chorizo　(Sp.)　A spicy sausage used in Spanish cooking, made of pork meat and fat and flavored with garlic and spices.

Choron　(Fr.)　In classical French cuisine, **béarnaise** sauce colored pink with a little tomato puree.

chou　(Fr.)　Cabbage.

choucroute　(Fr.)　**Sauerkraut.**

chou farci　(Fr.)　Stuffed cabbage.

chou-fleur　(Fr.)　Cauliflower.

choux de Bruxelles　(Fr.)　Brussels sprouts.

choux pastry　See **pâte à choux.**

chow-chow　A Chinese-American vegetable pickle flavored with mustard; the original Chinese condiment consisted of orange peel in a thick syrup, flavored with ginger and other spices.

chowder　A thick soup, made from various foodstuffs; the word comes from the French *chaudière,* the iron cauldron in which it was cooked, which in turn derives from the Latin word for "warm." Today, chowder is usually made of seafood or perhaps vegetables, with a milk base.

chuck　Cut of beef from the forequarter, between the neck and shoulder, usually best for stewing or braising.

chuleta (Sp.) Chop.

chūn juăn (Chin.) Spring roll; a thin, round **lumpia** wrapper made from flour and water, stuffed with various fillings, such as shrimp, pork, and black mushrooms, wrapped up, and deep-fried to a golden brown; this authentic Chinese food is served at the spring festival to celebrate the Chinese New Year, and its elegant appearance is said "to resemble a bar of gold"; not to be confused with **cai juan.**

chutney (Ind.) See **chatni.**

ciboulette (Fr.) Chives.

cicely, sweet cicely A fragrant herb of the parsley family little used today, whose anise-flavored leaves and seeds contribute to salads and **bouquets garnis.**

cider Apple juice, or sometimes another fruit juice, either fermented or not. In the U.S., sweet cider is unfermented, while hard cider is slightly alcoholic; in Europe, fermented cider can range widely in alcoholic content and is often sparkling. Cider can also be made into apple brandy or vinegar and is often used in cooking in any of its many forms.

cigala (Sp.) Saltwater **crayfish,** a small lobster; the British call it a Dublin Bay prawn, the French *langoustine,* the Italian *scampo.*

cilantro (Sp.) Fresh **coriander** leaf.

ciliègia (It.) Cherry.

Cincho (Sp.) A ewes' milk cheese, from Spain; hard and pungent, similar to **Villalón.**

cinnamon A spice from the dried bark of an evergreen tree indigenous to Asia and used since the Egyptians (third millennium B.C.); cinnamon was one of the most desirable eastern spices from ancient to medieval times, but is now mainly relegated to flavoring desserts, at least in the west. Cinnamon is often confused with its close relative **cassia,** especially in powdered form.

cioccolata (It.) Chocolate.

cioppino A fisherman's stew, often made with tomatoes; originally the *ciuppin* of Genoa, by way of San Francisco, where it is a favorite.

cipolla (It.) Onion.

cisco A North American lake **whitefish,** usually smoked.

ciseler (Fr.) To cut into julienne strips or shred as for a **chiffonnade;** to score a whole fish to hasten cooking.

citron A fruit of the citrus family, resembling a large, lumpy lemon; cultivated for its thick rind, which is candied or pressed; its oil is used in making liqueurs, perfume, and medicine.

citron (Fr.) Lemon; *citron vert* means lime.

civet (Fr.) A stew of furred game, cooked with red wine, onions, mushrooms, and **lardons,** and thickened with the animal's blood.

civette (Fr.) Chives.

clabber Buttermilk—soured, thickened milk that has not yet separated.

clafouti (Fr.) A pudding from Limousin made of small fruit, such as cherries or plums, with a thick egg batter poured over and baked.

clam A saltwater bivalve **mollusk** in many varieties, generally divided into hard-shell (see **quahog**), which are eaten raw or cooked, and soft-shell, usually eaten cooked.

Clamart, à la (Fr.) Garnished with peas.

clambake See **New England clambake.**

claret The British term for red **Bordeaux** wine.

clarified butter Butter that has been heated to separate the impurities, thus allowing their easy removal; butter so treated has a higher burning point and clearer color but less flavor; also called drawn butter.

clarify To remove all impurities from stock or jelly (usually with egg white) or from fat.

classed or **classified growth** Wine, especially from the French **Bordeaux,** that has been officially ranked, usually by the Classification of 1855 for Médoc. At that time, the best vineyards and estates were ranked *Cru Classé* ("Classed Growth"), including the five official Growths— *Premier Cru* (First Growth) through *Cinquième Cru* (Fifth Growth)— and various lower rankings, such as *Cru Exceptionnel, Cru Bourgeois Supérieur,* and *Cru Bourgeois.* (These latter were often fine wines and not "inferior" at all in the usual sense.) Since only Médoc and Sauternes were included in the 1855 Classification, many excellent wines were omitted altogether.

clementine A hybrid produced by crossing the orange with the tangerine; small, sweet, and seedless.

clos (Fr.) A specific vineyard, usually one of distinction, such as *Clos de Vougeot* of the **Côte d'Or** in Burgundy.

clotted cream (Brit.) Cream skimmed from scalded milk and slowly warmed until it thickens; a specialty of Devonshire, England.

cloud ear See **yún ěr.**

clou de girofle (Fr.) Clove; *clouté* means studded.

clove The dried bud of an east Indian evergreen tree known since ancient times and a desirable commodity in the medieval spice trade; the name derives from the Latin word for nail, *clavus.*

club steak A cut of beef from the **loin** between the **T-bone** and **rib** section; tender and flavorful, it is the same as a **strip loin** unboned.

cobbler A deep-dish fruit pie with a thick top crust of biscuit dough.

cocada (Sp.) Coconut custard.

cochineal See **carmine.**

cochino (Sp.) Pig; a suckling pig is *cochinillo.*

cochon (Fr.) Pig; the culinary term, like that in English, is *porc.*

cocido (Sp.) Stew; also means cooked, as opposed to fresh.

cock-a-leekie (Scot.) A soup made from chicken broth, leeks, and sometimes prunes and pieces of chicken.

cocoa The remaining nibs in chocolate manufacture after the chocolate butter is liquefied; the pods of the **cacao** tree are fermented, roasted, and ground until the chocolate butter is liquefied, leaving the nibs, which are then powdered to make cocoa. Cocoa is thus much lower in fat than chocolate proper.

cocotte (Fr.) Casserole; a cooking pot with a closely fitted lid for slow braising or stewing.

cod A fish with great historic importance for its economic value in centuries past and an essential part of the triangle that supported the slave trade. Cod meat is lean, firm, white, and mild, with a large flake, suitable fresh for diverse cooking methods and with many flavors. Salted, smoked, or dried, it can be preserved for long periods; as *morue,* **brandade,** *bacalao, bacalhau,* **lutefisk,** and **finnan haddie** it is often preferred to fresh cod. Haddock, hake, and pollock are members of the cod family.

coda di bue (It.) Oxtail.

codorniz (Sp.) Quail.

coeur à la crème (Fr.) A cream-cheese dessert from provincial France in which heavy cream and cream cheese are combined and molded in a heart-shaped form that allows the whey to drain off, then turned out and garnished with strawberries or other berries.

Cognac Brandy, blended and aged, from the French town of the same name in the Charentes district north of Bordeaux.

coing (Fr.) Quince.

Cointreau A colorless orange-flavored French liqueur, formerly called Triple Sec White **Curaçao.**

col (Sp.) Cabbage.

Colbert, à la (Fr.) Fish dipped in egg, breadcrumbed, and fried; *Colbert* butter is a chicken or meat glaze made of butter, chopped parsley, and perhaps tarragon.

Colby An American variety of Cheddar cheese; a washed-curd cheese, originally from Colby, Wisconsin.

colcannon (Ir.) A peasant dish of cabbage, potatoes, leeks, and milk, traditionally eaten at Halloween with a "treasure," such as a ring, coin, thimble, or button hidden within.

colère, en (Fr.) Fish, usually whiting, cooked with its tail in its mouth, giving it a so-called "angry" look; often dipped in egg, breadcrumbed, and deep-fried, and served *à la française,* with a tomato sauce.

coliflor (Sp.) Cauliflower.

colin (Fr.) Hake.

collage (Fr.) **Fining.**

collard, collard greens A type of cabbage whose leaves do not form a head; highly nutritious and able to withstand very hot and very cold temperatures; it is a favorite country vegetable in the southern U.S., where it is called collard greens.

collé (Fr.) With gelatin added.

collop (Brit.) A thin slice of meat; an old term that has been used variously but now usually means a **scallop** of meat or fish.

colza See **rape.**

comal (Mex.) A cast-iron griddle or earthenware plate for making **tortillas.**

commis (Fr.) Apprentice.

commune (Fr.) A township or village and its surrounding land; frequently used to describe wine-producing regions.

composé(e) (Fr.) A term describing a salad that is arranged or composed in its serving dish or plate, rather than tossed.

compote (Fr.) A dish of fresh or dried fruit stewed slowly in syrup to keep its shape, often flavored with liqueur and spices and served cold.

compound butter Butter combined with other seasonings such as herbs, shallots, and wine.

concasser (Fr.) To pound in a mortar or chop roughly; often applied to tomatoes that have been peeled, seeded, and chopped for sauce; *concassé* is the adjective.

conch A gastropod mollusk usually eaten in chowder or salad, mostly in Florida and the Caribbean. Conch is also the name of the curved trough, resembling the shell, in which refined chocolate particles are churned with **cocoa** butter to a smooth liquid; this process, essential to high-quality melting chocolate, is called conching.

conchiglia (It.) Shellfish; pasta in the shape of a conch shell.

concombre (Fr.) Cucumber.

Condé (Fr.) With rice; also a pastry strip covered with almond icing and many other sweet or savory dishes, often with rice.

condensed milk Milk with its water content reduced by slightly more than half, sterilized, homogenized, and canned; sweetened condensed milk has sugar added as a preservative and may not be sterilized; both types taste sweeter than regular milk.

condiment Relish, pickle, or seasoning, highly aromatic, that accompanies food at the table and stimulates the appetite.

conejo (Sp.) Rabbit.

confectioners' sugar Powdered white sugar, not crystallized like superfine sugar, useful for its ability to dissolve quickly.

confectionery The art of sugar working or candy making.

confiserie (Fr.) Confectionery, confectioner's shop; *confiseur* means confectioner in French.

confit (Fr.) Pork, goose, duck, or other meat, cooked and preserved in its own fat; a specialty of Gascony in southwestern France; also fruits and vegetables cooked and preserved in a brandy or liquor syrup.

confiture (Fr.) Preserve, jam.

cōng (Chin.) Scallion; *yáng cōng* (literally, "Occidental scallion") means onion.

coniglio (It.) Rabbit.

consommé (Fr.) Clear broth; meat, chicken, game, or fish stock flavored with vegetables, strained, reduced, and usually clarified.

copeaux en chocolat (Fr.) Chocolate shavings.

coq au vin (Fr.) Chicken cut up and braised with onions, mushrooms, and lardoons in red wine.

coquillage (Fr.) Shellfish.

coquille de (Fr.) Served in a scallop shell.

coquille Saint-Jacques (Fr.) Scallop.

coral Lobster roe, which turns red when cooked; used for sauces and butters.

coratèlla (It.) Organ meats.

cordero (Sp.) Lamb; a suckling or milk-fed lamb is *cordero lechazo* or *lechal.*

Cordon Bleu The "blue ribbon" awarded to outstanding women chefs, a tradition going back to a story, perhaps apocryphal, of Madame de Pompadour and Louis XV; the name also designates a dish of chicken or veal scallops cooked with cheese and ham, which came from the Cordon Bleu cooking school in Paris in the early twentieth century.

coriander An herb valued both for its dried seeds and fresh leaves; used extensively in Oriental, Indian, and Spanish cooking; the Spanish word for fresh coriander is *cilantro.*

corn A new-world grain from Central America, upon which the pre-Columbian cultures were founded; still the main food crop on the American continent (in the U.S. indirectly, through livestock and dairy feed). Columbus brought corn, or maize, to the Old World, where it has slowly gained acceptance. Corn, of which there are countless varieties, cannot sow itself and is therefore unknown in the wild. In Europe, corn is the generic name for whatever grain is dominant in a particular area. See also **polenta.**

corned beef Salted and spiced brisket of beef, the traditional ingredient of **New England boiled dinner.** "Corned" means granulated; hence, corning means to preserve with salt.

cornet (Fr.) A horn-shaped pastry stuffed with sweetened whipped cream; a slice of meat, such as ham, rolled into a cone and often filled, for a garnish or hors d'oeuvre.

corn flour (Brit.) See **cornstarch**.

Cornish hen   See **Rock Cornish game hen.**

Cornish pasty   (Brit.)   A pastry turnover enclosing a meat or vegetable filling; originally from Cornwall.

corn pone   Cornmeal dough shaped into ovals and deep-fried or baked; a southern American bread served with butter and sometimes **pot liquor;** the word *pone* is of American Indian origin.

corn salad   See **lamb's lettuce.**

cornstarch   Very fine white flour milled from corn; used as a thickening agent for sauces and sometimes for baking; used extensively in Chinese cooking; sometimes called corn flour.

Corton   (Fr.)   Excellent red and white wines from the village of Aloxe-Corton in the Côte de Beaune region of Burgundy.

cos   Romaine lettuce.

coscetto   (It.)   Leg of lamb.

còscia   (It.)   Thigh, as of chicken; leg, as of lamb.

cosciotto, coscetto   (It.)   Leg of lamb; haunch.

costata   (It.)   Rib chop.

costoletta, cotoletta   (It.)   Chop or cutlet.

côte   (Fr.)   Rib or chop.

cotechino   (It.)   A large fresh sausage made with pork meat and rind and seasoned with nutmeg and cloves; sometimes delicate, sometimes very spicy.

Côte de Beaune   (Fr.)   See **Côte d'Or.**

Côte de Nuits   (Fr.)   See **Côte d'Or.**

Côte d'Or   (Fr.)   A narrow strip of hillside along the Saône River Valley in Burgundy, southeast of Paris, comprising the *Côte de Dijon* in the uppermost part, the *Côte de Nuits* in the middle, and the *Côte de Beaune* in the southernmost part; in the latter two most of the greatest French wines are produced, hence the meaning of its name, "golden slope."

côtelette   (Fr.)   Cutlet.

Côte Rôtie   (Fr.)   A famous red wine from steep slopes overlooking the Rhône River.

Côtes de Provence   (Fr.)   Red, white, and rosé wines produced on the southern coast of France between Nice and Marseilles; light, pleasant, fairly inexpensive, and popular.

Côtes du Rhône   (Fr.)   Pleasant but undistinguished wines, mostly red, from the Rhône Valley between Vienne and Avignon; the finer wines of the region are sold under more specific **appellations.**

cotriade   (Fr.)   A fish soup from Brittany.

cottage cheese   Fresh lumpy cheese made from skimmed pasteurized cows' milk in which the curds are washed; its taste is bland and slightly acid, lending itself to various flavorings; also used in salads, cheesecake, and even with fruit; it is high in protein but low in fat.

còtto (It.) Cooked.

coulibiac (Russ.) See **kulibyaka.**

coulis (Fr.) An old culinary term of some confusion; originally the strained juices from cooked meat, then a puree of chicken, game, or fish; now it usually means a **bisque** or thick sauce or puree, such as tomato.

Coulommiers (Fr.) A whole-milk cows' cheese from **Brie,** usually eaten fresh but sometimes molded and aged like Brie; shaped in wheels smaller than Brie, with a white rind flora; the interior is creamy white and increasingly flavorful with age.

country style spareribs A cut of pork—the backbones from the shoulder end of pork loin, cooked like breast **spareribs.**

courge (Fr.) Marrow, squash.

courgette (Brit.) Zucchini.

couronne, en (Fr.) In the shape of a crown; in a ring.

court bouillon (Fr.) Flavored acidulated stock for cooking food, primarily fish, but also vegetables and meat.

couscous A dish from Morocco, Tunisia, and Algeria prepared variously, but usually consisting of **semolina** steamed on top of a special two-part pot over meats and vegetables boiled below, served all together with a hot sauce.

couverture (Fr.) High-grade chocolate used especially for coating and ornamental work; it is semisweet and high in cocoa butter, giving it a glossy surface.

cozza (It.) Mussel.

crab A large and varied family of clawed crustaceans with delicate white meat; all true crabs are edible, and some of them are separately entered.

crackling The crisp brown skin of pork or sometimes poultry with all its fat rendered; sometimes baked into breads.

crapaudine, à la (Fr.) Poultry, especially small birds, trussed to look like toads.

crayfish A crustacean with many species, usually freshwater, varying widely in size but most often smaller than a lobster; these "dainties of the first order," as Audubon called them, are prized delicacies in many cuisines but largely ignored in the U.S., except for the **Creole** and **Cajun** cooking of Louisiana. The freshwater crayfish is sometimes called crawfish or (in French) *écrevisse;* the saltwater crayfish is also called crawfish, rock or spiny lobster, *langouste, langoustine* (in French), Dublin Bay prawn (in Britain), Norway lobster, and *scampo* (in Italy). There is considerable confusion among these terms.

cream The fatty part of milk, which rises to the surface unless homogenized. Single cream is 45 percent butterfat, measured by the percentage of dry matter rather than volume; double cream is 60 percent butterfat;

triple cream is 75 percent. In cheesemaking, additional cream must sometimes be added to the milk to bring it up to the degree of butterfat required.

cream cheese   Fresh unripened whole-milk cows' cheese, with a high fat content (varying with different types); in the U.S. this cheese is usually factory made, with stabilizers added to keep the whey from draining further, but there are many versions throughout the world.

cream puff pastry   See **pâte à choux.**

Crécy, à la   (Fr.)   With carrots; from the town of the same name, where the finest French carrots are grown.

crema   (Sp.)   Custard, cream.

crème à l'anglaise   (Fr.)   Custard.

crème brûlée   (Fr.)   Rich custard topped with a brittle layer of sugar (usually brown sugar), caramelized under the broiler just before serving.

crème Chantilly   (Fr.)   See **Chantilly.**

crème chiboust   (Fr.)   **Crème pâtissière** lightened with **Italian meringue,** usually stabilized with a little gelatin.

crème fraîche   (Fr.)   Heavy cream with a lactic culture introduced; the culture acts as a preservative and gives a characteristic tangy flavor; see also **fleurette.**

crème pâtissière   (Fr.)   Pastry cream—a custard of eggs, flour, milk, and sugar used to fill cream puffs, line tarts underneath fruit, and garnish various pastries.

crème pralinée   (Fr.)   **Crème pâtissière** flavored with powdered **praline;** used to fill **Paris-Brest** and other French pastries.

crème renversée   (Fr.)   Custard baked in a caramel-lined mold, chilled, and inverted for serving.

Creole   In Louisiana, food cooked in the Creole style usually begins with sautéed tomatoes, onions, celery, and sweet peppers, and often includes rice; it combines the many local influences—French, Spanish, Black, and Indian—in a unique way; see also **Cajun.** In classic French cuisine, *à la créole* designates a dish garnished with rice and containing sweet peppers, onion, and tomatoes cooked in oil.

crêpe   (Fr.)   A pancake made thin, light, and surprisingly strong from the eggy batter; invariably stuffed, spread, or served with moist mixtures, either savory or sweet.

crêpes Suzette   (Fr.)   **Crêpes** heated in a chafing dish at table with a sauce of orange juice and zest, butter, and orange-flavored liqueur, and flambéed.

crépinette   (Fr.)   A small French sausage wrapped in **caul** rather than casing, usually made of pork, and occasionally truffled; *crépine* is pig's **caul.**

Crescenza   See **Stracchino.**

crespella (It.) A pancake, usually stuffed like a **crêpe.**

crevette (Fr.) Shrimp.

croaker A large family of fish, sometimes called drum, found mostly in temperate western Atlantic waters; it is named for the noise it makes during spawning season; croaker is excellent in various culinary preparations but should not be eaten raw.

croissant A light yeast-dough pastry layered like puff pastry, rolled into a "crescent" shape, sometimes stuffed, and baked; an indispensable part of the French breakfast. In 1686 the bakers of Budapest heard the Turks tunneling into the city by night and sounded the alarm. The grateful city gave them the privilege of making this pastry, whose shape comes from the emblem on the Ottoman flag.

croquembouche (Fr.) Bite-size cream puffs piled high into a pyramid and cemented together with sugar glaze or caramel; other pastries and fruits arranged in a highly ornamented pile.

croque monsieur (Fr.) The French version of a grilled ham and cheese sandwich, often cooked in a special device; a *croque madame* is a cheese and chicken sandwich.

croquette Chopped meat or vegetables bound with a sauce, crumbed, and fried into a crisp, brown cylindrical shape; originally French.

cròsta, crostata, crostatina (It.) Crust, pie, tart.

crostacei (It.) Shellfish.

crostino (It.) **Crouton** or **croûte;** a small piece of toast.

Crottin de Chavignol (Fr.) A goats' milk cheese from Berry; semihard to hard, shaped in very small discs; aging brings out its goaty flavor, an acquired taste that is favored by connoisseurs; *crottin* literally means "dung."

croustade (Fr.) Hollowed bread or pastry that serves as a base for a savory puree or ragoût.

croûte (Fr.) A crust, shell, or piece of bread or dough used in various savory preparations; *en croûte* means encased in pastry.

croûton (Fr.) A small piece of bread or dough used for garnish; sautéed bread cubes.

crown roast Loin of pork or two loins of lamb from the rib section, tied into a crown, trimmed, and roasted; the ends of the rib bones are often decorated with paper frills, the center filled with a vegetable or starch stuffing.

cru (Fr.) Growth; that is, a specific vineyard and its wine; a vineyard of superior quality. See also **classed growth.**

crudités Raw food, usually vegetables, eaten before a meal to assuage hunger and stimulate the appetite.

crudo (It. and Sp.) Raw, fresh.

crustacean A class of arthropods, mostly water-dwelling, with a hard shell; includes all members of the **lobster, shrimp, crayfish,** and **crab** families.

cú (Chin.) Vinegar.

cuaresmeño (Mex.) A green chili pepper sometimes confused with the **jalapeño,** but actually darker, rounder, hotter, and less flavorful.

cube To cut food into cubes about ½ inch across; larger than **dice** or **mirepoix.**

cuisine minceur (Fr.) Light and healthful cooking for dieters, devised and advocated by three-star French chef Michel Guérard, substituting low-calorie ingredients in haute cuisine; not to be confused with **nouvelle cuisine.**

cuisse (Fr.) Drumstick; *cuisseau* means leg, usually of veal.

cuissot (Fr.) Haunch of venison or boar.

culotte (Fr.) Rump of beef.

Cumberland sauce Red-currant jelly dissolved with port and flavored with shallots, orange zest, and mustard—a traditional accompaniment to venison and other game.

cumin A spice made from the dried and ground seeds of the cumin plant; a relative of parsley, cumin is used in sweet and savory preparations in Germanic, Mediterranean, Middle Eastern, and Asian cooking, especially curries.

cuore (It.) Heart.

Curaçao (Neth.) A Dutch liqueur made from the dried peel of the green sour oranges found on the island of Curaçao in the Dutch Antilles; **Cointreau, triple sec,** and **Grand Marnier** are similar to Curaçao.

curd The solid residue of coagulated milk that separates from liquid whey after acidification in the cheesemaking process.

cure To age a food product, such as cheese, wine, vegetable, fish, or meat, in order to preserve it by methods such as drying, salting, or smoking.

curly endive See **chicory.**

Curnonsky The pen name of French gastronome, journalist, and food critic Maurice-Edmond Sailland (1872–1956); he encouraged interest in regional French cuisine and the development of the restaurant as we know it.

currant A small, black, seedless raisin originally grown near Corinth, Greece, from which its name is derived; no relation to the fruit of the same name.

curry A mixture of spices widely used in Indian cooking for thousands of years, originally as a preservative. Ground on a special stone, the particular spices vary according to individual taste, a specific dish, or regional preferences (those of the south tend to be hotter). The *masala,* or spice mixture, can be either wet (in which case it is ground with vinegar, coconut milk, or water and must be used immediately) or dry (in which case it is ground to a powder that can be kept for quite a while). The many spices (most entered separately) include turmeric, cumin, coriander, fenugreek, fennel seed, saffron, mace, nutmeg, cardamom, clove, cinnamon, poppy and sesame seeds, tamarind, onion, garlic, and chilies. See also **garam.**

custard apple   A general term for various tropical fruits, including the **cherimoya.**

custard marrow   See **chayote.**

cut in   To mix particles of fat, such as butter or lard, throughout flour with two knives or a pastry blender.

cutlet   A **scallop** of meat—usually a slice from the leg and preferably from one muscle.

cuvée   (Fr.)   A particular blend, lot, or batch of a certain wine.

cygne   (Fr.)   A swan made from **pâte à choux** and filled with **crème Chantilly.**

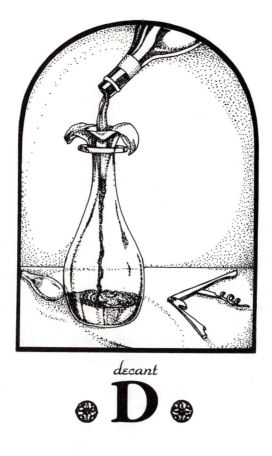

decant

❖ D ❖

---

dab See **flounder.**

dacquoise (Fr.) A pastry made of **meringue** combined with finely ground nuts, baked in discs, and filled with flavored whipped cream or buttercream and often fresh berries.

dahchini (Ind.) Cinnamon or cassia.

daikon (Jap.) A large radish used extensively in Japanese cooking, either in raw or cooked form.

daizu (Jap.) Dried soybeans.

dal (Ind.) Legumes of all sorts.

Dampfnudeln (Ger.) Yeast dumplings sweetened and served with fruit.

dàn (Chin.) Egg.

Danablu (Den.) A Danish blue cheese of whole raw cows' milk, made in the **Roquefort** style.

Danish pastry A yeast pastry filled with nuts, fruit, custard, or cheese, and iced; originally from Denmark, but much traveled since.

Daõ (Port.) Red and white table wines produced in the Daõ river valley in the town of Viseu in Portugal; they are full-bodied, deep in color, and made from the same grape varieties as **port.**

dariole   (Fr.)   A cylindridal mold, usually small; also a cake baked in such a mold.

Darjeeling   (Ind.)   A variety of tea from the Indian province of the same name.

darne   (Fr.)   Fish steak; a thick cross section of fish.

dashi   (Jap.)   Fish stock made of dried bonito and seaweed; used extensively in Japanese cooking.

dàttero   (It.)   Date.

daube, en   (Fr.)   Meat, usually beef, slowly braised in red wine and seasonings; stew; a *daubière* is a tight-lidded casserole for cooking *daubes,* originally with indentations in the lid for charcoal.

Daumont, à la   (Fr.)   A large fish garnished with quenelles, roe, mushrooms, and crayfish, served with **Nantua sauce.**

dauphine, à la   (Fr.)   Potato puree mixed with **pâte à choux** and deep-fried in balls or piped shapes.

dauphinois   (Fr.)   Usually means with walnuts; potatoes *à la dauphinoise* are sliced and baked with milk, egg yolk, nutmeg, **Gruyère,** and garlic.

daurade   (Fr.)   Gilthead **bream;** *dorade* is another type of bream.

débourbage   (Fr.)   Clearing of the sediment from newly pressed grape juice, especially white, by allowing it to settle for twenty-four hours before starting fermentation; this technique must be closely controlled.

debrecziner   (Hung.)   A sausage similar to a **Frankfurter** but spicier and coarser in texture.

decant   To transfer wine from bottle to carafe or decanter, in order to remove sediment before serving; decanting is practiced primarily with old red wines, whose bottles are held against the light of a candle to show sediment as it first appears.

découper   (Fr.)   To cut up, to carve.

deep-fry   To cook food immersed in a large amount of fat, thus sealing the outside while keeping the inside moist.

déglacer   (Fr.)   To deglaze by dissolving, with wine, stock, or other liquid, the sediment left in the pan after meat, poultry, or fish has been cooked in a small amount of fat.

dégorger   (Fr.)   To soak a food, such as sweetbreads, in cold water in order to cleanse it; also an important final step in making Champagne, whereby the sediment is removed from the bottle before the **dosage** and final cork are added.

dégraisser   (Fr.)   To remove grease from the surface of liquid, by skimming, or from a large piece of meat, by scraping or cutting.

dégustation   (Fr.)   Tasting or sampling.

Deidesheim A town in the German Palatinate producing excellent white wines, mostly Rieslings, with full body, fine bouquet, and varying sweetness.

Delmonico A boneless cut of beef from the rib section, roasted or cut into steaks; also called Spencer steak.

Demeltorte (Aus.) A pastry filled with candied fruit, from Demel's Café in Vienna.

demerara sugar Partially refined raw cane sugar, naturally light brown in color from the molasses.

demi, demie (Fr.) Half.

demi-deuil, à la (Fr.) Poultry and other pale-colored foods garnished with truffles to resemble "half-mourning"; with poultry, the truffle slices are slipped between the skin and breast meat.

demi-feuilletage (Fr.) See **rognures.**

demi-glace (Fr.) Brown sauce reduced by half—nearly to a glaze—with veal stock.

demijohn A large, narrow-necked wine bottle or jug of varying size, sometimes in a wicker or straw jacket; from the French *Dame Jeanne.*

demi-sec (Fr.) A term for Champagne and sparkling white wines denoting them as sweet, even though the literal meaning is "half-dry"; this is the sweetest category of Champagne.

demi-sel (Fr.) Soft, fresh, whole-milk cows' cheese from Normandy, in a small square.

Demi-Suisse See **Petit-Suisse.**

dénerver (Fr.) To remove gristle, tendons, membrane, etc., from meat.

denominazione controllata (It.) The Italian equivalent of **appellation contrôlée;** recently implemented.

dente, al (It.) Literally, to the bite; refers to pasta or vegetables cooked only until firm and crunchy, not soft and overdone.

dépecer (Fr.) To cut up, to carve.

deposit See **sediment.**

dépouiller (Fr.) To skim the fat or scum from the surface of a sauce or stock.

Derby or **Derbyshire** (Brit.) Cows' milk cheese, uncooked and hard, pale and mild, made in large flat rounds by a method similar to that of **Cheddar; Sage Derby** is flavored and colored with the herb.

deshebrar (Sp.) To shred.

désosser (Fr.) To bone.

détrempe (Fr.) Dough of flour and water in which a layer of butter is encased in the making of **pâte feuilletée.**

Devonshire cream (Brit.) See **clotted cream.**

diable, à la (Fr.) Deviled—food, usually meat or poultry, spiced with mustard, vinegar, or hot seasoning, coated with breadcrumbs, and grilled; *sauce diable* is **demi-glace** with white wine or vinegar and cayenne pepper.

diablotins   (Fr.)   Cheese-flavored **croûtes** or **choux** for garnishing soup.

dice   Small squares of food, technically smaller than a cube.

dicke Bohnen mit Rauchfleisch   (Ger.)   A Westphalian dish of broad beans with bacon and smoked pork belly.

dieppoise, à la   (Fr.)   Saltwater fish garnished with mussels and crayfish in a white-wine reduction sauce.

Dijon   The capital of Burgundy; Dijon mustard has a white-wine base; *à la dijonnaise* means with a mustard-flavored sauce.

dill   An herb whose seeds and leaves flavor sweet and savory foods, especially in northern and eastern European countries; in the U.S. it is commonly used with vinegar for pickling cucumbers.

dím sàm   (Chin.)   Small dishes, such as various dumplings, fried shrimp balls, spare ribs, or fried spring rolls, eaten for snacks during the day; served in restaurants specializing in these dishes, which are from Canton; commonly spelled *dim sum,* it means "little heart."

dim sum   See **dím sàm.**

dinde   (Fr.)   Turkey hen; *dindon* is a cock, *dindonneau* a young turkey.

Dionysus   See **Bacchus.**

diplomat pudding   (Brit.)   A molded dessert of ladyfingers soaked with candied fruit in liqueur or brandy and layered alternately with custard; diplomat sauce is **sauce normande** with lobster butter, garnished with diced lobster and truffles.

disossato   (It.)   Boned.

Dobostorte   (Hung.)   Thin layers of sponge cake spread with chocolate cream, stacked, and glazed with hot caramel; created by the Austrian *pâtissier* Josef Dobos.

dodine   (Fr.)   See **ballotine.**

dolce   (It.)   Sweet; the plural, *i dolci,* means desserts.

Dolcelatte   (It.)   A mild blue-veined cheese, a younger and sweeter type of **Gorgonzola.**

Dolcetto   (It.)   A grape variety, grown in Piedmont, used in Italian red wines; soft and early-maturing.

dolma   (Turk.)   A stuffed leaf or other vegetable; usually a blanched grape leaf filled with rice and ground lamb and braised in stock, oil, and lemon juice.

domaine   (Fr.)   Vineyards comprising a single property, whether or not they are contiguous; in Bordeaux and Provence, the word means *château;* the German word is *Domaene.*

Dom Perignon   A Benedictine monk, cellar-master at the Abbey of Hautvilliers, whom tradition credits with the invention of the process for making Champagne; now the brand name of the best wine produced by Moët et Chandon.

donburi (Jap.) A bowl of rice topped with a mixture of leftovers.

dōng gū (Chin.) Dried black mushrooms with a strong smoky flavor.

Doppelbock (Ger.) Extra strong **Bock** beer.

dorage (Fr.) See **dorure.**

dorato (It.) Dipped in egg batter and fried to a golden color.

dorée (Fr.) **John Dory** or *Saint-Pierre.*

Doria (Fr.) In classical French cuisine, a garnish for fish of cucumbers that are shaped into small ovals and simmered in butter.

Dorsch (Ger.) Cod.

dorure (Fr.) Egg wash for "gilding" pastry, made by beating together egg or egg yolk and a little water and brushing a thin layer on the surface of the pastry to color during baking.

dosage (Fr.) Sugar syrup added to bottled wine after the *dégorgement* (during the Champagne process), the amount of which determines the degree of sweetness of the finished wine.

dòu (Chin.) Bean.

double boiler See **bain-marie.**

Double Gloucester (Brit.) Cows' milk cheese with a rich, mellow flavor, dense almost waxy texture, and deep yellow color from **annatto** dye, made in large flat rounds; so named because this English cheese, made from the whole milk of two milkings of the Gloucester cow, is twice as large as **Single Gloucester.**

dòu fu (Chin.) Bean curd or **tōfu;** the Chinese *dòu fu* is drier and firmer than the Japanese **tōfu.**

dough Flour or meal mixed with water, milk, or other liquid, for making bread or pastry.

Douro Valley River valley in Portugal where **port** is made.

doux, douce (Fr.) Sweet; as a wine term it implies sweetening by an agent rather than by nature.

dòu zhī (Chin.) Black beans; *chǐ zhī* is black bean sauce, made from fermented black beans, which are rinsed and chopped before being added to sauces.

Dover sole See **sole.**

dragée (Fr.) Sugar-coated almond; sugarplum.

dragoncello (It.) Tarragon.

Drambuie (Scot.) A liqueur made from Scotch malt whisky flavored with heather honey.

drawn Refers to a whole fish scaled and gutted but with head and fins left on.

drawn butter See **clarified butter.**

dredge To coat food with a dry ingredient such as flour, cornmeal, or breadcrumbs, shaking off the excess.

drum See **croaker.**

dry Wine term meaning not sweet.

Dubarry, à la (Fr.) Garnished with cauliflower shaped into balls, coated with Mornay sauce, and glazed with **château potatoes.**

Dublin Bay prawn (Brit.) Saltwater **crayfish;** the French *langoustine,* the Italian *scampo,* the Norway lobster.

duchesse, à la (Fr.) Potatoes boiled and pureed with eggs and butter and often piped as a garnish or border; a *duchesse* is a small cream puff stuffed with savory puree, coated with a **chaud-froid** sauce, and served as an hors d'oeuvre.

duck sauce (Chin.) See **suan mei jiāng.**

Dugléré (Fr.) Sole poached and served in a sauce of tomatoes, shallots, herbs, and white wine reduced and finished with cream; named for the famous eighteenth-century French chef, Dugléré.

dulce (Sp.) Sweet.

dulse A coarse but edible seaweed from the North Atlantic, especially around Britain, used mostly for its gelatin.

Dumas, Alexandre, père (1802–1870) A prolific French dramatist and novelist (*The Three Musketeers*) and author of the *Grand Dictionnaire de Cuisine,* published posthumously; Waverly Root has called him "an author more picturesque than accurate," and his dictionary indeed makes for lively reading.

dumpling A round lump of dough steamed on top of a savory soup or stew, or stuffed and baked with a sweet fruit filling; the variety is infinite.

Dundee cake (Scot.) A rich fruit cake topped with almonds.

Dungeness crab Pacific rock crab, very popular, weighing up to four pounds.

dunkeles Bier (Ger.) Dark beer.

Dunlop A Scottish cows' milk cheese, similar to **Cheddar** but moister, softer, and blander.

dünsten (Ger.) To steam, to stew.

durazno (Sp.) Peach.

durian The fruit of a Malaysian tree with prickly rind and edible pulp and seeds; its highly offensive smell keeps most Westerners from tasting its flesh, considered exquisite by its advocates.

Dürkheim A town in the Rhine Valley producing a very large amount of red and white wine, mostly unremarkable.

durra See **sorghum.**

durum wheat The hardest species of **wheat,** usually made into **semolina** flour.

dust Finely broken tea leaves, inferior in grade, yielding a quick, strong brew.

Dutch oven A large, heavy cast-iron or metal kettle with a close-fitting lid, used for cooking stews, pot roasts, etc.; originally, coals could be put on top to heat food from above as well as below.

duxelles   (Fr.)   Finely chopped mushrooms and shallots slowly cooked in butter to form a thick, dark paste that is used for seasoning sauces, as a spread for toast, and in other preparations; often said to be the invention of **La Varenne,** who worked for the Marquis d'Uxelles, but the story is probably apocryphal since he gives no such recipe in his books.

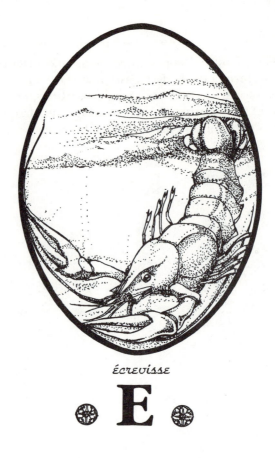

écrevisse

❂ E ❂

eau de vie (Fr.) Fruit brandy, literally "water of life," often called *alcool blanc* ("white alcohol"); colorless *eau de vie* retains its clarity because it is aged in crockery rather than wood, unlike most brandies. Alsace, Germany, and Switzerland produce many *eaux de vie,* flavored with a wide variety of fruits, **Kirschwasser** being the best known.

ebi (Jap.) Shrimp.

Eccles cake (Brit.) A small traditional cake, originally from Lancashire, of puff pastry filled with currants and sprinkled with sugar.

échalote (Fr.) Shallot.

échaudé (Fr.) Pastry whose dough is first poached in water, then baked in the oven.

éclair **Choux pastry** piped into finger shapes and filled with flavored cream; originally French.

écrevisse (Fr.) Freshwater **crayfish.**

Edam (Neth.) A round yellow Dutch cheese from the town of the same name, made of partly skimmed cows' milk and slowly fermented;

the finished cheese is coated with linseed oil and, if for export, covered with red wax.

edamame (Jap.) Fresh soybeans in the pod.

Edelfäule (Ger.) **Noble rot.**

eel A snakelike fish that migrates from the ocean to tidelands and rivers in spring; eel tastes best taken from fast-moving rather than brackish water and killed soon before eating; a rich and fatty fish, eel is excellent smoked, stewed, jellied, baked, and grilled; its shape may account for its unpopularity in the U.S., but until the eighteenth century it was considered a delicacy in England and still is in many countries.

Eger A town in Hungary that produces two famous red wines, *Egri Bikavér* ("bull's blood") and *Egri Kadarka;* both are full-bodied, deep in color, and slow-maturing.

egg-and-breadcrumb To dip food into beaten egg and then into bread crumbs before frying to give it a crisp coating.

eggnog A nutritious milk punch made of milk, egg yolks, sugar, spices (such as nutmeg), and usually some kind of liquor.

egg roll See **cai juan.**

égrappage (Fr.) The process of removing stems from grapes before pressing, thus reducing the **tannin** content of the wine.

Ei, Eier (Ger.) Egg, eggs.

eingelegte (Ger.) Pickled, preserved.

eingemacht (Ger.) Pickled, preserved, bottled, canned; also preserves, jam, pickles.

Eintopf (Ger.) "One-dish" stew or meal containing various meats and vegetables and possibly even fish.

Eis (Ger.) Ice cream.

Eisbein (Ger.) Pickled pork hocks, usually accompanied by mashed potatoes and sauerkraut.

Eiswein (Ger.) Wine made from very ripe grapes caught by an early hard frost and only partially frozen because of their high sugar content.

elaichi (Ind.) **Cardamom.**

elder A shrub whose cream-colored flowers are delicious in fruit compotes and fritters, and whose deep purple berries contribute to fruit soups, jellies, and homemade wines.

elote (Mex.) Corn.

Eltville A town in the Rheingau region of West Germany producing many consistently good white wines.

émincé (Fr.) Thinly sliced cooked meat, usually leftover, covered with sauce and reheated.

Emmental, Emmentaler (Switz.) A whole-milk cows' cheese from German-speaking Switzerland; the cheese is cooked, pressed, and shaped into large wheels with a hard light brown rind and golden interior with large holes; its taste is mellow, rich, and nutty, excellent for eating or cooking, the quintessential Swiss cheese; incorrectly spelled Emmenthal or Emmenthaler.

empanada, empanadilla (Sp.) A pie or tart with various savory fillings, originally from Galicia.

empandita (Sp.) A pastry turnover whose shape—square, round, tri-angular, or rectangular—indicates the specific type of filling, such as meat, seafood, or vegetable.

emulsion A stable liquid mixture in which one liquid is suspended in tiny globules throughout another, as with egg yolks in oil or butter for **mayonnaise** or **hollandaise** sauce.

enchilada (Mex.) A **tortilla,** fried and filled variously, often with meat, chilies, or cheese.

endive See **Belgian endive.**

enokidake (Jap.) Wild mushrooms with long thin stems and tiny caps, either white or tan; the stems should be trimmed before using these mushrooms fresh in salads or cooked in soup, stir-fried, or in **tempura** dishes; mild in flavor, they are available fresh and canned.

ensalada (Sp.) Salad.

Ente (Ger.) Duck.

Entrammes (Fr.) See **Port-Salut.**

entrecôte (Fr.) Steak cut from between the ribs.

entrecuisse (Fr.) Thigh or second joint of poultry and game birds, as opposed to drumstick (*cuisse*).

Entre-Deux-Mers A region "between two rivers," the Dordogne and Garonne, in Bordeaux, that produces a large quantity of wine; those using the name *Entre-Deux-Mers* are fairly good white wines, gradually becoming drier and better.

entrée In the United States, this word today usually means the main course, but in France it retains its original meaning of first course.

entremeses (Sp.) Appetizers, hors d'oeuvre.

entremets (Fr.) Literally "between courses," this vague term can denote side dishes, such as vegetables and salads, and desserts served after the cheese course.

entremettier (Fr.) Vegetable cook.

épaule (Fr.) Shoulder.

éperlan (Fr.) Smelt.

épice (Fr.) Spice.

Epicurus A Greek philosopher who espoused the pursuit of pleasure, often interpreted as indulgence in luxury and sensual pleasure; an epicure, with regard to food, can mean either a gastronome or a voluptuary.

épigramme (Fr.) A preparation of lamb in which a cutlet or chop and a slice of breast are dipped in egg and breadcrumbs and fried or grilled.

épinard (Fr.) Spinach.

éplucher (Fr.) To peel; *épluchoir* is a paring knife.

éponger (Fr.) To drain vegetables cooked in water or oil on towels.

Erbsen (Ger.) Peas, usually dried and split.

Erdapfel (Ger.) Potato, especially in southern Germany and Austria. See also **Kartoffel.**

Erdbeere (Ger.) Strawberry.

escabeche (Sp. and Port.) Cooked fish, sometimes poultry, marinated in vinegar or wine (which pickles it) and other seasonings; served cold in the earthenware container in which it was pickled; often confused with **seviche.**

escalibada (Sp.) Mixed vegetables—sweet peppers, eggplants, tomatoes, and onions—grilled over charcoal; from Catalan.

escalope (Fr.) Scallop of meat or fish; a thin slice possibly flattened by pounding.

escargot (Fr.) Snail.

escarole A type of chicory with broader, less delicate leaves and a more bitter taste than lettuce; excellent for winter salads.

Escoffier, Auguste (1847–1935) A great French chef who codified classical French cuisine with *Le Guide Culinaire* and other books. Escoffier, who worked with the great hôtelier César Ritz at the London Savoy, Connaught, and Carlton hotels, and the Ritz in both London and Paris, improved the organization and working conditions of the professional kitchen.

espadon (Fr.) Swordfish.

espagnole (Fr.) A basic brown sauce that serves as the basis for many others in classic cuisine; made from brown **roux,** brown stock, browned **mirepoix,** tomato puree, and herbs cooked together slowly, skimmed, and strained.

espresso (It.) Strong Italian coffee made with a special machine that forces steam through the coffee grounds.

essence A concentrated substance, usually volatile, extracted by distillation, infusion, or other means, such as fish essence, coffee essence, vanilla extract; see also **extract.**

estate-bottled See **château-bottled.**

estilo de, estilo al (Sp.) In the style of, **à la.**

estofado (Sp.) Stew.

estouffade (Fr.) A dish cooked by the **étouffer** method; also a brown stock used to dilute sauces and moisten braised dishes.

estragon (Fr.) Tarragon.

estufa See **Madeira.**

étamine   (Fr.)   A cloth for straining stocks, sauces, etc; see **tamis.**

étouffer, étuver   (Fr.)   A method of cooking food slowly in a tightly closed pan with little or no liquid; *estouffade* refers to the dish itself.

evaporated milk   Milk with its water content reduced by half and sterilized; this causes it to taste caramelized, but no sugar is actually added.

extract   Concentrated stock, juice, or solution produced by boiling and clarification (as for vegetables, fish, poultry, game, and meat, when the extract may be reduced to a jelly or *glace*) or by distillation (as for fruits, seeds, or leaves, such as vanilla, almond, rosewater, and peppermint essence). Fish extract is usually called *fumet.*

eye of round   See **round.**

fennel

● F ●

---

fabada asturiana (Sp.) A hearty peasant stew of dried **fava** beans cooked slowly with salt pork, ham, sausages, and onions.

fagioli (It.) Beans, usually white *haricot* or kidney beans; *fagiolini* are green string beans.

faisan (Fr.) Pheasant; the Spanish term *faisán* sometimes includes other game birds.

falafel, felafel (Mid. E.) Dried **fava** beans or **chick-peas** minced, spiced, shaped into balls, and deep-fried; eaten throughout the Middle East with slight variations.

fàn (Chin.) Rice; *bai fàn* is plain rice, *chǎo fàn* is fried rice, and *zhōu fàn* is congee rice.

fannings Tea made from broken leaves, yielding a quick, strong brew.

farce (Fr.) Stuffing, forcemeat; *farci* means a stuffed dish, such as cabbage, breast of veal, or flank steak stuffed and braised.

farcito (It.) Stuffed.

farfalle (It.) Butterfly-shaped pasta.

farfel (Jew.) Egg dough grated, dried, and cooked in soup as a garnish.

farina (It.) Flour.

farinaceous Made of flour or meal; from cereal grains, starchy.

Farmer, Fannie Merritt (1857–1915) A cooking teacher and author of *The Boston Cooking School Cook Book* (1896), which achieved great and lasting popularity; its main innovation was precise measurements for ingredients, but Farmer has been blamed as "the maiden aunt of home economics."

farmer cheese Cheese made from whole or partly skimmed cows' milk, similar to **cottage cheese.**

Fasnacht, Fastnacht A potato doughnut deep-fried in pork fat; the diamond-shaped yeast pastry, Pennsylvania German in origin, is traditionally eaten on Shrove Tuesday (*Fastnacht* in German), to use up the fat before Lent.

fatto in casa (It.) Homemade.

fava Broad or faba bean, of Mediterranean origin; important as a nutritional component of the diet and as a rotation crop; fava beans can be eaten raw, cooked fresh, or dried, and though esteemed for their distinct flavor in the Mediterranean are largely ignored in the U.S.

fegato (It.) Liver; *fegatelli* means pork liver; *fegatini* means chicken livers.

feijoa A fruit native to South America and now grown commercially in New Zealand; deep green with a white pulp, it is eaten fresh in salads or made into preserves.

feijoada (Braz.) A robust dish halfway between a soup and a stew, made of pork trimmings, sausage, beef, **black beans,** rice, and **manioc** meal, seasoned with peppers and garnished with oranges.

Feingebäck (Ger.) Pastry.

fennel A vegetable and herb in many varieties whose bulbous stems, leaves, and seeds are edible; anise-flavored, it is favored in Mediterranean countries where it originated; Italians call it *finocchio,* the English refer to it as Florentine fennel; it is no relation to Chinese anise (see **ba jiao**).

fenouil (Fr.) Fennel; *au fenouil* means grilled over dried wild fennel stalks.

fěn sī (Chin.) Cellophane or translucent noodles made from mung beans, softened in a liquid before being used in Chinese cuisine.

fenugreek A leguminous plant from western Asia whose slightly bitter leaves are consumed fresh in salads and whose celery-flavored seeds are eaten by people and cattle; usually added to curries, fenugreek is eaten mostly in India, the Near East, and Northern and East Africa; in the U.S. it is used as the main flavoring in imitation maple syrup.

fermentation A chemical process in the making of bread, cheese, wine, beer, and other foods, in which yeast, mold, or bacteria act upon sugar and bring about a transformation.

fermière, à la (Fr.) In the style of the farmer's wife; with mixed vegetables.

ferri, ai (It.) Grilled over an open fire; also *ferri alla griglia.*

Feta (Gr.) A goats' or ewes' milk cheese from Greece, pressed, then cured in brine or its own salted whey; crumbly, salty, white, and rindless, it is often used in salads and cooking; generic feta is increasingly made with cows' milk or a mixture of cows' and goats' milk, especially by large commercial producers outside Greece.

fetta (It.) Slice, fillet.

fettucine (It.) Long, flat, thin strips or "ribbons" of egg pasta; this is the Roman and southern Italian name for **tagliatelle,** almost the same, but slightly narrower and thicker.

feuilletage (Fr.) Puff pastry, **pâte feuilletée.**

fiambre (Sp.) Cooked meats served cold; cold cuts.

fiasco (It.) A flask or wine bottle, thin and round-bottomed, with a woven straw covering for strength and support; the plural is *fiaschi;* Chianti has the most familiar *fiasco.*

fico (It.) Fig.

fiddlehead The young shoots of certain ferns, such as bracken, harvested in spring as they unfurl, at which time they resemble violin ("fiddle") heads.

Figeac, Château A large and fine vineyard from **Saint-Émilion** in Bordeaux; several lesser-known vineyards nearby have *Figeac* as part of their names.

filbert A cultivated hazelnut, so called because the nuts ripen around St. Philbert's Day, August 22; used in confectionery and hazelnut butter.

filé powder Dried ground sassafras leaves used to thicken **gumbos** in Creole cooking.

filet (Fr.) Fillet; a boneless cut or slice of meat, poultry, or fish, especially beef tenderloin.

filet mignon (Fr.) A small, boneless, tender slice of beef from the thick end of the **tenderloin.**

filo See **phyllo.**

financière, à la (Fr.) Meat or poultry garnished with cocks' combs and kidneys, sweetbreads, mushrooms, olives, and truffles; sometimes these ingredients are encased in **vol-au-vent** pastry.

fines herbes (Fr.) A mixture of chopped herbs such as parsley, chervil, tarragon, and chives used to flavor omelets, salads, chops, etc.; occasionally the term means chopped parsley alone.

fining The process of clarifying wine by adding various substances and removing sediment.

finnan haddie (Brit.) Smoked haddock; originally from the Scottish town of Findon, hence the name.

fino   Pale, light, dry sherry, generally used as an apéritif and considered the best type of sherry.

finocchio (It.) **Fennel.**

Fior di Latte (It.) A cows' milk cheese of the spun-curd type, similar to **Mozzarella;** originally from southern Italy.

fiorentina, bistecca alla (It.) T-bone steak charcoal grilled in the Florentine style—rare and plain but moistened after grilling with a few drops of olive oil.

fiori di zucca (It.) Squash blossoms dipped in batter and fried.

Fior Sardo (It.) A whole, raw ewes' milk cheese—the original Sardinian **Pecorino** and still produced in Sardinia; this Italian cheese is good for the table when young and excellent for grating when mature.

firm-ball stage   Sugar syrup that has reached a temperature of 243°F. (117°C.) and that forms a firm ball between the fingers when immersed in cold water.

first-growth wine   See **classed growth.**

five-spice powder   See **wu hsiang fun.**

flageolet (Fr.) A small pale green bean, fresh or dried, similar to the **haricot** or kidney bean.

flamande, à la (Fr.) Garnished with braised cabbage, carrots, turnips, sliced pork belly, sausage, and potatoes.

flambé (Fr.) The French word for flamed; used to describe food that is ignited with a small amount of heated liquor poured over it, the burning alcohol enveloping the dish in flames.

flameado (Sp.) **Flambé.**

flan   An open tart made in a ring mold, usually filled with custard, either sweet or savory; in Spanish, *flan* is a caramel cream custard, a very popular dessert.

flank   A cut of beef from the lower hindquarter that, well trimmed, is true **London broil.**

flatbrød (Nor.) "Flat bread," very thin and crisp, traditionally made in Norway of rye, barley, and wheat flours.

flatfish   Any saltwater fish with both eyes on one side of the head; this includes **sole, flounder, turbot, halibut,** and **plaice.**

Fleisch (Ger.) Meat.

Fleischkäse (Ger.) Meat loaf.

flétan (Fr.) Halibut.

fleurette (Fr.) French sweet cream that has not been cultivated with lactic acid to make **crème fraîche.**

fleuron (Fr.) A small ornament, such as a crescent, cut from flaky pastry to garnish hot food.

floating island   See **île flottante.**

flor (Sp.) Literally "flower," it is the name for the yeast that naturally forms after fermentation on Spanish **fino** and **amontillado** sherries and on those of other countries by inoculation, and which greatly improves the wine.

florentine, à la (Fr.) With spinach; a garnish, especially for eggs and fish, of a bed of spinach; the whole dish is often masked with **Mornay** sauce.

Florentine fennel See **fennel.**

flounder A flatfish member of the **sole** family in many varieties, including plaice, brill, halibut, sanddab, turbot, and so-called gray, lemon, rock, and petrale sole. The flounder's shape is rounder than that of sole and though an excellent fish for eating, many of the names under which it is marketed are merely intended to make it more attractive to the consumer.

flummery (Brit.) An oatmeal or custard pudding, thick and sweet; in the United States, it has come to mean a fruit pudding thickened with cornstarch.

flute To make a grooved or furrowed pattern in certain fruits and vegetables, especially mushrooms, or in the edges of a pie crust; also the name of a Champagne glass shaped in a deep slender cone.

focaccia (It.) A flat, round peasant bread flavored with sage and **pancetta** and originally baked on hot stones on the hearth.

foie gras (Fr.) The enlarged livers of force-fed geese and ducks, especially the geese of Toulouse and Strasbourg.

fold To combine a frothy light substance, such as beaten egg whites or cream, with a heavier one by using a gentle circular motion, in order not to lose air and reduce volume and lightness.

Folle Blanche (Fr.) A French grape variety yielding a pale, light, clean, and acidic wine, productive but vulnerable; also called *Picpoul* in the Armagnac country, where it produces an excellent brandy but a mediocre table wine.

foncer (Fr.) To line a cake or pie tin; **pâte brisée** and **pâte sucrée** are types of *pâte à foncer.*

fond, fonds de cuisine (Fr.) See **stock.**

fondant (Fr.) An icing mixture used as a coating in confectionery and pastry.

fond d'artichaut (Fr.) Artichoke heart.

fondre, faire (Fr.) To "melt" vegetables, especially onions, leeks, and garlic, by cooking them very gently until softened.

fondue (Fr. and Switz.) From the French word for melted, *fondue* has several meanings: in Switzerland, it refers to Swiss cheese, melted with white wine and seasonings in a special earthenware pot over a flame, for dipping bread cubes into; *fondue bourguignonne* is cubes of raw beef speared and cooked in a pot of oil heated over a flame, then eaten with various sauces; in French cooking, it refers to minced vegetables, such as tomatoes, cooked in butter or oil until they disintegrate; also a dish of eggs scrambled with melted cheese and butter.

fonduta (It.) A dish of melted **Fontina** cheese with eggs, butter, milk, sliced truffles, and white pepper; from the Piedmont region.

Fontal A pasteurized whole-milk cows' cheese from northern Italy and eastern France, similar to **Fontina** but without its distinction.

Fontina (It.) Raw whole-milk cows' cheese, semicooked and pressed, originally from the Aosta Valley near the Swiss border; it is pale yellow with a brown crust, about one foot across (in wheels), firm but creamy, mild yet nutty; true Fontina is a fine cheese, but there are many inferior imitations.

fool (Brit.) A puree of fruit, such as rhubarb or gooseberry, mixed with cream; the word apparently does not come from the French *foulé,* meaning crushed, but is akin to the English folly or **trifle.**

forcemeat Stuffing.

Forelle (Ger.) Trout.

forestière, à la (Fr.) Garnished with sautéed morels or other mushrooms, diced bacon, and diced potatoes sautéed in butter.

formaggio (It.) Cheese.

fortified Refers to wines (such as port, sherry, and Madeira) that have had brandy or another spirit added to them before bottling, thus strengthening their alcoholic content.

fouet (Fr.) Whisk; *fouetté* means whisked.

four, au (Fr.) Baked in the oven.

Fourme d'Ambert (Fr.) Tall cylindrical cheese from the Auvergne, made from raw, partly skimmed cows' milk; it is creamy, with blue veins and a dry rind.

fourrage (Fr.) Filling or stuffing, as for pastry.

fragola (It.) Strawberry; *fragoline di bosco* are wild strawberries.

frais, fraîche (Fr.) Fresh.

fraisage (Fr.) A technique for kneading dough by smearing it across the workboard with the heel of the hand and then regathering it.

fraise (Fr.) Strawberry; *fraises des bois* are wild strawberries.

framboise (Fr.) Raspberry.

frambuesa (Sp.) Raspberry.

Franconia A wine-producing region of West Germany in the upper Main Valley around Würzburg; its white wines, of Sylvaner and Riesling varieties, are bottled in the characteristic squat flat-sided green flagons called *Bocksbeutels.*

frangipane (Fr.) A type of **choux pastry,** originally Italian; *frangipane* cream is a **crème patissière** flavored with almonds.

Frankfurter (Ger.) A sausage from which the hot dog is descended.

frappé (Fr.) Chilled; iced; surrounded by crushed ice.

Frascati, à la (Fr.) A classical garnish of sliced **foie gras,** truffles, fluted mushroom caps, asparagus, and **duchesse** potato crescents, with veal stock; also a pleasant dry white wine produced in the town of the same name near Rome.

freddo (It.) Cold.

fresa (Sp.) Strawberry.

fresco (It. and Sp.) Fresh.

Fresno chili (Mex.) A small cone-shaped chili pepper, fairly hot in flavor.

friandise (Fr.) **Petits four** or other small confection.

fricassée (Fr.) A stew of white meat, usually poultry or veal, in a white sauce, such as a **blanquette.**

Friese (Neth.) A whole or partly skimmed cows' milk cheese from the Netherlands, uncooked and very hard; it is spiced with cloves and cumin, giving it a strong flavor.

frijoles (Sp.) Beans; in Mexican cooking, *frijoles negros* are black beans; *frijoles refritos* are refried beans—that is, beans that are boiled, mashed, and fried with **piquín** chilies for filling tacos, etc.

Frikadellen (Ger.) Meatballs of beef, breadcrumbs, and egg, often served cold.

frío (Sp.) Cold.

frire (Fr.) To fry.

frit (Fr.) Fried; *friture* means fried food or frying.

frito (Sp.) Fried; *fritúra* means fried food.

frittata (It.) An open-faced omelet.

frittèlla (It.) Fritter.

fritter Food, either savory or sweet, dipped into batter and deep-fried.

fritto misto (It.) Mixed food, deep-fried in batter; can be very elaborate and include a wide variety, such as meat, offal, and vegetables served together.

frizzante (It.) A wine term meaning slightly sparkling or effervescent, due to some additional fermentation in the bottle.

froid (Fr.) Cold.

fromage (Fr.) Cheese; *fromager* means to add grated cheese, usually **Gruyère** or **Parmesan,** to a sauce, dough, or stuffing, or to sprinkle it on top of food for browning in the oven.

fromage de tête de porc (Fr.) **Head cheese,** pork brawn.

Frucht (Ger.) Fruit.

fructose The form of sugar found in many plants, especially fruits, and also in honey; fructose tastes sweeter than sucrose and contains half as many calories but is not necessarily more healthful or "natural" than other forms of sugar, especially when crystallized.

Frühlingsuppe (Ger.) A soup of spring vegetables in meat stock.

Frühstück (Ger.) Breakfast.

fruits de mer   (Fr.)   Seafood, usually shellfish.

frumenty   (Brit.)   A porridge of oatmeal or wheat berries and milk with raisins, sugar, and spices—a traditional Old English Christmas food; spelled variously.

frutta fresca de stagione   (It.)   Fresh seasonal fruit.

frutti di mare   (It.)   Seafood, usually shellfish.

fry   To cook in hot fat, either a large (see **deep-fry**) or small (see **sauter**) amount.

fuki   (Jap.)   Coltsfoot; a vegetable similar to celery.

Füllung   (Ger.)   Stuffing.

fumé   (Fr.)   Smoked.

fumet   (Fr.)   A concentrated liquid that gives flavor and body to stocks and sauces; made by completely reducing stock that may contain wine; see also **essence** and **extract.**

fungo   (It.)   Mushroom; the plural is *funghi.*

furai   (Jap.)   To fry.

fusilli   (It.)   Thin, spiral-shaped pasta.

game

❖ G ❖

galantine (Fr.) Boned poultry, or occasionally fish or meat, stuffed, rolled or shaped, poached in gelatin stock, and served cold surrounded by its own aspic; often confused with **ballotine,** which is similar in construction but braised or roasted and served either hot or cold.

galette (Fr.) A thin broad cake usually of flaky pastry or **feuilletage;** *Galette des Rois* is the Twelfth Night cake, baked with a bean and perhaps other emblems to symbolize good fortune for the finder; its shape and decoration vary according to the traditions of particular French regions.

gallina (Sp.) Hen.

Gamay A grape variety that yields an especially excellent red wine in Beaujolais; also grown in Burgundy and California.

gamba (Sp.) Shrimp.

gambero (It.) Shrimp; *gamberetti* are small shrimp; *gamberi di fiume* are freshwater crayfish.

game Wild animals, either furred, feathered, or finny, that are pursued for sport and whose flesh is edible; except for fish, game is often hung and marinated in vinegar or wine and oil to break down tough muscular tissue and develop flavor.

Gammelost (Nor.) A blue cheese made from skimmed cows' milk with interior and exterior molds; apparently the Vikings made this cheese.

gammon (Brit.) Ham; the bottom part of a side of bacon.

ganache (Fr.) A rich chocolate filling for French pastry, made of semi-sweet chocolate melted with heavy cream, that sets when cool.

Gans (Ger.) Goose; *Gansleber* is goose liver.

garam (Ind.) Hot, warm; *garam masala* is a mixture of ground spices—such as cinnamon, cloves, cardamom, cumin, nutmeg, coriander, and black peppercorns—that is sprinkled over a dish just before serving.

garbanzo (Sp.) **Chick-pea.**

garbure (Fr.) A thick soup from Béarn, varying widely but usually containing cabbage, beans, potatoes, vegetables, and pork, sausage, or ham; usually served with toasted bread.

garde manger (Fr.) A pantry or cold storage area for foodstuffs where the cold buffet in a hotel dining room is prepared; the *chef garde manger* oversees this area and is responsible for **pâtés,** salads, **galantines, chaud-froids,** etc., and for fancy display garniture.

garganelli (It.) Homemade macaroni made with egg pasta, rolled with a comblike tool.

Garibaldi In classic cuisine, a **demi-glace** sauce seasoned with mustard, cayenne, garlic, and anchovy butter.

garlic An herb of the onion family widely used in Eastern, Middle Eastern, and Latin cooking, but disdained by Anglo-Saxons until quite recently; aside from its odor, which is strongest when chopped raw and disappears with gentle slow cooking, garlic has many healthful properties recognized by the ancients.

garnacha (Mex.) See **sope.**

Garnele (Ger.) Shrimp, prawn.

garni (Fr.) Garnished.

garnish An edible trimming or embellishment added to a dish, usually enhancing its flavor as well as visual appeal; in classic cuisine the name of the dish, such as *Sole à la florentine* or *Sole florentine,* designates its particular garnish; care must be given to choose appropriate garnishes; see also **à la.**

garniture (Fr.) **Garnish.**

gasconne, sauce (Fr.) Veal velouté with white wine, herbs, and anchovy butter; *gasconne* sometimes means flavored with Armagnac.

gastronomy The science and art of fine food and drink; the connoisseurship of the culinary arts.

gâteau (Fr.) Cake.

gâteau Saint-Honoré (Fr.) A pastry dessert of a crown of **choux** puffs on a **pâte brisée** base filled with **crème patissière** lightened with beaten egg whites, the whole topped with caramel; Saint Honoré is the patron saint of bakers.

Gattinara A fine Italian red wine, from the **Nebbiolo** grape, produced near Lake Maggiore in the Piedmont; big, slow-maturing, and long-lasting.

gaufre (Fr.) Waffle; *pommes gaufrette* are potato chips cut like waffles in a **mandoline.**

gauloise, à la (Fr.) A garnish for clear soup made of cocks' combs and kidneys.

gayette (Fr.) A sausage from Provence of pork liver and bacon wrapped in **caul** and baked.

gazpacho (Sp.) A light, refreshing but thick peasant soup from Andalusia, made of tomatoes, garlic, olive oil, and vinegar, and sometimes bread crumbs mashed together and thinned with ice water; *gazpacho* is traditionally served with a garnish of diced fresh vegetables, hard-boiled eggs, and croutons, with many regional variations.

Gebäck (Ger.) Pastry; *gebacken* means baked.

gebraten (Ger.) Roasted.

gebunden (Ger.) Thickened.

gedämpft (Ger.) Steamed.

gefilte fish (Jew.) Balls of mashed fish, onion, **matzo** meal, egg, and spices cooked variously; originally, the fish mixture was stuffed back into the skin of the fish.

Geflügel (Ger.) Poultry.

gefüllt (Ger.) Filled, stuffed.

Geisenheim A town in the Rheingau region of Germany known for its excellent Rieslings and for its outstanding wine school.

gekocht (Ger.) Cooked.

gelatin, gelatine A glutinous substance found in animal bones, cartilage, and tendons which, when dissolved in water, heated, and chilled, turns to jelly.

gelato (It.) Ice cream; a *gelateria* is an ice cream parlor.

gelée, en (Fr.) In aspic.

gemischt (Ger.) Mixed.

Gemüse (Ger.) Vegetables.

Gênes, pain de (Fr.) See **pain.**

genevoise (Fr.) A classic sauce of salmon stock reduced with red wine and herbs and flavored with anchovy butter.

genièvre (Fr.) Juniper berry; also, gin that is flavored with the berry; the Italian is *ginepro.*

génoise (Fr.) A basic sponge cake made with well-beaten eggs to produce a dry, light base for buttercream icings, petits fours, lining for molds, and various other elaborate pastries.

genovese, alla (It.) In the style of Genoa, the northwestern maritime city in Liguria, whose cuisine stresses fresh herbs, vegetables, and seafood.

geräuchert (Ger.) Smoked.

German sauce See **allemande.**

geschabt (Ger.) Ground, grated, scraped.

geschmort (Ger.) Pot-roasted, stewed.

Gevrey Chambertin A *commune* in the **Côte d'Or** producing extraordinary Burgundy wines, including first-growth and *grand cru* vintages, most of which carry the name of *Chambertin* as part of their title.

Gewächs (Ger.) Growth or **cru,** usually meaning an estate-bottled wine.

Gewürz (Ger.) Spice, condiment, seasoning.

Gewürztraminer A grape variety producing a spicy and refreshing white wine quite unusual in quality; planted widely in Alsace, also in Germany, the Tyrol, and California.

ghee (Ind.) Clarified butter; in India, *ghee* is usually made of buffalo butter. *Vanaspati ghee* is vegetable *ghee*—hydrogenated cooking fat, for everyday use; *usli ghee* is pure fat or butter.

gherkin A small cucumber—the young specimen of certain varieties—used especially for pickling and garnishing.

ghiaccio (It.) Ice; *ghiacciato* means iced.

giardiniera, alla (It.) With mixed sliced vegetables.

gibier (Fr.) Game.

giblets The heart, liver, gizzard, neck, wing tips, feet, leg ends, and sometimes cocks' combs and kidneys of poultry, cooked separately in stocks and stews; goose and duck livers, as special delicacies, are not considered giblets.

gigot (Fr.) Leg of mutton; *gigot d'agneau* is leg of lamb; *manche à gigot* is a special attachment to the *gigot* bone that facilitates carving.

gigue (Fr.) Haunch of venison or boar.

gilthead A type of sea bream from the Mediterranean, with a gold spot on each side of the head; its fine, firm, white flesh is excellent grilled over fennel stalks and in numerous other aromatic preparations.

gingembre (Fr.) Ginger.

ginger The rhizome of a plant native to tropical Asia and used as a spice either fresh, preserved, or dried and ground; pervasive in Far and Middle Eastern cooking, important dried in medieval European cooking, it is enjoying a new popularity used fresh in American **nouvelle cuisine.**

gingerbread A cake flavored with ginger (and often with other spices) and molasses; also a cookie cut into imaginative shapes and decorated.

ginkgo nut The seed or nut of a tree native to China and considered a delicacy in the Orient; eaten raw or cooked, it is high in starch.

ginnan (Jap.) Ginkgo nut.

giorno, del (It.) Of the day, *du jour* (Fr.).

giri (Jap.) A cut, or stroke, of the knife.

girolle (Fr.) See **chanterelle.**

gîte à la noix (Fr.) **Silverside** of beef.

Gjetost (Nor.) A cheese made in Norway from leftover goats' milk whey that is boiled down for some hours; the milk sugar caramelizes and produces a rich brown color and sweet flavor; shaped in a brick, it can be soft or hard and, strictly speaking, is not a cheese.

glaçage (Fr.) Browning or glazing; see **glaze.**

glace (Fr.) Ice cream; cake icing; see **extract.**

glacé (Fr.) Glazed, iced.

glacier (Fr.) Ice cream maker—usually a pastry cook in a large kitchen.

glassato (It.) Glazed.

Glasse, Hannah (1708–1770) Author of *The Art of Cookery, Made Plain and Easy* (1747), a best-seller for a century despite Dr. Johnson's remark that "Women can spin very well; but they cannot make a good book of cookery." The clarity of her writing ensured her posthumous popularity among servants and mistresses alike.

glaze To give a shiny appearance to various preparations both hot and cold in one of several ways: to brown meat in its own stock in the oven or under the **salamander;** to brush extract over meat or other food; to coat chilled food with aspic jelly; to cover fish or eggs in a light sauce; to coat hot vegetables with a butter sauce with a little sugar; to coat sweets with sprinkled sugar or strained jam and caramelize them quickly under intense heat; to ice confections.

glögg (Swed.) Hot spiced wine with **akvavit** or brandy, almonds, and raisins.

Gloucester See **Double Gloucester** and **Single Gloucester.**

glucose Natural sugar, found in fruit and other foods, which is easily absorbed by the body.

Glühwein (Ger.) Mulled wine.

gluten A substance formed when certain flours, especially hard wheat, are combined with water and yeast into an elastic dough, which rises due to trapped air bubbles produced by the yeast; if dough is put under running water or well chewed, the starch is removed, leaving the viscous gluten behind.

glycerin, glycerine, glycerol A sweet, clear, syrupy liquid used to retain moisture in certain kinds of confectionery, such as cake icing, and to sweeten and preserve foods.

gnocchi (It.) Small dumplings made from **choux** paste, semolina flour, or pureed potatoes, poached in water, and served covered with cheese or other sauce or in a soup.

goats' milk cheese See **chèvre.**

gobō (Jap.) Burdock root.

gohan, gohanmono (Jap.) Rice.

golden buck (Brit.) Poached eggs on toast with **Welsh rarebit.**

golden oak mushroom See **shiitake.**

goma (Jap.) Sesame seeds.

goober Peanut; the term derives from an African word for the peanut.

gooseberry A thorny shrub whose tart fruit, mostly small and green or larger and purple, but sometimes white or yellow, is especially popular in France and England for pies, compotes, or preserves; gooseberry sauce is a traditional accompaniment to mackerel in France.

goosefish See **monkfish.**

gordita (Mex.) Cornmeal and potato dough flavored with cheese, fried in lard, and served with ground pork and **guacamole.**

Gorgonzola (It.) A blue cheese from whole cows' milk, either raw or pasteurized, from the village of the same name near Milan; shaped in twenty-five-pound drums, it has a rough reddish rind and creamy white interior streaked with blue; milder and less salty than **Roquefort,** it is one of the great blue cheeses, but made from a different mold than most.

Gouda (Neth.) A round whole-milk cows' cheese from the town of the same name near Amsterdam; creamy yellow and firm, its taste becomes more pronounced with age. Gouda is sometimes flavored with cumin or caraway seeds; young cheeses are covered with yellow wax, older cured cheeses with black wax.

gougère (Fr.) A savory ring of **choux pastry** flavored with cheese, often eaten as a light meal with red wine.

goujonette (Fr.) Fillet of sole cut into strips, floured or breaded, and deep-fried, to resemble little fishes or "gudgeons."

goulash See **gulyás.**

gourmand (Fr.) One who appreciates fine food and drink, a gastronome; in English the term has come to mean glutton, but this association is foreign to France.

goût (Fr.) Taste in both senses—flavor and discriminating style.

graham flour Whole-meal flour made from unbolted wheat; invented in 1840 by the American social reformer Sylvester Graham, who also advocated vegetarianism and sexual abstinence; the crackers sold in supermarkets today under his name, which include among their ingredients sugar, salt, and preservatives, would horrify him.

grana (It.) Hard granular cheese sometimes eaten when young as table cheese but more often aged and used grated on pasta or minestrone or in cooking; dry, crumbly, and long-lasting, several of this type, such as **Parmesan,** are separately entered.

granada (Sp.) Pomegranate.

granadilla See **passion fruit.**

granchio (It.) Crab.

Grand Cru (Fr.) For **Burgundy** wine, the highest classification, including thirty vineyards in all; their individual appellations usually exclude the name of the **commune.**

Grand Marnier (Fr.) A liqueur with a **Cognac** base, flavored with bitter orange peel.

grand' mère, à la (Fr.) Garnished with sautéed pearl onions, potatoes cut into olive shapes, parsley, lemon juice, and browned butter.

grandville (Fr.) A classic white wine sauce with truffles, mushrooms, and shrimp.

granita (It.) Fruit ice or sherbet to which no **Italian meringue** is added, so that its ice crystals intentionally form a grainy texture.

grappa (It.) **Marc.**

gratin de, au gratin, gratiné (Fr.) Topped with a crust of bread-crumbs and sometimes grated cheese and browned in the oven or under a grill.

Graves A wine region on the left bank of the Garonne River southwest of Bordeaux producing mostly dry white wines; the best reds are sold under their estate names and, except for **Château Haut-Brion,** were omitted from the 1855 classification; an excellent sweet wine similar to **Sauternes,** usually named *Cérons,* is also produced in Graves.

gravlaks, gravlax (Scand.) Raw salmon fillets cured for a day or so in sugar and salt and seasoned with dill.

grecque, à la (Fr.) Vegetables, particularly Greek ones such as artichokes and mushrooms, stewed in olive oil, lemon juice, water, and seasonings.

green onion See **scallion.**

green sauce See **mayonnaise verte.**

gremolada (It.) A mixture of chopped parsley, garlic, and grated lemon zest sprinkled over **osso buco** as an aromatic garnish.

Grenache A grape variety, productive and good in quality, planted extensively in southern France, the Rioja region of Spain, and California.

grenadine Pomegranate syrup; used to color and flavor cocktails.

grenouille (Fr.) Frog; *cuisses de grenouille* are frog legs.

gribiche (Fr.) A sauce for chilled fish, based on mayonnaise with capers, chopped gherkins and herbs, and hard-boiled egg whites.

griglia, alla (It.) Grilled.

grill To cook over flames or embers or under a broiler in intense direct heat.

grillade (Fr.) Grilled meat; grilling or broiling.

Grimod de La Reynière, Alexandre Balthazar Laurent (1758–1838) French gastronome, critic, and author of the *Almanach des Gourmands,* with a mordant sense of humor; he organized a jury to taste and approve the meals sent by willing tradesmen seeking favorable publicity.

grissino (It.) Breadstick.

grits   See **hominy.**

groats   Hulled grain, usually broken up or coarsely ground, as with grits (see **hominy**).

groseille   (Fr.)   Currant; *groseille à maquereau* means **gooseberry,** the traditional French garnish for mackerel.

grouper   Several varieties of fish, all members of the **sea bass** family; the lean, firm, moist meat can be cooked in a wide variety of ways.

grouse   A large family of wild game birds, prepared in various ways, depending on age and species; one bird usually serves one person.

gruel   A thin cereal, usually oatmeal, cooked in milk or water.

grunt   Stewed fruit topped with dumplings; an early American dessert similar to **slump.**

Gruyère   (Switz.)   A cows' milk cheese, cooked and pressed, from the valley of the same name in French-speaking Switzerland; originally of skimmed or partially skimmed milk but now made with whole milk; the pale yellow cheese with a golden brown rind is made in rounds of over a hundred pounds and aged; those for the export market are made less salty and with little holes; an excellent table or cooking cheese with fine melting properties.

guacamole   (Mex.)   Avocado mashed with onion, chilies, lime juice, seasonings, and perhaps tomato, and served as a dip, filling, or sauce.

guajillo   (Mex.)   A long, thin, dried chili pepper, reddish brown and smooth, very hot, about 4 inches long and 1 inch wide; it is sometimes called **cascabel** because it resembles the tail, rattle, and bite of a rattlesnake, but should not be confused with that chili.

guajolote   (Mex.)   Wild turkey.

guarnito   (It.)   Garnished.

guava   A tropical shrub whose odiferous berrylike fruit is made into pinkish orange jams and jellies; a poor traveler, this delicious fruit is inadequately appreciated outside its native habitat.

güero   (Mex.)   A greenish yellow chili pepper, about 4 inches long and 1 inch wide, and pointed; it is fairly hot, with some variation, and is generally used fresh and toasted or canned, but never dried; also called Californian pepper or sweet green pepper.

Gugelhupf   (Aus.)   Austrian dialect for **Kugelhopf.**

guisantes   (Sp.)   Peas.

guiso, guisado   (Sp.)   Stew, stewed.

gulyás   (Hung.)   A stew of beef or sometimes veal or pork, onions, potatoes, and dumplings, seasoned with plenty of **paprika;** it varies widely according to the region and individual, from delicate to hearty. The English spelling is *goulash.*

gum arabic, gum tragacanth   Vegetable gums used as emulsifiers and thickeners in certain processed foods such as ice cream, candy, and commercial sauces.

gumbo   A thick Creole soup or dish thickened with okra or **filé powder;** the word *gumbo* is derived from an African word for okra.

Gumpoldskirchen   An Austrian town south of Vienna known for its fine white wine, which is pale, clean, fruity, and pleasing.

Gurke   (Ger.)   Cucumber.

gyū   (Jap.)   Beef.

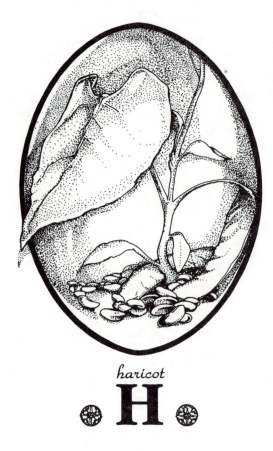

haricot

• H •

haba (Sp.) Fava or broad bean; *habas secas* are dried beans.

habañero (Mex.) A very hot green chili pepper, smooth-skinned and oval, smaller than the **jalapeño;** sometimes available yellow and red.

hachée (Fr.) A classic sauce of chopped shallots and onions reduced in vinegar, mixed with **demi-glace** and tomato puree, and flavored with **duxelles,** capers, diced ham, and parsley.

hacher (Fr.) To chop or mince; *hachis* means hash.

Hackbraten (Ger.) Meat loaf.

haddock A small variety of **cod,** usually sold fresh or smoked but not salted.

haggis (Scot.) A traditional dish of sheep's stomach stuffed with chopped lamb's liver and heart, onions, and oatmeal, well steamed like a pudding; celebrated by the Scots poet Robert Burns.

Hahn (Ger.) Cock.

hǎi shēn (Chin.) A spineless marine creature, called a sea cucumber or sea slug; a delicacy relished for its gelatinous texture and saved for special occasions.

hake   A small variety of **cod.**

hakusai   (Jap.)   Chinese cabbage.

haldi   (Ind.)   Turmeric.

half-mourning   See **demi-deuil, à la.**

halibut   A large flatfish of the **flounder** family.

Hallgarten   A village in the German Rheingau producing very good full-bodied white wines.

halvah   (Turk.)   Candy made of crushed sesame seeds and honey.

hamaguri   (Jap.)   Hard-shell clams.

Haman's ears   (Jew.)   Pastries, deep-fried and ear-shaped, served with sugar or honey at Purim.

Hamantaschen   (Jew.)   Triangular pastries stuffed with poppy seeds and apple, apricot, or prune filling, traditionally eaten for Purim.

Hammelfleisch   (Ger.)   Mutton.

Handkäse   (Ger.)   A pungent acid-curd cheese made from skimmed cows' milk, in small round or oblong shapes; originally made by hand. In Hesse, the cheese is served "mit Musik"—onion relish—which produces flatulence, hence the name.

Hangtown fry   A dish, apparently from the California Gold Rush, of breadcrumbed oysters, fried bacon, and beaten eggs cooked together like an omelet until set.

hard-ball stage   Sugar syrup that has reached a temperature of 250–268°F. (121–130°C.) and that forms a firm ball between the fingers when immersed in cold water.

hard-crack stage   Sugar syrup that has reached a temperature of 300–320°F. (150–160°C.) and that, when immersed in cold water, forms brittle threads and sheets that break easily between the fingers.

hard sauce   Butter creamed with sugar and flavored with liquor; served with dessert puddings such as plum pudding.

hardtack   A hard cracker that was often used for military rations because of its excellent keeping qualities; also known as ship biscuit and pilot biscuit.

hare   A large wild cousin of the rabbit, relished for its dark rich meat with gamy flavor; hare is usually hung, skinned and drawn, marinated, and then roasted or stewed; see also **jugged hare.**

hareng   (Fr.)   Herring.

haricot   (Fr.)   Bean, either fresh (*frais*) or dried (*sec*).

haricot blanc   (Fr.)   White kidney bean, fresh or dried.

haricot de mouton   (Fr.)   Mutton stew with turnips and potatoes but no beans at all.

haricot flageolet   (Fr.)   Pale green bean, usually fresh in France and rare in the U.S.

haricot rouge   (Fr.)   Red kidney bean, fresh or dried.

haricot vert   (Fr.)   Green string bean.

harina (Sp.) Flour.

hartgekocht (Ger.) Hard-boiled.

Hase (Ger.) Hare; *Hasenpfeffer* is a hare stew flavored with pepper and other spices and braised in red wine.

Haselnuss (Ger.) Hazelnut.

hash Chopped meat, often with vegetables, usually combining leftovers, seasonings, and gravy; from the French word *hacher,* meaning to chop.

hashi (Jap.) Chopsticks.

hasty pudding See **Indian pudding.**

Hattenheim A village in the German Rheingau whose vineyards produce excellent white wine.

Hauptgerichte (Ger.) Main course.

Hausfrauen Art (Ger.) Housewife's style, meaning with sour cream and pickles.

hausgemacht (Ger.) Homemade.

Haut-Brion, Château A very famous red Bordeaux wine, ranked a first growth in the 1855 classification (the only **Graves** included) because of its superlative quality.

Haut-Médoc The southern and more elevated half of the Médoc, north of Bordeaux, including Margaux, Saint-Julien, Pauillac, and Saint-Estèphe; its wines are superior to those from the Bas-Médoc to its north.

Havarti (Den.) A cheese made from partially skimmed cows' milk, semihard and containing many small holes; pale and mild, sometimes flavored with herbs, it grows sharper with maturity.

hazelnut See **filbert.**

head cheese Meat from a pig's or calf's head and other scraps boiled, molded into a loaf, and served in its own jelly with condiments.

heavy syrup Two parts sugar to one part water, dissolved; this is a *sirop à trente* with a density of 30 degrees on the Baumé scale. A light syrup has an approximately equal sugar-to-water ratio.

Heilbutt (Ger.) Halibut.

heiss (Ger.) Hot.

helado (Sp.) Ice cream.

helles Bier (Ger.) Light beer.

Hendel (Aus.) Chicken, in Austrian dialect.

Henne (Ger.) Hen.

Henry IV (Fr.) Garnished with artichoke hearts filled with potato balls and **béarnaise** sauce mixed with meat glaze—a classical garnish.

hermetical seal Airtight closure of a casserole or container with bread dough or flour and water paste, designed to keep steam inside during cooking.

Hermitage A celebrated Rhône wine from a large steep slope south of Lyons; most of this full-bodied, richly colored and flavored wine is red, from the Syrah grape; the white wine is pale gold, dry, and also full-bodied, if not so fine.

herring   A flavorful and nutritious fish, until recently abundant in the Pacific and Atlantic Oceans and very important economically; herring is particularly appreciated in northern Europe and, with its high fat content, lends itself to smoked or pickled preparations (separately entered).

herring rollmop   Filleted herring rolled around a pickle or onion, marinated, and served as an appetizer.

Herve   (Bel.)   A whole-milk cows' cheese, soft, rich, and pungent, made in 3-inch cubes with a reddish brown rind; named for the town of Herve, near Liège.

hervir   (Sp.)   To boil.

Hessia   A region in western Germany delineated on the north and east by the Rhine, on the west by the Nahe, and on the south by the Pfalz, which produces a large quantity of white wine; the best, from the Riesling grape, comes from particular towns along the Rhine, while the rest, from the Sylvaner grape, is quite ordinary.

hibachi   (Jap.)   A small open charcoal grill.

hickory   A tree native to North America whose nut was eaten by the Indians and which we still eat, especially the **pecan;** the word hickory comes from the Algonquin Indian language.

hígado   (Sp.)   Liver.

higo   (Sp.)   Fig.

Himbeer   (Ger.)   Raspberry.

Himmel und Erde   (Ger.)   Apples and potatoes with onions and sausage or bacon (literally "heaven and earth"); a very popular dish.

hinojo   (Sp.)   Fennel.

hirame   (Jap.)   Flounder.

Hirn   (Ger.)   Brains.

Hirsch   (Ger.)   Stag, venison.

hiyashi   (Jap.)   Cold, chilled.

hochepot   (Fr.)   A thick stew, sometimes more of a soup, made from less desirable cuts of meat and winter vegetables; the English and Scottish hotch-potch, hodge-podge, and hot pot are all derivatives.

Hochheim   A town in the northeast corner of the German **Rheingau** producing distinctive and characteristic Rhine wine even though situated on the Main River; hock, designating Rhine wine to an Englishman, is derived from its name.

hock   See **Hochheim.**

hodge-podge   See **hochepot.**

hoecake   **Johnny cake,** originally cooked over an open fire, using the hoe as a griddle, when kitchen equipment was less readily available than now; early American in origin.

hói sìn jeung (Chin.) A thick, rich, dark brown sauce made from fermented soy beans, garlic, sugar, and salt, and used to flavor sauces and marinades; it is a Cantonese version of **sweet bean sauce.**

hollandaise (Fr.) In classic cuisine, a thick emulsion sauce of reduced vinegar whisked with egg yolks, into which melted butter is gradually beaten in. It is then flavored with lemon juice and kept warm in a **bain-marie;** one of the basic sauces, it is used primarily with fish, eggs, and vegetables; in modern cooking there are many shortcuts in technique and ingredients.

Holsteiner Katenschinken (Ger.) Smoked raw ham.

Holsteiner mit Spiegelei; Holstein Schnitzel (Ger.) Veal chop garnished with a fried egg and smoked salmon.

homard (Fr.) Lobster.

hominy Corn kernels with the bran and germ removed either by a lye bath, as for whole kernels in lye hominy, or by crushing and sifting, as for pearl hominy; hominy grits, a Southern favorite, are often served as porridge for breakfast or as starch for dinner seasoned with cheese; the word *hominy* is American Indian in origin.

hongroise, à l' (Fr.) Meat garnished with cauliflower flowerets, glazed with Mornay sauce, paprika, and sautéed potatoes cut into olive shapes.

Honig (Ger.) Honey.

hoogli See **ugli fruit.**

Hoppelpoppel (Ger.) Scrambled eggs with potatoes and bacon.

hopping John A dish of rice and beans—usually black-eyed peas; a staple of Black cooking in the southern U.S. and Caribbean, traditional for New Year's Day.

hops Ripe conical female flowers of the hop vine, used in brewing to impart a bitter flavor to beer, in order to balance the sweetness of the malt; in continental Europe the young male shoots of the hop vine are eaten as a vegetable.

horchata (Sp.) A drink, usually of pumpkin seeds or almonds.

horehound A fragrant Old World herb of the mint family used to flavor candy and medicine; also spelled hoarhound.

hōrensō (Jap.) Spinach.

hornear (Sp.) To bake.

horno (Sp.) Oven; *al horno* means baked.

hors d'oeuvre (Fr.) Light and stimulating finger food eaten before the main meal (literally, "outside the works") as an appetizer; the term is often misspelled: when used as a collective noun it has no final *s,* but a group of specific appetizers takes the plural *s.*

horseradish A vegetable related to mustard, whose pungent root is grated and mixed with vinegar, then folded into a cream or tomato sauce and served as a condiment or sauce; the tender leaves can be used for salad; native to southeastern Europe.

Hospices de Beaune A fifteenth-century charitable hospital in Beaune, France, endowed and maintained with some forty **Côte de Beaune** vineyards; at the auspicious annual auction the wine, all very good, often sets Burgundy prices for that year.

hotch-potch See **hochepot** and **Lancashire hot pot.**

hot cross buns (Brit.) A yeast roll, round, slightly sweet, and traditionally iced with a white cross; eaten on Good Friday or during Lent.

hot pot See **hochepot.**

huachinango (Mex.) Red snapper.

huā jiāo (Chin.) Hot peppercorns from Sichuan, reddish brown in color; when roasted, crushed, and added to salt as a dipping sauce they become *huā jiāo yen.*

huckleberry A small black berry, similar to the blueberry but with a darker color, lacking the blueberry's silvery sheen, larger seeds, and tarter taste; the low shrub grows wild in North America, was praised by Thoreau, and chosen by Mark Twain for the name of his greatest fictional character.

huevo (Sp.) Egg.

huevos a la flamenco (Sp.) Eggs baked on a bed of peas, peppers, onions, tomatoes, ham, and sausage.

huevos asturian (Sp.) Scrambled eggs with eggplant, tomatoes, and **fava** beans.

huevos pasados por agua (Sp.) Soft-boiled eggs.

huevos rancheros Tortillas "country style"; that is, with eggs and a hot spicy sauce.

huevos revueltos (Sp.) Scrambled eggs.

Huhn (Ger.) Chicken, hen, fowl.

huile (Fr.) Oil.

huitlacoche (Mex.) A fungus that grows on green corn cobs, making a favorite stuffing for **quesadillas** or soup; the fungus makes the kernels grow large, black, and deformed, but tastes delicious.

huître (Fr.) Oyster.

hull To husk or remove the outer covering of a seed or fruit, as of a nut, or the interior pith, as of a strawberry.

Hummer (Ger.) Lobster.

hummus (Mid. E.) Chick-peas mashed to a paste with lemon juice and garlic, flavored with **tahini,** and eaten with **pita** bread as an appetizer.

hún tún (Chin.) Wonton: a pastalike dough wrapper.

huǒ guō (or shuàn yáng ròu) (Chin.) Mongolian hot pot.

hush puppies Deep-fried cornmeal dumplings, sometimes flavored with chopped onions, usually eaten as a savory accompaniment to fried fish; from the southern U.S.

Indian pudding

I

ice See **water ice.**

ice cream A frozen dessert of cream that is sweetened, flavored variously, and beaten during freezing to keep ice crystals from forming; a custard base is frequently, though not necessarily, used for rich flavor and smooth texture.

icing A confectionery mixture made of sugar, egg white, butter, flavorings, etc., used to cover or decorate cakes and other pastries; the various types, both cooked and uncooked, differ according to purpose.

icing sugar (Brit.) **Confectioners' sugar.**

ika (Jap.) Squid.

Île de France A region around Paris, the original Frankish kingdom, famous for its fine produce, cheeses, bread, pastry, game, meat, and fish; the Île de France also lays claims to the culinary creations of Paris's many fine restaurants.

île flottante (Fr.) A dessert of meringue "islands" on a sea of custard; also sponge cake sliced, sprinkled with liqueur, spread with jam, nuts, and dried fruit, reshaped and covered with **crème Chantilly,** with custard or fruit puree poured over all.

imam bayildi (Turk.) A cold vegetable dish of eggplant sautéed in olive oil with onions, tomatoes, garlic, and parsley; the name in Turkish means "the priest fainted"; spelled variously.

imbottito (It.) Stuffed.

impanato (It.) Breaded.

impériale, à l' (Fr.) Garnished with truffles, **foie gras,** cocks' combs and kidneys, sweetbreads, and Madeira sauce.

Indian fig See **prickly pear.**

Indian pudding Cornmeal pudding sweetened with molasses and spiced, made by early English settlers; also called hasty pudding.

indienne, à l' (Fr.) Served with boiled rice and sauce flavored with curry powder.

infuse To steep or soak herbs, spices, or vegetables in a liquid to extract their flavor.

Inglenook A distinguished California vineyard in the Napa Valley that concentrates on **varietal wines.**

insalata (It.) Salad.

interlard To lard: to thread strips of pork fat or **lardons** through meat or other flesh in order to baste it during cooking.

involtine (It.) Scallops of meat, usually veal, or fish, pounded thin, stuffed, and rolled up; veal birds.

iota See **jota.**

Irish coffee Coffee laced with Irish whiskey, usually flavored with sugar, spices, and cream.

Irish Mist (Ir.) A liqueur made with Irish whiskey flavored with heather honey.

Irish moss See **carrageen.**

Irish soda bread A traditional Irish bread, usually baked in free-form rounds, whose leavening agent is baking soda with buttermilk rather than yeast.

Ischlertörtchen (Ger.) A biscuit spread with jam.

isinglass Gelatin, obtained from the air bladder of sturgeon and other fish, which is pure and transparent.

Ismaîl Bayaldi (Fr.) A classic French garnish, originally from Turkey, of sliced fried eggplant, crushed tomatoes, rice pilaf, and sauce **portugaise.**

Italian meringue Meringue made by whipping hot sugar syrup into stiffly beaten egg whites; used to frost pastries, to lighten pastry and buttercreams, in soufflés, and in sherbets.

italienne, sauce (Fr.) A classic sauce of finely chopped mushrooms with diced ham and chopped parsley.

ivoire, sauce (Fr.) *Sauce suprême* with meat glaze, colored white.

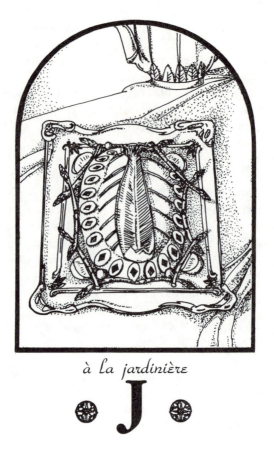

à la jardinière

J

Jack See **Monterey Jack.**

Jäger, Jäger Art (Ger.) Hunter's style—with mushrooms and usually in a wine sauce.

jaiba (Mex.) Crab.

jalapeño (Mex.) A green chili pepper, very hot, about $2\frac{1}{2}$ inches long, generally used fresh.

jalousie (Fr.) **Feuilletage** pastry strip with a sweet filling, whose top layer is cut into parallel strips like a Venetian blind (hence its name).

jambalaya A dish from **Cajun** cuisine of rice with ham, shellfish, sausage, chicken, and beans, seasoned with **Creole** vegetables and spices; the ingredients vary widely.

jambon (Fr.) Ham.

jamón (Sp.) Ham.

japonaise, à la (Fr.) Garnished with Chinese or Japanese artichokes and potato croquettes.

jardinière, à la (Fr.) Garnished with various fresh vegetables cooked and arranged separately around the main piece of meat or poultry.

Jarlsberg (Nor.)   A hard cows' milk cheese, made from partially skimmed milk, nutty and sweet, made in large wheels, and similar to **Emmental.**

jarret (Fr.)   Knuckle or hock.

Jerez de la Frontera   A city in southern Spain whose outlying vineyards produce sherry (the name is an anglicization of *Jerez).*

jerky   Preserved meat, usually beef and originally sometimes buffalo, that is cut into thin strips and dried in the sun; used by the American Indians and early settlers as a staple for its keeping powers.

jeroboam   A large wine bottle with the capacity of six ordinary bottles (about $\frac{4}{5}$ of a gallon); named for the first king of the Hebrews.

Jerusalem artichoke   A tuberous vegetable of the sunflower family, native to North America, whose knotty root is a versatile and nutritious foodstuff; also called sunchoke; "Jerusalem" is a corruption of the Italian *girasole,* meaning "sunflower."

jī (Chin.)   Chicken; *jī rou* designates chicken meat.

jiāng (Chin.)   Sauce; the word also means ginger root.

jiāng yóu (Chin.)   Soy sauce in light, medium, and dark grades; light soy sauce, saltier and thinner, is used with seafood and chicken; dark soy sauce, thick, rich, and strong, is best with red meat roasts, stews, and barbecues.

jícama (Mex.)   A root vegetable, crisp and slightly sweet, that resembles the turnip; used both raw and cooked.

jigger   A volume measure of $1\frac{1}{2}$ ounces for making cocktails.

jitomate (Mex.)   Tomato.

Johannisberg   A German village in the Rheingau that produces fine wine; that from the Schloss Johannisberg, overlooking the Rhine, deserves its venerable reputation.

Johannisberg Riesling   A fine white grape variety from Germany cultivated increasingly in California.

John Dory   A saltwater fish found mainly in European waters, especially the Mediterranean, with two yellow rings on either side of the body, said to be the fingerprints of St. Peter (hence its French name, Saint-Pierre); its delicate, white, flavorful flesh is valued in many recipes, either in fillets or chunks, as for **bouillabaisse.**

johnny cake, jonny cake   A hearth- or pancake of cornmeal, sometimes mixed with other grains, cooked in the ashes or in a griddle or pan; the name is often said to be derived from Shawnee and the cake originally from Rhode Island, but what is certain is that early American settlers adapted the native cornmeal to a familiar cooking method.

Joinville, à la (Fr.)   Garnished with finely diced shrimp, truffles, mushrooms, and bound in *sauce normande.*

jota (It.)   A robust soup of beans with sauerkraut, potatoes, and bacon cooked slowly; *jota* comes from Trieste, its unusual spelling a holdover from the Austro-Hungarian influence (the Italianized spelling is *iota*).

judía   (Sp.)   Kidney bean, string bean; *judiás verdes* are green string beans.

jugged hare   Hare (or other furred game) that is stewed in an earthenware pot or jug to which some of the animal's blood is added along with the cooking liquid.

jujube   The fruit of a tropical Asian plant, sometimes called Chinese date, which is picked ripe, dried, and used to sweeten cough medicines; also the name of a candy.

julienne   (Fr.)   Vegetables or other foodstuffs cut into fine matchsticks; a clear consommé garnished with sautéed vegetables cut into matchsticks.

juniper   An evergreen tree whose purple berries flavor gin, marinades, sauerkraut, and game dishes.

junket   Milk curds formed with **rennet** and served as a custardlike dessert.

Jurançon   An unusual and renowned wine from the foothills of the Pyrenees in southwestern France, possessing a gold color and a sweet, spicy taste.

jus   (Fr.)   Juice; *au jus* means meat served with its natural juices; *jus de viande* means gravy.

kale

◉ **K** ◉

Kabeljau (Ger.) Cod.

Kabinett (Ger.) Superior or special reserve unsweetened wine, usually estate-bottled and from the Rheingau.

kabocha (Jap.) Pumpkin, squash.

kabu (Jap.) Turnip.

Kaffee (Ger.) Coffee; afternoon coffee in Germany can include elaborate cakes and sandwiches, a social occasion not unlike the English high tea.

Kahlúa (Mex.) A coffee-flavored liqueur.

kailkenny A Scottish version of **colcannon.**

kake (Jap.) Noodles.

kaki (Jap.) Persimmon; several European languages, including French, have borrowed the word *kaki* for persimmon; it also means oyster in Japanese.

Kalb (Ger.) Veal.

Kalbschnitzel (Ger.) Veal cutlet cooked simply in butter.

Kalbshaxe (Ger.) Veal shanks or knuckles, very popular in Bavaria.

kale   A loose, green leafy vegetable of the cabbage family, highly nutritious; its hardiness in frost and snow makes it a winter staple in cold rural areas, where it appears in such country dishes as **colcannon** and **kailkenny.**

kalt   (Ger.)   Cold.

kamaboko   (Jap.)   Fish paste or sausage in many varieties.

kampyō   (Jap.)   Dried gourd shavings.

kani   (Jap.)   Crab.

Kaninchen   (Ger.)   Rabbit.

kanten   (Jap.)   **Agar-agar** seaweed.

kǎo   (Chin.)   To roast or bake.

Kapaun   (Ger.)   Capon.

Kaper   (Ger.)   Caper.

karashi   (Jap.)   Mustard.

Karfiol   (Aus.)   Cauliflower, in Austrian dialect. See also **Blumenkohl.**

kari   (Ind.)   Curry, seasoned sauce; also the aromatic leaves of the *kari* plant.

kari-kari   (Phil.)   Oxtail stew flavored with garlic and onion, the sauce thickened with crushed peanuts and rice flour.

Karotte   (Ger.)   Carrot.

Karpfen   (Ger.)   Carp—a very popular fish in Germany and traditional for Christmas Eve.

Kartoffel   (Ger.)   Potato; *Kartoffelbrei* means mashed potatoes, *Kartoffelklösse* means dumplings, and *Kartoffelpuffer* means potato pancakes.

Käse   (Ger.)   Cheese.

Käseteller   (Ger.)   Cheese plate.

Käsetorte   (Ger.)   Cheesecake.

kasha   (Russ.)   Hulled, crushed, and cooked groats, usually buckwheat.

Kasnudeln   (Ger.)   Noodles stuffed with savory meat and cheese filling or fruit and poppy seed filling for dessert.

Kasseler Rippenspeer   (Ger.)   Cured and smoked pork loin served on a bed of sauerkraut, mashed potatoes, and apples or red cabbage and potato dumplings, with a red wine and sour cream gravy; a great favorite in Germany.

Kastanie   (Ger.)   Chestnut.

katch   (Ind.)   Lamb.

Katenschinken   (Ger.)   Smoked country ham, originally from Schleswig-Holstein; *Katenwurst* means smoked sausage from the same area; the word *Katen* means peasant hut or cottage, where these meats were originally cured.

katsuo-bushi   (Jap.)   Dried bonito flakes, essential in making **dashi.**

kebab   (Turk.)   Small pieces of meat seasoned and often combined with vegetables, sometimes skewered, and grilled over an open fire.

kedgeree (Ind.) See **kitcheri.**

kéfir Fermented milk, slightly effervescent and alcoholic, widely consumed in the Middle East and Russia; the *kéfir* bacteria sours the milk (usually cows'), making it thick, frothy, and healthful.

Keks (Ger.) Biscuit.

Kellerabfüllung (Ger.) See **Original-Abfüllung.**

Kellerabzug (Ger.) See **Original-Abfüllung.**

kelp See **konbu.**

ketchup Savory sauce or condiment, Chinese in origin, made from a variety of foodstuffs, such as mushrooms, anchovies, or oysters pickled in brine; our commercially manufactured tomato ketchup is a sorry comedown; also spelled *catchup, catsup,* and *katsup.*

Key lime pie A pie originally made from a variety of lime grown on the Florida Keys that is no longer commercially cultivated; the pie has a pastry or graham-cracker crust with an egg yolk, **condensed milk,** and lime-juice filling, with a meringue topping.

khoya (Ind.) Milk "fudge," very thick and reduced.

kibbeh (Mid. E.) **Bulghur** and ground lamb, onions, and pine nuts, deep-fried or served raw; its origin is Lebanese and it has many variations.

kidney A pair of organs embedded in white fat; excellent for various culinary preparations trimmed of exterior membrane and interior gristle, then sautéed or broiled quickly or braised slowly in stews or meat pies; veal and lamb kidneys are considered best.

kielbasa (Pol.) Sausage made of pork, sometimes beef or veal, flavored with garlic, smoked, and cooked; its links are very long.

Kiev, chicken à la See **chicken à la Kiev.**

kiku (Jap.) Edible chrysanthemum.

kikurage (Jap.) **Cloud ear** or **wood ear** mushroom, usually dried.

kim chee (Kor.) A pungent Korean condiment of pickled shredded vegetables, including Chinese cabbage, radishes, cucumbers, greens, onions, garlic, and chili peppers, seasoned with fermented shellfish and salt; the condiment varies widely in its strength and is especially common in winter, when fresh vegetables are unavailable; also spelled *keem chee* and *kim chi.*

king crab A large variety of **crab** living in northern Pacific waters and growing up to twenty pounds; the meat is usually sold cooked and frozen; also called Alaska king crab and Japanese crab.

king salmon See **salmon.**

Kipferl (Ger.) A crescent-shaped roll, sweeter and doughier than a **croissant.**

kippered herring, kipper (Brit.) Herring that has been split, lightly salted, dried, and smoked to preserve it; a favorite breakfast dish.

Kir See **cassis.**

Kirsch (Ger.) Cherry.

Kirschwasser (Ger.) A colorless liqueur distilled from the fermented mash of wild cherries, especially those grown in the French Alsace and the German Black Forest; often used as a flavoring in confectionery and pastry; sometimes called simply *Kirsch*.

kissel (Russ.) A berry pudding, often made with pureed strawberries, thickened with potato flour; also used as a dessert sauce.

kitcheri (Ind.) Kedgeree; cooked rice, lentils, and spices, of Hindi origin; when the English anglicized this dish they often served it with leftover fish, hard-boiled eggs, and curry, which is how it survives as a breakfast dish in England today.

kited fillet Fish cut through along the backbone and filleted but left attached at the belly.

kiwi A small tree of Chinese origin whose plum-shaped fruit is covered with a thin layer of brownish fuzz; once peeled, the soft green interior with small black seeds radiating from a pale green center is entirely edible, tasting somewhere between a strawberry and melon; also called Chinese gooseberry, but recently marketed as kiwi.

Klopse (Ger.) Ground meatballs usually containing two or three kinds of meat; *Königsberger Klopse* are poached meatballs of pork with veal or beef, flavored with anchovies and served with a lemon, sour cream, and caper sauce; from the Slavic northeast.

Klösse (Ger.) Dumplings or meatballs; the singular is *Kloss*.

Kloster Eberbach See **Steinberg.**

Knackwurst (Ger.) Sausages similar to hot dogs but thicker.

knädlach (Jew.) Dumplings of **matzo** meal, egg, ground almonds, and chicken fat dropped into chicken broth; spelled variously.

knead To work dough with the fingers and heels of the hand in order to distribute ingredients uniformly, develop the gluten, and produce an even texture ready for rising.

knish (Jew.) Chopped chicken livers or **kasha** wrapped in a pastry of mashed potatoes, flour, and chicken fat; from Eastern Europe.

Knoblauch (Ger.) Garlic.

Knödel (Ger.) Dumpling.

Kobe beef (Jap.) Japanese steer raised and pampered to an impeccably high standard for its delectably tender meat which, in accordance, is exorbitantly expensive.

kofta (Ind.) Meatballs of ground lamb, beef, or veal, variously seasoned and spelled, eaten throughout the Balkans, North Africa, Middle and Far East.

Kohl (Ger.) Cabbage; *Kohlrouden* is cabbage stuffed with ground meats and braised.

kohlrabi A vegetable in the cabbage family whose stem swells just above the ground into a bulbous knob; this bulb, the long stems, and the leaves are edible and taste like cabbage and turnip, which together give it its name; favored in central and eastern Europe and Asia.

koi-kuchi shōya (Jap.) Dark soy sauce, thicker and heavier but less salty than light soy sauce (*usu-kuchi shōya*).

Kompott (Ger.) Compote of stewed fruit.

konbu (Jap.) Dried kelp, essential in making **dashi;** sometimes spelled *kombu.*

Konditorei (Ger.) A pastry shop, where coffee and hot chocolate are offered to sample pastries with.

Königenpastete (Ger.) Pastry filled with meat and mushrooms or other savory fillings.

konnyaku (Jap.) Literally, "devil's tongue jelly"; a translucent cake made from arum root.

Kopfsalat (Ger.) Lettuce salad, head of lettuce.

korma (Ind.) To braise, braised; the word also designates a spicy stew, often of lamb or mutton, braised with a thick yogurt and cream sauce.

Korn (Ger.) Grain, cereal; the word means the dominant grain in a specific region, whether rye, wheat, or barley—not necessarily corn.

kosher (Jew.) According to Jewish dietary laws, the *kashruth,* as set forth in the *Talmud.*

Kotelett (Ger.) Cutlet, chop.

Krabbe (Ger.) Crab; the plural *Krabben* often means shrimp.

Krakauer (Ger.) Polish ham sausage.

Krapfen (Ger.) Sweet Bavarian fritters, similar to doughnuts.

Kraut (Ger.) Plant, herb, greens; on a menu the word usually means cabbage.

kreatopita (Gr.) A meat pie wrapped in **phyllo** dough.

Krebs (Ger.) Crab, crayfish.

Kren (Ger.) Horseradish; *Krenfleisch* is top round of beef boiled, sliced, and served with bread, gherkins, and horseradish, from Bavaria.

kreplach (Jew.) Small dough turnovers with savory filling, often served in soup.

Kreuznach A town on the Nahe River, west of the Rhine, that is the center of the valley's wine industry; a good wine school is located there.

Kronsbeer (Ger.) A berry similar to the cranberry.

krupnik (Jew.) Mushroom barley soup.

kuài zi (Chin.) Chopsticks.

Küche (Ger.) Kitchen, cooking.

Kuchen (Ger.) Cake, tart, pastry.

kudamono (Jap.) Fruit.

kugel (Jew.) A baked casserole or pudding.

Kugelhopf (Ger.) A yeast cake, sometimes made from **brioche** dough, flavored with currants steeped in brandy and baked in a special fluted mold strewn with almonds; now a specialty of Alsace, it is originally from Austria where it is called *Gugelhupf,* each region having its traditional molds.

kulibyaka (Russ.) A pie filled with layers of salmon or fish, rice or kasha, herbs, mushrooms, onion, etc., oval in shape, large or small in size; French *haute cuisine* has adapted it as *coulibiac.*

kulich (Russ.) A tall cylindrical cake in the shape of a priest's hat, flavored with fruit, almonds, and saffron; this is the Russian Orthodox ceremonial dessert for Easter, decorated with the letters XB, signifying "Christ is Risen," and traditionally served with **paskha.**

kümmel (Russ.) A Russian liqueur made from caraway and, according to some authorities, cumin seeds.

kumquat A small oval citrus fruit, native to China, eaten whole, either fresh or preserved in syrup, and often used as a garnish; its rind is sweeter than its pulp; the name means "golden orange" in Cantonese.

kuri (Jap.) Chestnuts.

Kutteln (Ger.) Tripe.

kvass (Russ.) A fermented drink similar to beer, made from yeast, rye, and barley; it is used to flavor **borsch, chlodnik,** and other soups; sometimes spelled *kwas.*

kyūri (Jap.) Japanese cucumber.

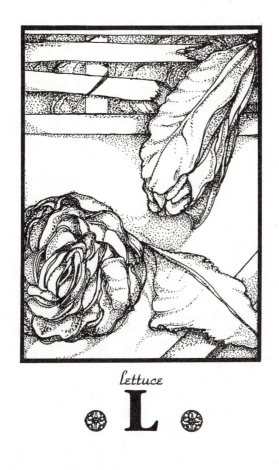

lettuce

❖ L ❖

labna, labneh (Mid. E.) Yogurt whose whey has been drained off, shaped into balls, rolled in herbs or spices, and preserved in olive oil; eaten with bread.

Labskaus (Ger.) "Seaman's stew" from Hamburg, of pickled pork or beef cooked with onions and potatoes, sometimes with pickled fish, beets, or gherkins as garnish.

Lachryma Christi A white wine from the vineyards on Mt. Vesuvius near Naples, Italy, pale gold and fairly dry; the name means "tears of Christ"; a sparkling white wine with the same name is made elsewhere in Italy.

Lachs (Ger.) Salmon.

lacón con grelos (Sp.) Cured pork shoulder with turnip tops—a famous dish from Galicia.

lactic acid The acid in sour milk produced by bacterial starter culture, which turns lactose (milk sugar) into lactic acid, causing the coagulation of the milk and the first step in the cheesemaking process; lactic acid is also present in rested muscle tissue and acts as a natural preservative in slaughtered meat.

Lafite, Château A great Bordeaux vineyard, from Pauillac in the Haut-Médoc, which fully deserves its fame; ranked a first growth in 1855, it is owned by the Rothschild family; the wine is full-bodied and long-lived, with remarkable bouquet and depth—perhaps the greatest red wine of all.

lager Bottom-fermented beer that has been aged; most American beers are lager.

lait (Fr.) Milk.

laitue (Fr.) Lettuce.

là jiāo jiàng (Chin.) Hot chili sauce; a condiment made from chili peppers, vinegar, and seasonings; red in color, red hot in taste.

lal mirch (Ind.) Red pepper.

Lambrusco A slightly effervescent red wine, fruity, fragrant, and pleasant, made near Modena from the *lambrusco* grape.

lamb's lettuce A plant indigenous to Europe, whose dark green, nutty-flavored leaves are used for winter salads; it is prized by the French; also called corn salad and *mâche.*

lampone (It.) Raspberry.

lamprey A salt- or freshwater fish similar to the **eel;** its fatty flesh is eaten in various ways, most often stewed.

Lancashire (Brit.) A creamy white cows' milk cheese from England, cooked and pressed yet still soft and crumbly; true farmhouse Lancashire has a full flavor and excellent melting qualities for **Welsh rarebit** and other dishes, but travels poorly or not at all; the factory-made variety is a pale comparison.

Lancashire hot pot (Brit.) A traditional English stew of secondary cuts of lamb, especially neck, stewed with layered potatoes and onions, lamb kidneys and oysters often included; a relative of the French **hochepot.**

Landjäger (Ger.) A smoked sausage from Swabia.

langouste (Fr.) Rock or spiny lobster (U.S.), called saltwater crayfish or crawfish in Britain; found in the Mediterranean and Pacific, its claws are small, so most of the meat comes from the tail; when cooked its color is paler than lobster; the Spanish word for this crustacean is *langosta.*

langoustine (Fr.) A small lobster, a saltwater crayfish; also called Dublin Bay prawn (Brit.), Norway lobster, and scampo (It.).

langue (Fr.) Tongue.

langues-de-chat (Fr.) Long, thin cookies whose shape resembles a cat's tongue, hence the name; because they are light and dry, they often accompany simple desserts and sweet wines.

Languedoc A region in southeastern France along the Mediterranean, a former province, with wonderful produce and an excellent gastronomic tradition; some of its specialties are **cassoulet, confit, brandade de morue, Roquefort,** Bouzigues oysters, and other seafood, to name just a few.

languedocienne, à la (Fr.) Meat or poultry garnished with eggplant rounds, *cèpes,* and tomatoes *concassés,* all sautéed in oil, with chopped parsley.

lapin (Fr.) Rabbit; *lapin de garenne* is wild rabbit; *lapin en gibelotte* is rabbit stew with onions, mushrooms, and **lardons,** in white wine sauce.

Lapsang Souchong See **Souchong.**

lard Rendered pork fat, excellent for flaky pastry because of its solidity and for deep-frying because of its high smoke point and purity; as a saturated fat high in cholesterol, however, it is not very healthful. See also **interlard.**

lard de poitrine fumé (Fr.) Bacon.

larder (Fr.) To lard, to interlard.

lardo (It.) Salt pork; *lardo affumicato* is bacon.

lardon (Fr.) Lardoon; larding fat cut into long strips and threaded through lean cuts of meat by a special larding needle in order to moisten the meat as it cooks; the term also includes pork or bacon, diced, blanched, and fried, used to flavor and moisten braised dishes and stews.

largo (Mex.) A long, thin chili pepper, pale yellow green in color, fairly hot; often used in soups and stews.

lasagne (It.) Large flat ribbons of pasta about $4\frac{1}{2}$ inches wide, baked in layers with sauce, cheese, or other filling; *lasagne* is usually made with egg and often pureed spinach as well to color it green.

lassam (Ind.) Garlic.

lassi (Ind.) Yogurt flavored with rosewater and sugar.

latkes (Jew.) Potatoes grated and fried in pancakes, traditionally eaten at Hanukkah.

Latour, Château A great and renowned Bordeaux vineyard in Pauillac in the Haut-Médoc; ranked a first growth, it deserves its place next to Margaux and Lafite; the wine is robust, deep-colored, and long-lived.

latte (It.) Milk.

lattuga (It.) Lettuce.

Lauch (Ger.) Leek.

lauro (It.) Bay leaf.

La Varenne, François Pierre de Seventeenth-century chef and author of *Le Cuisiner Français* (1651), a landmark cookbook which, breaking with the Middle Ages, began the culinary tradition of the golden age to follow; La Varenne set up a system of ready stocks, **liaisons** (**roux** first appeared in his book), **forcemeats,** and herb and spice mixtures to be drawn upon as needed.

laver   Thin, black seaweed used in Japanese cooking and called **nori** in Japan; in Wales it is often called laverbread.

leavening   Any agent that produces gas in dough or batter by means of **fermentation,** thus raising and lightening it. **Yeast, baking powder,** and **baking soda** are all common forms of leavening; beaten egg whites, although they do not involve fermentation, are another kind of leavening.

Leber   (Ger.)   Liver.

Leberkäs   (Ger.)   Meat loaf or pâté of mixed ground meats, from Bavaria.

Leberknödelsuppe   (Ger.)   Soup of clear meat broth with liver dumplings, from Bavaria.

Leberwurst   (Ger.)   A smoked sausage made from ground pork liver and (usually) pork or veal meat.

Lebkuchen   (Ger.)   Spiced honey cake traditionally eaten at Christmas.

leche   (Sp.)   Milk; the word can also mean custard.

lechecillas   (Sp.)   Sweetbreads.

lechuga   (Sp.)   Lettuce.

Leckerli   (Switz.)   Rectangular biscuit, flavored with cinnamon, honey, dried citrus peel, and almonds; from Basel.

leek   An ancient member of the lily family, originating in the Mediterranean; its flavor, more subtle than that of other onions, lends itself to soups, stews, and braised dishes; because the leek lacks a well-defined bulb, dirt gets well down into its leaves, necessitating careful washing.

lees   The sediment that settles in the wine barrel before bottling.

legumbres   (Sp.)   Vegetables; *legumbres secos* are dried vegetables.

legume   The seed pod of leguminous plants whose peas or beans are eaten fresh (sprouted or not) and dried for their high protein and carbohydrate value; legumes are an important staple food crop in much of the world.

légumes   (Fr.)   Vegetables.

legumi   (It.)   Vegetables.

Leicester   (Brit.)   A whole-milk cows' cheese, cooked and pressed, made in large cylinders; it has a hard brownish red rind and a yellow, flaky but moist interior; similar to **Cheddar,** English farmhouse Leicester has a tangy, rich flavor.

lekach   (Jew.)   A honey and spice cake, traditional for Rosh Hashanah.

lemon balm   A Mediterranean herb whose leaves, faintly lemon-scented, are used in salads, compotes, drinks, tea, and in the making of **Chartreuse.**

lemon curd Lemon juice, sugar, butter, and egg yolks mixed together and cooked slowly until the yolks thicken (but do not curdle); used for pastries.

lemon grass See **sorrel.**

lemon thyme See **thyme.**

lemon verbena An herb whose lemon-scented leaves flavor teas and salads; native to South America.

lengua de ternere (Sp.) Calf's tongue.

lenguado (Sp.) Sole.

lenticchie (It.) Lentils.

lentil A legume that originated in Southwest Asia; high in nutrients, it has been a staple in the Middle East and Central Asia for millennia and is cultivated in many varieties.

lepre (It.) Hare; *lepre in salmi* is **jugged hare.**

lesso (It.) Boiled, especially boiled meat.

levée, pâte (Fr.) See **pâte levée.**

leveret (Fr.) Young hare.

Leyden (Neth.) A hard Dutch cheese similar to Edam, made from partially skimmed cows' milk; the curd is cooked, flavored with cumin, caraway, and spices, molded, and pressed.

liaison (Fr.) Binding or thickening of soup or sauce by means of egg yolk, blood, or starch such as flour (see **beurre manié** and **roux**), arrowroot, cornstarch, or tapioca.

lichi, lichee See **lychee.**

licorice, liquorice A plant, native to the Middle East, whose name derives from the Greek for "sweet root"; the ancients used the root for medicinal purposes, while today its anise flavoring is used primarily for candy; before sugar cane, strips of the raw root were chewed as a kind of candy.

licuado (Sp.) Fruit drink, especially citrus.

Liebfraumilch A catchall name for Rhine wine, almost all very ordinary; the name means "milk of the Blessed Mother."

Liederkranz A pasteurized cows' milk cheese invented by a Swiss immigrant in the U.S. and named after a choral society; it is a soft, mild, surface-ripened cheese shaped in rectangles.

liégeoise, à la (Fr.) Garnished with juniper berries.

lier (Fr.) To blend.

lièvre (Fr.) Hare.

lights The lungs of an animal, used in the U.S. for pet food but in other countries combined with other organs and meat in stews, pâtés, etc., for human consumption.

li jiàng (Chin.) Oyster sauce, consisting of oysters, salt, and seasonings concentrated into a thick paste; used mostly in Cantonese cooking.

lima (Sp.) Lime; the Mexican *lima agria* is a sour lime from the Yucatán.

limande (Fr.) Lemon sole.

Limburger A pasteurized cows' milk cheese, originally Belgian but now German; soft, surface-ripened, creamy yellow, dense, with a strong and characteristic smell.

lime, limette (Fr.) Lime.

limon (Fr.) Lime.

limón (Sp.) Lemon.

limone (It.) Lemon.

limousine, à la (Fr.) Garnished with red cabbage.

lingua di bue (It.) Ox tongue.

lingue di passero (It.) Very thin, flat, eggless pasta; literally, "sparrows' tongues."

linguiça (Sp.) Pork sausage flavored with garlic; similar to **chorizo.**

linguine (It.) Thin flat eggless pasta.

Linse (Ger.) Lentil.

Linsensuppe (Ger.) Lentil soup with sausage.

Linzertorte (Aus.) An Austrian tart of ground hazelnut pastry filled with raspberry jam and covered with a latticework crust.

Liptauer A ewes' milk cheese, originally German, now made in Hungary; soft, dense, rindless, and strong, it is made in small blocks.

litchi See **lychee.**

Livarot (Fr.) A whole-milk cows' cheese from the town of the same name in Normandy, made in one-pound discs; the cheese is soft, even-textured, and tangy in flavor, with a hard, shiny surface; colored yellow or dyed deep red with **annatto,** it is a fall or winter cheese.

lobster A family of marine crustaceans, including the saltwater **crayfish,** rock or spiny lobster, Spanish lobster, and American or Maine lobster; its delicate, lean, flavorful meat—concentrated in the large tail and sometimes the claws—its coral (roe), and tomalley (liver) all are prized in cooking.

locust bean See **carob.**

loganberry A hybrid cultivar of the blackberry, developed by Judge James Logan in California; the fruit is darker, larger, and more prolific than the raspberry and milder in flavor; excellent for cooking.

loin A cut of beef from the hindquarter, between the **rib** and **round;** the full loin contains the tenderest cuts within the **sirloin** and **short loin.**

Loire The longest river in France, flowing northwest from near Lyons to the Atlantic at Nantes; there are many diverse vineyards in its valley, mostly white and some quite fine, including **Pouilly-Fumé, Sancerre, Vouvray, Saumur,** and **Muscadet.**

lombo, lombata (It.) Loin; the Spanish word is *lomo.*

London broil   A cut of beef from the **flank**—one thin, flat muscle that is usually either braised or broiled and sliced on an angle; other cuts from different sections of beef are sometimes loosely called London broil.

longanzia   (Sp.)   A large pork sausage flavored with garlic, marjoram, and pimiento.

longe de veau   (Fr.)   Loin of veal.

lonza   (It.)   Loin; the word often means cured loin of pork.

loquat   A plum-shaped golden fruit from a small Oriental tree, sometimes called the Chinese or Japanese medlar; because it ripens in March, it was very popular in Europe before air travel, as it is the first fruit to ripen in spring; now that fresh fruit is flown from the other side of the globe, the bland but juicy loquat is mostly used in jams and jellies.

Lorraine   A region in northeastern France (a former duchy) bordering on Germany, Luxembourg, and Belgium; its excellent cuisine and wines, like Lorraine's political history, show the influence of Germany, with many distinguished dishes using pork, veal, geese, crayfish, apples, eggs and cream, and pastries.

lorraine, à la   (Fr.)   Garnished with braised red cabbage balls and olive-shaped potatoes sautéed in butter.

lotte   (Fr.)   Monkfish.

loup   (Fr.)   Sea bass; the word also means wolf.

lovage   An herb once popular but little used today, whose unusual and strong celery flavor seasons meat stews and stocks; its leaves, stems, roots, and seeds can all be used; it is indigenous to the Mediterranean and resembles overgrown celery in appearance.

lox   (Jew.)   Salmon, usually from the Pacific Ocean, cured (but not smoked, as it used to be) with salt, then soaked in water to remove some of the salt; often eaten with cream cheese on **bagels;** see also **nova.**

lubina   (Sp.)   Sea bass.

luganeaga   (It.)   Mild, fresh pork sausage flavored with Parmesan cheese, made in long tubes without links.

lumaca   (It.)   Snail; the plural is *lumache.*

lumpia   (Phil.)   A thin pastry wrapper enclosing a savory filling, either fresh and wrapped in a lettuce leaf or deep-fried like a **spring roll.**

lutefisk   (Scand.)   Dried cod soaked in a lye bath of potash, eaten with cream sauce or pork drippings.

lychee   (Chin.)   The fruit of a small tree, also called the Chinese plum, often used in Oriental cuisine; the exterior of the nutlike fruit is a thin red scaly shell; the soft, white, fleshy interior surrounds a stone; the fruit is eaten fresh, dried, canned, or preserved in syrup both as a fruit dessert and as an accompaniment to savory foods; spelled variously.

Lymeswold (Brit.) A new English cheese recently developed on a large commercial scale; it is essentially a mild blue **Brie,** combining the delicate white rind and soft creamy paste with blue veining. The name has no particular meaning but was devised by marketing specialists; called Westminster for export.

Lyonerwurst (Ger.) Ham sausage flavored with garlic.

lyonnaise, à la (Fr.) With onions; *lyonnaise* sauce in classic cuisine is chopped onions sautéed in butter, reduced with white wine and vinegar, **demi-glace** added, and strained; the city of Lyons, located near Beaujolais, where the Rhône and Saône Rivers flow together, has a renowned gastronomic tradition.

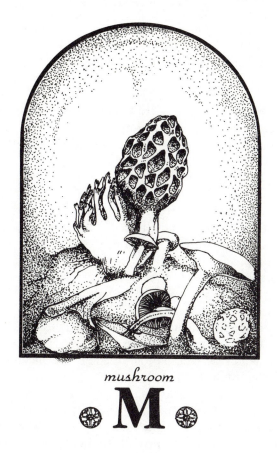

mushroom

❖ M ❖

maanz (Ind.) Meat.

maatjes herring (Neth.) See **matjes herring.**

macadamia nut Nut from a tree native to Australia but now cultivated mostly in Hawaii; usually shelled and roasted before purchase, the round nut is white, sweet, and high in fat, making it prized as a dessert nut.

macaroni See **maccheroni.**

macaroon A small, light, round cookie made of almond paste, sugar, and egg whites; in Italy, where they probably originated, these pastries are called *amaretti.*

maccarèllo (It.) Mackerel.

maccheroni (It.) Macaroni, tube-shaped pasta; except in Naples (where it is spelled *macaroni*), Italians spell this type of pasta thus. In eighteenth-century England, young dandies who on their return from Italy affected continental dress and style were called *macaronis,* hence the famous "stuck a feather in his hat and called it macaroni."

mace A spice made from the lacy covering of the nutmeg seed, dried to an orange brown color and usually powdered; mace tastes like nutmeg with a hint of cinnamon and is used more widely in savory dishes than is nutmeg.

macédoine (Fr.) A mixture of fruits or vegetables served hot or cold; its name refers to the racial variety of Macedonia.

macerate To steep food in liquid; usually refers to fresh fruit steeped in liqueur.

mâche (Fr.) **Lamb's lettuce.**

machi (Ind.) Fish.

Mâcon A town in southern Burgundy on the Saône River and the center of its wine trade; Mâcon wines are red, white, and rosé, strictly limited according to grape variety; Mâconnais is the large wine-producing region encompassing Mâcon.

Madeira A Portuguese island in the Atlantic famous for its fortified wines, which are 18–20 percent alcohol; aged and blended in **soleras** like **sherry,** the special character and longevity of Madeira comes from the long and gradual heating process called *estufa;* Madeira wines range from very dry to very sweet, so they are suitable for **apéritif** and dessert wines as well as for cooking; specific types of Madeira are separately entered.

madeleine (Fr.) A small cake made of flour, sugar, butter, and eggs baked in a special shell mold; its origin is uncertain, but the town of Commercy is famous for *madeleines,* Louis XV favored them, and Proust gave them immortality with the beginning of *A la Recherche de Temps Perdu.*

madère (Fr.) A classic French sauce of **demi-glace** flavored with **Madeira.**

maderisé (Fr.) Wine that is partially spoiled by oxidation; a maderized wine has acquired a brownish color and the special aroma of **Madeira** due to the effects of excessive heat.

madrilène (Fr.) Beef consommé flavored with tomato.

mafalde, mafaldine (It.) Long pasta strips with fluted edges, in medium and narrow widths.

maggiorana (It.) Marjoram.

magnum A double-sized wine bottle that helps exceptional Bordeaux or Burgundies mature to their fullest, but not advantageous to the development of other wines.

magret, maigret (Fr.) Breast of duck cooked rare.

maiale (It.) Pork; suckling pig is *maigletto.*

maigre (Fr.) An adjective denoting thin, lean, low-fat; food suitable for fast days, as prescribed by the Roman Catholic Church. At first only vegetable dishes were allowed during Advent, Lent, and days before important feasts; gradually, butter, milk, eggs, and cold-blooded animals, including fish and eventually waterfowl, were allowed, with many dispensations. The Italian word is *magro*.

maionese (It.) Mayonnaise; the Spanish word is *mahonesa*.

maison (Fr.) Literally, "house"; designates a dish made by a restaurant's own special method, such as *pâté maison*.

maître d'hôtel (Fr.) The person in charge of a restaurant dining room, who must command every aspect of service to patrons; originally, in royal or noble households, it was a position of great importance; the informal *maître d'* is often used. *Maître d'hôtel* butter is seasoned with chopped parsley and lemon juice.

maize Corn; the French word *maïs* actually means sweet corn, while the Spanish word *maíz* means dried corn.

makhan (Ind.) Butter.

maki (Jap.) Rolled.

mako See **shark.**

Málaga A sweet, heavy, dark **sherry** from the region north of the southern Spanish city of the same name, where it is blended.

malai (Ind.) Cream (all kinds).

Malbec (Fr.) A red-wine grape variety used for some better Bordeaux wines; faster-maturing than Cabernet.

Malmsey (Brit.) The English name for Malvasia, a grape variety producing very sweet, heavy, golden **Madeira** that turns amber with age; the wine, originally Greek, is produced elsewhere, but that of Madeira is the most famous.

malt Germinated barley used in brewing and distilling; malt extract, highly nourishing, is used to make food for children and invalids. In a malted milk, the malt powder is dissolved in milk, and other flavorings, such as chocolate, are sometimes added.

maltagliati (It.) "Badly cut" flat pasta about $\frac{1}{2}$ inch thick and cut on the bias; used mainly for bean soups.

maltaise (Fr.) A classic sauce of **hollandaise** flavored with grated orange zest and blood orange juice; the cold sauce *maltaise* is **mayonnaise** similarly flavored.

Malvasia See **Malmsey.**

Malzbier (Ger.) Dark, sweet, malty beer, low in alcohol.

mamé (Jap.) Bean.

mamey See **mammee.**

mammee A tall tropical tree that grows in Central and South America; its round fruit, with smooth orange pulp, is eaten fresh and in ice creams.

manche (Fr.) The projecting bone on a chop; a *manchette* is a frill used to cover the bone; for *manche à gigot* see **gigot.**

Manchego (Sp.) A pale, golden, dense ewes' milk cheese from Spain;

the curd is molded, pressed, salted in brine, and cured; the rind has a greenish black mold that is sometimes brushed off and replaced with a thin smearing of olive oil. *Manchego* also means in the style of La Mancha.

mandarine (Fr.) Tangerine.

Mandel (Ger.) Almond; the Italian word is *mandorla.*

mandoline (Fr.) A tool, somewhat resembling the musical instrument, used to cut vegetables evenly and quickly into thick or thin, furrowed or smooth slices.

mange-tout (Fr.) A pea or bean, such as the snow pea or sugar-snap, whose pod and seeds are literally eaten all together.

mango A tropical evergreen tree, Indian or Malayan in origin, whose fully-ripened fruit is perhaps the most luscious of all fruits; varying in size, shape, and color, it is usually a deep orange color and pear shaped, with smooth golden flesh; mangoes are eaten fresh or cooked in preserves and chutneys, still green.

manicotti (It.) Flat circular sheets of pasta stuffed variously and baked in a sauce.

manié See **beurre manié.**

manioc See **tapioca.**

Manteca (It.) A spun-curd cows' milk cheese from southern Italy wrapped around a pat of butter; the name comes from the Spanish word for butter, *mantequilla;* this small cheese is also called *Burro, Burrino,* or *Butirro,* locally.

mantecado (Sp.) Rich vanilla ice cream with whipped cream folded in.

mantequilla (Sp.) Butter.

manzana (Sp.) Apple.

Manzanilla An extremely dry pale Spanish **sherry** with a special, almost bitter, taste; drunk mostly in Spain, especially in Seville.

manzanilla (Sp.) Camomile, camomile tea.

manzo (It.) Beef.

maple syrup Syrup made from the sap of sugar maples and certain other maple trees in northeastern North America. The trees are tapped with a spigot set into the tree trunk. The sap begins to run in late winter in a natural process not entirely understood by scientists, but recognized by the American Indians and certain animals; the sap is boiled down into syrup and even further into maple sugar.

maquereau (Fr.) Mackerel.

maraschino A liqueur made from the *marasca* cherry and its crushed stones, originally from Yugoslavia and now from Italy as well. Maraschino cherries are cooked in artificially colored syrup and flavored with imitation liqueur—a far cry from the original.

marbled A term used to describe meat, especially beef, that has small flecks of fat throughout the muscle tissue. Such meat is generally considered high quality for its juiciness and flavor when cooked. Marbled pastry has light and dark dough swirled together so that it resembles marble stone.

marc (Fr.) Pomace: usually grape or sometimes apple skins and seeds, remaining after the juice has been pressed; *eau de vie de marc* (often shortened to *marc*) is the strong brandy distilled from these residual solids; known in Italy as *grappa.*

marcassin (Fr.) Young wild boar.

marchand de vin (Fr.) A classic sauce for grilled meats, similar to **Bercy** or **bordelaise:** red wine is flavored with chopped shallots and parsley and well reduced; butter is then beaten in. The name means wine merchant.

Marcobrunn A well-known vineyard from the German **Rheingau** producing one of the very best white wines.

maréchale, à la (Fr.) Small cuts of meat or poultry, egg-and-bread-crumbed, fried in butter, and garnished with sliced truffles, asparagus tips, or green peas.

marée (Fr.) All saltwater fish and shellfish.

Marengo, à la (Fr.) Chicken pieces browned in olive oil, braised with tomatoes, garlic, and brandy, and garnished with fried eggs, crayfish, and sometimes croûtons. This famous dish was devised by Napoléon's chef Dunand after the defeat of the Austrians at Marengo in 1800, when no other food could be found.

margarine A butter substitute, originally made from animal fats and now from vegetable fats, developed in 1869 by a French chemist.

Margaux A wine-producing **commune** in the French **Haut-Médoc** that produces exceptional Bordeaux, including some of the most famous: Châteaux Margaux, Brane-Cantenac, Palmer, Kirwan.

Margaux, Château A Bordeaux wine, from Margaux in the **Haut-Médoc;** a first-growth wine (see **classed growth**) and one of the world's very finest red wines.

Marguéry (Fr.) A classic sauce of **hollandaise** flavored with oyster liquor and garnished with poached oysters.

Maribo (Den.) A semihard pasteurized cows' milk cheese from the Danish island of Lolland; the large oblong cheeses have a yellow wax coating, a white paste with small holes, and a flavor that grows quite strong with age.

Marie Louise (Fr.) A classic garnish of artichoke hearts filled with mushroom puree and **Soubise.**

marignan (Fr.) A boat-shaped pastry made of rich yeast dough soaked in rum-flavored syrup, brushed with apricot jam, and filled with **crème Chantilly.**

marigold   A plant with bright golden flowers used fresh or dried as an herb or dye.

Marille   (Ger.)   Apricot.

marinade   A liquid, including seasonings and acid (vinegar or wine), in which food is steeped before cooking in order to flavor, moisten, and soften it.

marinara, alla   (It.)   Literally "sailor style"; a loose term often meaning a simple tomato sauce flavored with garlic and herbs, often served with **fettucine** or other pasta.

marinière, à la   (Fr.)   Literally "sailor style"; seafood cooked in white wine with chopped shallots, parsley, and butter and garnished with mussels; *moules marinière* is the classic example.

marinierter Hering   (Ger.)   Pickled herring.

mariscos   (Sp.)   Shrimp or scallops; shellfish.

marjolaine   (Fr.)   A famous pastry created by **Fernand Point** of almond and filbert **dacquoise** layered with chocolate, praline, and buttercream. *Marjolaine* also means sweet marjoram.

marjoram, sweet marjoram   An herb in many varieties, originally Mediterranean, from the mint family; it is used in diverse savory dishes.

marmalade   Citrus fruit jam, usually from bitter Seville oranges with the rind included, stewed for a long time and reduced to a thick preserve. Marmalade is indispensable to a proper British breakfast. The word derives from the Portuguese word for quince, *marmelo.*

marmelade   (Fr.)   A thick sweetened fruit puree (or occasionally onion), reduced to a jamlike consistency; not be be confused with **marmalade.**

marmite   (Fr.)   A large covered pot, usually earthenware but sometimes metal, for cooking large quantities of food; *Marmite* is a brand name for a type of yeast extract. See also **petite marmite.**

Maroilles   (Fr.)   A soft, uncooked cows' milk cheese, invented a thousand years ago by the monks at the Abbey of Maroilles in Flanders; square with a reddish rind and pale yellow interior, it is ripened up to six months with regular washings of the rind in brine; the flavor is creamy, rich, and tangy, the aroma attractively strong; also called *Marolles.*

marquise   (Fr.)   A fruit ice with whipped cream folded in.

marron   (Fr.)   A cultivated chestnut used as a vegetable, for stuffings, and for pastry; *marrons glacés*—whole peeled chestnuts poached for a long time and glazed in a thick syrup—are a choice delicacy.

marrow   A large summer squash similar to zucchini.

marrow bone   A large beef or veal bone cut into short segments and poached or braised to solidify the rich and nutritious interior marrow, which is then scooped out and spread or diced; marrow is prized in such recipes as **osso buco** and sauce **bordelaise.**

Marsala   An Italian **fortified** dessert wine, 17–19 percent alcohol, from the Sicilian city of the same name. The wine is a deep amber color, usually dry but sometimes sweet, roughly comparable to **sherry**; it is an important ingredient in **zabaglione.**

marshmallow A confection made from egg whites, sugar, and gelatin, originally flavored with the root of the marshmallow plant.

Marzenbier (Ger.) A strong, medium-colored beer traditionally brewed in March (hence its name) and drunk in spring and summer; any remaining beer is consumed at festivals such as Oktoberfest.

marzipan A paste of ground almonds, sugar, and egg white shaped and often colored to resemble fruits, vegetables, animals, etc.; the tradition of these decorative confections is very old, dating at least to the Middle Ages.

masa (Mex.) A dough of dried cornmeal and water, used in making tortillas and other preparations; *masa harina* is corn flour.

masala (Ind.) Spice or a blend of spices.

Mascarpone (It.) A soft cows' milk cheese made near Milan; the curd made from the cream is beaten or whipped to make a thick, velvety cheese with a rich sweet flavor; it is served with fruit and pastries like cream, layered with **Gorgonzola** to make *Torta di Gordenza,* and used in various other ways.

mask To cover food with sauce before serving.

masquer (Fr.) To mask.

massepain (Fr.) **Marzipan.**

Mastgeflügel (Ger.) Specially raised grain-fed poultry from the Vierlande region southeast of Hamburg, of fine quality.

matar (Ind.) Peas; chick-peas.

matelote (Fr.) A fish stew (usually of freshwater fish) made with red or white wine.

matjes herring High quality, lightly salted young "virgin" herring that have not yet spawned; very popular in Germany, the Netherlands, and Scandinavia.

matsutake (Jap.) "Pine" mushrooms.

matzo, matzoh (Jew.) Flat unleavened bread eaten during Passover to symbolize the Jews' hurried flight from Egypt, when there was no time for the bread to rise; *matzo* meal is used in other dishes such as **knädlach** and **gefilte fish.**

Maultaschen (Ger.) Ground veal, pork, and spinach wrapped in noodle dough and served in gravy or broth for Maunday Thursday; from Swabia.

mayonnaise (Fr.) The classic French **emulsion** of egg yolks seasoned with vinegar and mustard, with oil added very gradually to form a thick sauce; there are many variations of this basic cold sauce.

mayonnaise verte **Mayonnaise** flavored and colored green with finely minced herbs such as spinach, sorrel, watercress, parsley, chervil, and tarragon; the herbs may be **blanched** first.

May wine   A white-wine spring punch, lightly sweetened and flavored with the herb **woodruff** and served chilled in a bowl with strawberries; originally German.

meat birds   Scallops or slices of meat filled with a savory stuffing, rolled up and secured (usually with string), browned in fat, and braised; also called olives. The French term is **oiseaux sans tête,** the Italian *olivetti.*

médaillon   (Fr.)   Small round "medallion" or scallop of meat, such as beef, lamb, veal, or even a slice of **foie gras.**

medlar   See **loquat.**

Médoc   French wine-producing region north of Bordeaux bounded on the east by the Gironde River and on the west by the Atlantic Ocean; red wines so labeled come from the northern part, the *Bas-Médoc,* and are good though not as fine as those from the **Haut-Médoc** in the southern part of the region.

Meerrettich   (Ger.)   Horseradish.

meetha   (Ind.)   Sweet.

Mehlspeise   (Ger.)   A flour-based dish, especially popular in Bavaria— **dumplings,** pancakes, and **Strudel** are examples; in Austrian dialect this word means pudding.

mejillone   (Sp.)   Mussel.

mejorana   (Sp.)   Marjoram.

mela   (It.)   Apple.

melagrana   (It.)   Pomegranate.

mélanger   (Fr.)   To mix; the word *mélange* means mixture or blend.

melanzana   (It.)   Eggplant; the Greek word is *melidzanes.*

Melba toast   Very thin slices of toast, named for Dame Nellie Melba, the great Australian soprano; **pêche Melba** was also created for her by **Escoffier.**

melocotón   (Sp.)   Peach.

Melton Mowbray pie   (Brit.)   A pork pie encased in a pastry "coffin" or crust, served cold; an old and traditional convenience food that is easily transportable; named after the Leicestershire town of Melton Mowbray.

Mendocino   A wine-producing county in northern California, near Ukiah, with especially good **Zinfandels.**

menestra   (Sp.)   Stew.

menthe   (Fr.)   Mint; *crème de menthe* is a mint-flavored liqueur, either green or colorless.

menudo   (Sp.)   Tripe stew.

meringue   Pastry made of stiffly beaten egg whites with sugar, shaped variously, and baked in a slow oven. For *meringue italienne* see **Italian meringue.**

merlan (Fr.) Whiting; the Italian word is *merlango.*

Merlot A red-wine grape variety, productive and early-ripening, that yields soft, fruity, and graceful wines; Merlot combines well with the more astringent, later-maturing, and longer-lived **Cabernet;** widely planted in Bordeaux, California, parts of Switzerland, and northern Italy.

merluza (Sp.) Hake; the Italian word *merluzzo* means cod.

mero (Sp.) Rock bass.

mesclun (Fr.) A Provençal mixture of young salad greens whose seeds are sown together, traditionally including wild **chicory, mâche,** curly **escarole,** dandelion, **rocket,** and other tender lettuces; *mesclun* comes from the Niçoise word for mixture.

mesquite A scrub tree that grows wild in the southwestern U.S. and Mexico, whose wood has recently become very fashionable for grilling food in the **new American cuisine.**

metate (Mex.) A sloping slab of porous volcanic rock standing on three legs and used to grind corn and spices in Mexican cooking; similar to a **molcajete;** the stone that is rolled over the surface for grinding is called a *mano.*

methi (Ind.) **Fenugreek.**

Methuselah An oversized bottle of Champagne, holding up to eight regular bottles, named after the biblical patriarch said to have lived 969 years; spelled variously.

Mettwurst (Ger.) Smoked pork sausage with red skin and a coarse texture.

Meunier A fine grape variety, a subvariety of the Pinot Noir grape; planted extensively in Champagne, Alsace, and California.

meunière, à la (Fr.) Lightly dredged with flour, sautéed in butter, and served with melted butter and sliced lemon; *meunière* means "in the style of the miller's wife."

Meursault A village in the French **Côte d'Or** of Burgundy that produces a large quantity of distinguished white wine.

Mexican saffron See **safflower.**

mezzani (It.) Pasta in a long narrow tube.

microwave oven An oven that works on the principle of electromagnetic radiation; these high-frequency waves penetrate the food being cooked to a depth of two inches and heat the water inside very quickly and efficiently but without browning the outside; for this reason some microwave ovens include browning elements.

midollo (It.) Marrow.

mie (Fr.) The crumb or soft interior part of a loaf of bread; *pain de mie* is sandwich bread.

miel (Fr.) Honey; in Italian the word is *miele.*

mignonette (Fr.) Coarsely ground pepper; originally, this seasoning included various other spices, such as nutmeg, coriander, cinnamon, ginger, clove, and red pepper. A *mignonette* is also a **médaillon.**

mi jiú (Chin.) Chinese rice wine, yellow in color.

mijoter (Fr.) To simmer.

Mikado (Fr.) Japanese style.

mikan (Jap.) Tangerine.

milanaise, à la (Fr.) A classic garnish of julienne of tongue, ham, mushrooms and truffles with spaghetti, tomato sauce, and **Parmesan** cheese.

mille-feuille (Fr.) See **pâte feuilletée;** the Italian term is *mille foglie* or *pasta sfoglia.*

millet A grain native to Africa and Asia. Millet has been cultivated in dry, poor soil for millennia as an important high-protein staple, but in the U.S. it is used mostly for animal fodder; it has no gluten.

milt Fish sperm, prepared like roe, and sometimes euphemistically called roe or spleen.

Milzwurst (Ger.) Veal sausage from Bavaria.

mimosa A garnish of finely chopped hard-boiled egg yolk, sometimes including the white as well, that resembles the mimosa flower; also a drink of Champagne and orange juice, usually served with brunch.

mincemeat A preserve of chopped mixed foodstuffs much changed over the centuries. In fifteenth-century England it included small furred and feathered game, meat, spices, and gradually more fruit; in present-day England it consists mainly of fresh and dried fruits, nuts, spices, rum or brandy, with suet being the only vestige of meat. Mincemeat is cured and served in a piecrust for a traditional Christmas dessert.

minestra (It.) Soup or sometimes pasta served as the first course; *minestrina* means a thinner soup, while *minestrone* (literally, a "big soup," or meal in itself) means a thick vegetable soup in a meat broth with pasta, **Parmesan,** and various vegetables, depending on the region and season.

mint An aromatic herb, Mediterranean in origin, that includes basil, marjoram, oregano, peppermint, rosemary, sage, savory, and thyme in its large family. Common garden mint is spearmint or one of its many close relatives; it has wide culinary uses from mint julep to accompaniments for lamb (see **mint sauce**) to flavoring liqueurs, but has never been favored by the French.

mint sauce (Brit.) Chopped and lightly sugared fresh mint in vinegar, served with roast lamb; not to be confused with American commercial mint jelly, which is apple jelly flavored with mint and nowadays usually dyed bright green.

Mirabeau (Fr.) A garnish of anchovy fillets laid in a criss-cross pattern, pitted olives, tarragon and anchovy butter; for grilled meat.

mirabelle A small golden plum with a highly aromatic perfume, grown almost exclusively in Europe; used in stews, preserves, tarts, and a colorless **eau de vie** from Alsace.

mirchi (Ind.) Chili peppers.

mirepoix (Fr.) A mixture of diced vegetables—usually carrot, onion, celery, and sometimes ham or pork belly—used to flavor sauces and other preparations; see also **brunoise.**

mirin (Jap.) Rice wine, syrupy and sweet, used for cooking.

mirliton See **chayote.**

miroton (Fr.) A stew of meat with onions in brown sauce; the classic *sauce miroton* is a **demi-glace** with sautéed onion rings, sometimes flavored with tomato puree and mustard.

mise en place (Fr.) A term meaning that the preparation is ready up to the point of cooking.

miso (Jap.) Fermented bean paste—a high-protein staple used extensively and in many different forms; *miso-shiru* is a soup thickened with red bean paste, often eaten for breakfast and sometimes with other meals.

Mission-Haut-Brion, Château La An excellent first-growth wine of Pessac, Graves; an immediate neighbor of **Haut-Brion** and an exceptional red Bordeaux.

misto (It.) Mixed.

mithai (Ind.) Sweets.

Mittagessen (Ger.) Midday dinner, lunch; traditionally a substantial meal, the main one of the day.

mixed grill (Brit.) Various grilled meats, such as lamb chops, kidneys, bacon, and sausages, served with grilled mushrooms, tomatoes, and fried potatoes; the French *friture mixte* and Italian **fritto misto** are equivalents, including foods appropriate to those countries.

Mocha Originally, a very fine variety of coffee from the town of Mocha in Yemen, often blended with Java; today this is more likely to be a Mocha-style bean from Africa; *mocha* often means coffee-flavored and sometimes, more loosely, coffee- and chocolate-flavored.

mochi-gome (Jap.) Glutinous rice, used for special dishes such as red rice and sweet rice cakes (*mochi*); *mochiko* is the flour made from it.

mochomos (Mex.) Cooked meat, shredded and fried crisp.

mock turtle soup A clear soup made from a calf's head and often garnished with calf brains, originally intended to spare the expense and trouble of using real turtle. In Tenniel's illustration for *Alice in Wonderland,* the mock turtle is a calf beneath a turtle's shell with mock tears rolling down its cheeks.

mode, à la (Fr.) A large cut of braised beef with vegetables; in the United States, pie or other pastry served with ice cream.

moelle (Fr.) Beef marrow.

Mohn (Ger.) Poppy; *Mohnbeugel, Mohnkipferl,* and *Mohnstrudel* are popular poppy-seed pastries.

Möhre, Mohrrübe (Ger.) Carrot.

Mohr im Hemd (Aus.) A chocolate pudding, from Austria, literally, "moor in a shirt"; *Mohrenkopf* is chocolate meringue with whipped cream.

moka (Fr.) Mocha.

molasses The syrup remaining from sugarcane juice after sucrose crystallization, during the manufacture of sugar; the process is repeated three times, each yielding a lower grade of molasses with more impurities and darker color from the high heat; **blackstrap** is the third grade.

molcajete y tejolote (Mex.) Mexican mortar and pestle, made of heavy, porous stone, and balanced on three legs; indispensable for grinding spices.

mole (Mex.) A mixture or sauce, from the Aztec word for chili sauce; *mole* **poblano** *de guajolate* is a festive Mexican specialty of wild turkey (or pork or chicken) in a rich dark subtle smooth sauce of powdered **mulato, ancho,** and **pasilla** chilies simmered with vegetables, seasoning, and a little chocolate.

Molinara A fine Italian red-wine grape variety, used for **Valpolicella** and **Bardolino.**

mollusk, mollusc A class of shellfish: an invertebrate with a soft, unsegmented body, with a single or double shell; includes scallops, clams, oysters, mussels, squid, octopus, whelks, and one land-dweller, the snail.

Monbazillac A soft, sweet, golden dessert wine, not unlike **Sauternes,** produced east of Bordeaux in the Dordogne.

Mondeuse A good French red-wine grape variety, extensively grown in the Savoie and Upper Rhône regions and, to a lesser extent, in California.

monégasque, à la (Fr.) In the style of Monaco; a salad of **nonats,** tomatoes, and rice; also refers to numerous other preparations.

Monferrato A major Italian wine-growing region south of the Po Valley in the Piedmont; none of its many wines bears its name.

Mongolian hot pot (Chin.) See **shuàn yáng ròu.**

monkey bread A curious sweet bread, sometimes called bubble bread, made of separate clumps of dough piled and baked in a tube pan. Currants are sometimes added; no relation to the monkey "bread" that is the fruit of the **baobab** tree.

monkfish A voracious and odd-looking fish whose tail contains firm white flesh similar in flavor to lobster; the meat can be prepared in numerous ways but should be cooked longer than that of most fish; also called goosefish, anglerfish, and *lotte.*

monopole (Fr.) A wine-label term meaning that the entire vineyard belongs to one proprietor.

monosodium glutamate (MSG) A type of salt long used in Oriental cooking as a taste intensifier and enhancer. MSG was chemically isolated in 1908 but scientists do not fully understand how it works; often found in Chinese restaurant food and instant and canned soups in excessive amounts.

Montasio (It.) A firm, whole-milk cows' cheese from northeastern Italy; this pale yellow cheese with a smooth rind and scattered holes is made in large wheels; it is cooked, pressed, salted, and cured up to two years; when young it makes a mild and nutty table cheese, and when aged it makes a brittle and pungent grating cheese.

Mont Blanc (Fr.) A classic dessert of chestnut puree masked with **crème Chantilly;** the Italian version, *Monte Bianco,* includes chocolate and rum.

monter (Fr.) To whip egg whites or cream to give volume; *monter au beurre* means to enrich a sauce with a little butter.

Monterey Jack A semihard cooked cows' milk cheese first made in Monterey, California in 1892; a **Cheddar**-type of cheese, the whole-milk version, aged for three to six weeks, is pale, creamy, and bland, while the skimmed-milk version, matured for at least six months, is harder and stronger.

Montilla A Spanish wine from the villages of Montilla and Moriles, very similar to **sherry** and until recently sold as such, but now with its own appellation; Montilla, which is not fortified, makes an excellent **apéritif** or table wine, chilled.

Montmorency, à la (Fr.) With cherries.

montone (It.) Mutton.

Montpensier (Fr.) A classic garnish of green asparagus tips and sliced truffles, sometimes with artichoke hearts and Madeira sauce.

Montrachet A celebrated vineyard in the **Côte de Beaune** of Burgundy, straddling the **communes** of Puligny and Chassagne, whose dry white wine—made entirely from the **Chardonnay** grape—is one of the finest in the world; it lends its name to neighboring vineyards as well. *Montrachet* is also the name of a fresh goats' milk cheese, mild and creamy, usually shaped in logs and sometimes covered with vegetable ash.

Montreuil (Fr.) With peaches; also fish poached in white wine, served with large potato balls and shrimp sauce.

moong dal (Ind.) Yellow mung beans.

moo shu (Chin.) Shredded pork stir-fried with scallions, **cloud ears,** and egg, then rolled up in pancakes.

Morbier (Fr.) A hard, uncooked cows' milk cheese with a delicate flavor, from the Franche-Comté region; it is made in large rounds with a yellowish thin rind and an even paste marked by a traditional horizontal streak of black soot.

morcilla negra (Sp.) Blood sausage made with pork, garlic, spices, and pig's blood, the best coming from Asturias; *morcilla blanca* is a sausage containing chicken, bacon, hard-boiled eggs, and parsley.

morcón (Phil.) Beef roulade filled with vegetables, sausages, and hard-boiled eggs, braised and sliced into decorative rounds.

morel A wild fungus with a spongelike hollow cap, prized for its fine nutty flavor; this mushroom appears in springtime but can be dried successfully for other seasons; morels are never eaten raw.

morille (Fr.) Morel.

Mornay (Fr.) **Béchamel** sauce with butter, grated **Parmesan** and **Gruyère** cheeses, possibly with egg yolks beaten in—a classic sauce.

mortadella A large Italian sausage of ground pork with white cubes of fat, pistachio nuts, wine, and coriander; the best are from Bologna but should not be confused with American baloney.

morue (Fr.) Salt cod; see also **brandade.**

moscada (Sp.) Nutmeg.

Moselle A river in western Germany on whose banks, between Trier and Koblenz—where it flows into the Rhine—are many vineyards; Moselle wine, in its characteristic green bottle, comes from the **Riesling** grape. Some of these wines, especially those from the *Mittel-Mosel* or central section, are exceptionally fine, distinguished by their delicacy, fragrance, and spiciness. The German spelling is *Mosel.*

Most (Ger.) Fruit juice; cider; **must.**

mostarda di frutta (It.) Various fruits preserved in a syrup flavored with mustard; traditionally eaten with bread or cold meat, like chutney; from Cremona in Lombardy.

moulage (Fr.) Molding, as in molding a dessert; *moule* is mold.

moule (Fr.) Mussel.

mountain oyster Testicles of a bull, pig, or lamb, usually breaded and fried; sometimes called prairie oyster or Rocky Mountain oyster; this American slang term is as much descriptive as euphemistic.

moussaka, mousaka A Balkan dish, varying from one region to another, of vegetables layered with minced or ground meat, perhaps with a white sauce or cheese; the Greek version, with eggplant, lamb, tomatoes, and white sauce, is most familiar abroad.

mousse (Fr.) A sweet or savory dish lightened with beaten egg whites or cream; from the French word for froth or foam.

mousseline (Fr.) A dish or sauce with whipped cream or egg whites folded in; it often designates **hollandaise** or **mayonnaise** with whipped cream added. The term can also mean a "little mousse" in a small mold or in spoonfuls, especially for seafood preparations. See also **mousse.**

mousseux (Fr.) Sparkling or effervescent wine (literally "foaming"); does not include Champagne, which is considered a separate category.

moutarde de Meaux (Fr.) Mustard from the French town of Meaux made with partly crushed seeds, giving it a pleasantly grainy texture; **Brillat-Savarin** praised it.

mouton (Fr.) Mutton.

Mouton-Rothschild, Château An extraordinary Bordeaux wine from **Pauillac** in the **Haut-Médoc,** classified in 1855 as a second growth but unquestionably a great wine; it is large, robust, slow-developing but remarkably long-lived; from the **Cabernet Sauvignon** grape.

moyashi (Jap.) Bean sprouts.

Mozzarella (It.) A white spun-curd cheese originally made from buffalo milk; the uncooked curd is kneaded into a smooth mass from which small pieces are cut off (*mozzare* in Italian) and shaped into single cheeses, which are salted in brine. Mozzarella ripens fast, has a fresh, slightly acidulated flavor, and is sometimes smoked; it is widely imitated with cows' milk for pizza and other uses.

MSG See **monosodium glutamate.**

muffin A round individual pastry, either flat or raised, often served with butter. An English muffin is a flat yeast bread baked on a griddle, while its American counterpart is a raised quick bread made of any kind of flour and often including nuts or fruit, baked in a deep mold in the oven.

mulard (Fr.) A crossbreed duck bred for its meat and sometimes for its liver; as a hybrid it cannot reproduce.

mulato (Mex.) A dried chili pepper, large, brown, and pungent.

mulberry A tree originating in China and cultivated for the silkworms that feed upon its fruit (white berries only); a relative of the fig, it was known in ancient Greece and Rome and is still most appreciated in the Middle East; its berries are white, deep red, or black and are formed like raspberries.

Müllerin Art (Ger.) "In the style of the miller's wife"—dredged in flour and fried in butter—the German version of **à la meunière.**

mullet The name of several unrelated fish; the Mediterranean red mullet is the most distinguished, its liver and roe as prized as its flesh; the American striped and silver mullet, whose roe is used in **taramasalata,** are related to the European gray mullet.

mulligatawny (Ind.) An anglicized soup of East Indian origin; chicken or lamb poached in broth, flavored with curry and other spices, and served with rice, cream, lemon, and the diced meat.

mulling   A process in which wine, ale, or cider is warmed, sweetened, and spiced.

Münchner   (Ger.)   Literally, from Munich; used to designate the dark malty beers popular there.

mung bean   A variety of bean usually dried and used for **bean sprouts.**

Munster   (Fr.)   A pasteurized whole-milk cows' cheese first made by Benedictine monks in the Munster Valley of the Vosges mountains. The round cheese has a smooth orange rind and a pale yellow, fairly soft paste with cracks; its delicate salty flavor grows tangy with age. Alsatians eat their favorite cheese with rye or caraway bread, which complements it perfectly.

Murazzano   (It.)   A soft uncooked cheese from northwest Italy, made with a mixture of milks, mostly ewes'; the cylindrical cheese has no rind and a dense white paste that grows pale yellow with age.

mûre   (Fr.)   Blackberry or mulberry.

murgh, murghi   (Ind.)   Chicken.

Murol   (Fr.)   A hard cows' milk cheese, uncooked but pressed, from the Auvergne; the wheel-shaped cheese has a pinkish rind with a hole in the center.

Muscadet   A light, dry, fresh white wine from the lower Loire Valley; Muscadet tastes best drunk young and accompanies the seafood of neighboring Brittany exceptionally well.

Muscat   A grape whose many varieties are used for wine, raisins, and table grapes; it ranges widely in color, yield, and quality, but all types have the characteristic musky flavor; planted widely with different names, depending on the location.

Muschel, Jakobsmuschel   (Ger.)   Scallop.

mush   Cornmeal porridge; an American version of **polenta,** which can be sliced and fried.

mushi   (Jap.)   Steamed; *mushimono* means steamed food.

mushroom   The fruiting body of a fungus whose spores, if given the proper conditions, sprout up virtually overnight. Gastronomes for millennia have prized edible mushrooms for their delicate flavor and meaty texture, but their cultivation has been understood only since the early eighteenth century. In addition to the common field mushroom, many wild mushrooms (separately entered) can be gathered by those with the knowledge to distinguish between edible and poisonous species.

Musigny   An extraordinary red Burgundy wine from the Côte de Nuits; a **Grand Cru,** with great delicacy and refinement.

Muskatnuss   (Ger.)   Nutmeg, mace.

muskmelon A melon with netted skin, sometimes called nutmeg melon because of its resemblance to the spice, and orange or pale green flesh; the fruit that Americans call cantaloupe is really a muskmelon, while the true cantaloupe (not cultivated in the U.S.) has rough, scaly, or segmented—but never netted—skin. Muskmelons and cantaloupes have a separation layer in their stems, unlike **winter melons,** so that they cannot be harvested into frost.

muslin bag A bag filled with herbs, spices, or other flavorings and tied tightly, used for infusing liquids; it can be removed without leaving any solids.

mussel A bivalve **mollusk** with a blue black shell and a beard that attaches to rock or other solid objects (and should be removed before cooking); long popular in Europe in many preparations such as **Billy Bi** and **à la marinière,** mussels are gaining acceptance in the United States.

must Grape juice not yet fermented into wine.

mustard A plant related to cress, radish, horseradish, and turnip and sharing their pungent taste. Mustard seeds were eaten by prehistoric man, spread by the Romans, and today are consumed more than any spice but pepper; they are dried, crushed, powdered, moistened, and mixed with many seasonings. Mustard greens make a refreshing spring vegetable, and mustard oil is important in Indian cooking. See also **Dijon.**

mutton The flesh of mature sheep (over one year in age), dark red in color and rich in flavor; high-quality mutton is hard to find and generally unappreciated by Americans.

myrtille (Fr.) Bilberry, whortleberry, blueberry.

Mysost (Nor.) A hard uncooked cheese made from cows' milk whey; it is dark brown and sweet, usually firm and dense, and is made in several varieties; see also **Gjetöst.**

Nantua sauce

⊛ N ⊛

---

nabe   (Jap.)   Pot; *nabemono* means one-pot communal cooking.

nacho   (Mex.)   A small **tortilla** chip topped with melted cheese and chilies.

Nackenheim   A German wine-producing town overlooking the Rhine south of Mainz; the fruity white wines, from the **Riesling** and **Sylvaner** grapes, are of high quality.

naganegi   (Jap.)   Long onion, for which the leek can be substituted.

nage, à la   (Fr.)   Cooked in a **court bouillon** of white wine, carrots, onions, shallots, and herbs; *nage* means swimming.

Nahe   A German river flowing into the Rhine at Bingen; the Nahe Valley wines, from **Riesling** and **Sylvaner** grapes, produce a lot of good white wine.

naméko   (Jap.)   A mushroom appreciated for its slippery texture; usually canned.

nam pla   (Thai.)   Pungent salty fish sauce; *nam prik* is a hot variation with chilies, used as a dipping sauce.

Nantua sauce   In classic French cuisine, **béchamel** sauce reduced with cream, beaten with crayfish butter, and garnished with crayfish tails;

à la Nantua is a garnish of crayfish tails with Nantua sauce and sliced truffles.

Napa A valley northeast of San Francisco whose vineyards produce some of California's best wines, especially **Cabernet Sauvignon, Pinot Noir, Pinot Chardonnay,** and **Chenin Blanc.**

napoleon A dessert of **puff pastry** strips spread with **crème patissière** and stacked in layers, the top often iced; this pastry is not French.

napoletana, alla (It.) A meatless spaghetti sauce made with tomatoes, onion, garlic, and olive oil.

napolitain (Fr.) Originally a large ornamental cake—probably created by **Carême,** who delighted in such creations—of stiff almond pastry layers spread with different jams, piled high and elaborately decorated; nowadays it usually means a smaller-scale **génoise** filled with jam and spread with **Italian meringue** and more jam.

napolitaine, à la (Fr.) "In the style of Naples": veal scallops dipped in beaten eggs and breadcrumbs mixed with grated **Parmesan,** fried, and garnished with spaghetti, tomato sauce, and Parmesan—a classic preparation.

napper (Fr.) To coat or mask with sauce.

naranja (Sp.) Orange.

nasi goreng (Indon.) Fried rice cooked with various spices and ingredients, usually including chilies, garlic, onions, and shrimp paste and sometimes including meat, chicken, or shellfish; popular throughout Malaysia and Indonesia; when noodles replace the rice it is called *bami goreng* (or *bakmi goreng*).

nasturtium A plant whose blossoms and young leaves are eaten in salads and whose buds and seeds are pickled like **capers.**

nasu (Jap.) Eggplant.

natillas (Sp.) A soft runny custard, made from ewes' milk, sweetened and flavored with lemon and cinnamon; from the Basque country.

natural A term that is used by commercial producers to imply that no pesticides or additives have been used or that there has been no adulteration of any kind; however, the word has been given no specific definition by the Federal Trade Commission.

nature (Fr.) Plain, ungarnished; the Italian is *naturale,* the German *natur;* when used with wine the term means that nothing—in particular, sugar—has been added.

Naturschnitzel (Ger.) Unbreaded veal cutlet.

navarin (Fr.) A mutton stew with small onions and potatoes; in spring, when the dish is called *navarin à la printanière,* it is made with young vegetables such as carrots, turnips, new potatoes, and peas.

navarraise (Fr.) Tomato sauce flavored with garlic and chopped herbs.

navel orange A nearly seedless orange variety with a characteristic protuberance at the blossom end (hence its name), a thick skin, and sweet, flavorful flesh.

navet   (Fr.)   Turnip; the Spanish word is *nabo,* the Italian *navone.*

navy bean   A variety of common bean, small and white, widely used in dried bean dishes such as **cassoulet** and **Boston baked beans.**

neapolitan ice cream   Ice cream of various flavors, layered in a brick mold.

Nebbiolo   A red-wine grape variety that produces some of Italy's finest wines; it grows best in northern Italy and yields robust, full-bodied wines.

Nebuchadnezzar   A wine bottle, usually for Champagne, that holds twenty regular bottles; named for the superannuated biblical patriarch.

neck   See **chuck.**

négi   (Jap.)   Leek, scallion, onion.

négresse, négresse en chemise   (Fr.)   Chocolate mousse topped with whipped or iced cream; sometimes called by the Spanish term *negritas.*

negus   A wine punch flavored with sugar, lemons, and spices; served warm.

Nesselrode   A pudding of custard, whipped cream, and chestnut puree mixed with candied fruits, piled in a **charlotte** mold and frozen; apparently invented by Mouy, chef to Count Nesselrode, the nineteenth-century diplomat and chancellor of Russia.

nest   See **yàn cài.**

nettle   A prickly weed used in northern countries as a green similar to spinach; picked young and cooked, its sting disappears.

Neuchâtel   A well-known white wine produced on the northern shore of Lake Neuchâtel in Switzerland, from the **Chasselas** grape; it is pleasant and refreshing though unremarkable.

Neufchâtel   (Fr.)   A soft uncooked cheese from the town of the same name in Normandy; made in many shapes from pasteurized cows' milk, either skimmed or whole and sometimes enriched with cream; eaten fresh when delicate or ripe when pungent.

new American cuisine   A recent development in fashionable American restaurants, highly influenced by **nouvelle cuisine;** this style of cooking emphasizes American ingredients in imaginative new dishes usually made by classic French techniques, albeit lighter and fresher.

Newburg   A thick cream sauce for lobster meat, enriched with egg yolks and flavored with **sherry** and **cayenne pepper;** named after a Captain Wenberg who had the sauce made for him at Delmonico's restaurant in New York.

New England boiled dinner   A Yankee **pot-au-feu** of corned beef and salt pork, possibly a chicken, cabbage, potatoes, carrots, and other vegetables cooked together in one pot and usually served with mustard or horseradish.

New England clambake A traditional method of cooking seafood learned from the Indians: a pit is dug in the beach, layered with hot rocks, then covered with generous amounts of seaweed, clams, lobsters, chicken, unhusked corn (silk removed), potatoes, etc.; the food cooks by the heat of the steaming seaweed around it.

ni (Jap.) Braise, simmer; *nimono* is braised or simmered food.

niçoise, à la (Fr.) A classic preparation of tomatoes chopped and sautéed in olive oil with garlic, capers, sliced lemon, anchovies, and black olives; the popular *salade (à la) niçoise* contains, in addition to many of these ingredients, a variety of vegetables (usually including French beans and potatoes), seafood, especially tuna, and herbs.

Nieren (Ger.) Kidneys.

Nierstein An important wine-producing town in the German Rheinhessen, with many good or fine white wines, mostly from the **Riesling** grape.

niku (Jap.) Meat.

nimboo (Ind.) Lemon, lime.

ninjin (Jap.) Carrot.

níspola (Sp.) Persimmon.

niú ròu (Chin.) Beef.

nivernaise, à la (Fr.) Garnished with glazed carrots and turnips cut into olive shapes, onions, braised lettuce, and boiled potatoes.

noble rot A mold (*Botrytis cinerea*) that develops on grapes in certain regions, withering the grapes but concentrating the sugar and flavor; grapes so affected produce very fine—and expensive—wine; the French term is *pourriture noble,* the German *Edelfäule.*

nocchette (It.) Small pasta "bow ties" for soup.

noce (It.) Nut, walnut; *noce moscata* means nutmeg; *nocciòla* means hazelnut.

Nock (Ger.) Dumpling; in Austrian dialect, the word is *Nockerl.*

Noël, bûche de See **bûche de Noël.**

nogada (Mex.) Walnut sauce; traditionally served with **poblano** chilies stuffed with shredded pork and garnished with pomegranate seeds—a famous dish.

noisette (Fr.) Hazelnut. The word also means a cut of meat from the rib, usually of lamb, trimmed, rolled, tied in a small round, and served in an individual portion. *Noisette* potatoes are shaped like hazelnuts and browned in butter; *beurre noisette* is brown butter sauce.

noix (Fr.) Nut, walnut; *noix muscade* is nutmeg.

Nøkkelost (Nor.) A Norwegian cheese based on the Dutch **Leyden** and similarly flavored with cumin and caraway.

nonat (Fr.) A very small Mediterranean fish, usually deep-fried or served as an hors d'oeuvre.

nonpareille (Fr.) Small pickled capers from Provence—a superior variety "without equal."

nopales (Mex.) The fleshy oval joints of the *nopal* cactus, eaten with scrambled eggs or in salad; *nopalitos* are cactus leaves eaten in salad.

noques (Fr.) The Alsatian version of **gnocchi;** in Austria, *noques* are made into a sweet, light dessert similar to **snow eggs.**

noquis (Sp.) **Gnocchi.**

nori (Jap.) Thin black sheets of seaweed, used either toasted or untoasted for wrapping **sushi,** rice balls, and crackers, and for coating food to be deep-fried.

normande (Fr.) Fish **velouté** with mushrooms and oyster liquor, thickened with egg yolks and cream, and enriched with butter—a classic sauce; the garnish *à la normande* consists of oysters, mussels, crayfish, **goujonettes,** shrimp, mushroom caps, and truffle slices with **fleurons,** in *sauce normande.*

Normandy A northern French province renowned for its butter, cream, cheese, apples, seafood, and salt-meadow sheep; cider is drunk here instead of wine, and **Calvados** is the local brandy.

norvégienne (Fr.) A classic sauce of hard-boiled egg yolks mashed and seasoned with vinegar and mustard and beaten with oil for a mayonnaiselike texture; *omelette à la norvégienne* is **baked Alaska.**

Norway lobster See **Dublin Bay prawn.**

nostrale, nostrano (It.) Native or homegrown.

nougat A confection of roasted nuts (usually almonds or walnuts) with honey or syrup; there are many varieties. *Nougatine,* a vague term, can mean almond brittle or nougat combined with chocolate.

nouilles (Fr.) Noodles.

nouvelle cuisine (Fr.) Literally "new cooking," this culinary movement features fresher, lighter food often in innovative combinations, usually served in small portions with artful and striking presentations, but otherwise cooked primarily by classic French techniques.

nova (Jew.) Cold-smoked salmon, originally from Nova Scotia and now probably, but not necessarily, from the Pacific; traditionally eaten like **lox** with cream cheese and **bagels.**

Nudeln (Ger.) Noodles.

nuez (Sp.) Nut, walnut.

Nuits-Saint-Georges A town in the Côte de Nuits whose vineyards produce excellent red Burgundies.

nuoc mam (Vietnam) Fermented fish sauce, salty and pungent, related to **nam pla** and **patis.**

Nuss (Ger.) Nut, walnut.

nutmeg The oval seed of the tropical nutmeg tree, native to the Moluccas, which is dried, ground, and used to flavor a wide variety of sweet and savory dishes. Connecticut is known as the Nutmeg State because Yankee peddlers sold wooden "nutmegs" to unsuspecting customers.

nymphes à l'aurore (Fr.) Frog legs poached in white wine and served in a pink **chaud-froid** sauce with aspic.

oyster

O

oats, rolled Hulled oats ground into a meal, then steamed to gelatinize some of their starch (thus reducing spoilage), rolled into flakes, and dried; rolled oats are quicker to prepare as oatmeal than other kinds of oats, even if they have lost much of their texture.

Obst (Ger.) Fruit; *Obsttorte* is an open mixed fruit tart, glazed, and perhaps garnished with almonds, whipped cream, or meringue; *Obstsuppe nach Hamburger Art* is a soup of pureed fruits, from Hamburg.

oca (It.) Goose.

ocha (Jap.) Green tea.

octopus A marine mollusk whose flavorful but tough meat is appreciated mainly by Oriental and Mediterranean cultures, often smoked, marinated, or stewed.

oeil d'anchois (Fr.) Literally "eye of anchovy," this hors d'oeuvre is a raw egg yolk surrounded by anchovies and chopped onions.

oenology The science of wine-making.

oeuf (Fr.) Egg; *o. brouillés* means scrambled eggs; *o. en cocotte* means poached in a casserole; *o. à la coque* means soft-boiled; *o. durs* means

125

hard-boiled; *o. en gelée* means poached and chilled in aspic; *o. mollets* means soft-boiled; *o. au plat* or *sur le plat* means fried or baked; *o. pochés* means poached; *o. pochés bénédictine* means poached and served on a creamed salt-cod base (not eggs Benedict); *o. à la poêle* means fried.

oeufs à la neige   See **snow eggs.**

offal   So-called variety meats, consisting of organs or trimmings that the butcher removes from the skeletal meat. Offal includes brains, heart, sweetbreads, liver, kidneys, lungs, pancreas, spleen, tripe, tongue, headmeat, tail, blood, skin, feet, horns, and intestines. Offal can also mean inedible waste or carrion.

oie   (Fr.)   Goose; *oison* is a gosling.

oignon   (Fr.)   Onion; *oignon clouté* is an onion studded with cloves.

oiseau   (Fr.)   Bird.

oiseaux sans tête   (Fr.)   Meat birds; a meat scallop stuffed, rolled up, and cooked.

okra   A tropical plant of the mallow family, native to Africa or Asia and brought to the southern U.S. with the slave trade; its unripe seed pod, star-shaped in cross section, is used as a vegetable and a thickener for soups and **gumbos** because of its mucilaginous texture.

Öl   (Ger.)   Oil.

øl, öl   (Den., Nor., Swed.)   Beer.

oleo   See **margarine.**

olio   (It.)   Oil; in Italy, *olio* always means olive oil—*olio d'oliva.*

olives, meat   See **meat birds.**

Olivet   (Fr.)   A whole- or partially skimmed-milk cows' cheese similar to **Camembert,** from Orléans; it is eaten very fresh or matured for a month, when it develops a delicate blue rind and is called *Olivet Bleu.*

olivette di vitello   (It.)   Veal scallops filled with a savory stuffing, rolled up, and braised; veal birds.

olla podrida   (Sp.)   A stew, literally "rotten pot," made from many different meats (mainly pork) and vegetables, including cabbage, chickpeas, and tomatoes; similar to the **cocido** of Madrid; *olla* means stewpot and lends its name to other hearty dishes.

oloroso   (Sp.)   A type of Spanish **sherry** matured in **soleras** like **fino** but without **flor** yeast; its color is dark—deep gold to amber—its alcoholic content higher than *fino,* and it has a rich flavor and intense, characteristic bouquet; *olorosos* range from nearly dry to very sweet.

omelette   (Fr.)   Omelet: eggs beaten and cooked in butter in a special flat pan until set, often filled or flavored with a wide variety of other ingredients.

oolong   A partially fermented, amber-colored tea, mostly from Taiwan—a cross between black fermented tea and green unfermented tea.

Oporto A city in Portugal near the mouth of the Douro River; the fortified wine **port,** whose name comes from that of the city, must by law be shipped from Oporto or the town across the river.

Oppenheim A town in the German Rheinhessen whose many vineyards produce good white wines (although not so distinguished as those of its northern neighbor, **Nierstein**).

orange, sauce (Fr.) **Demi-glace** flavored with orange and perhaps lemon juice and julienne of orange zest.

orange flower water Liquid distilled during the extraction of essential oil from bitter orange blossoms and used as a flavoring; before **vanilla** was discovered it was the principal flavoring extract and remains so in the Middle East.

orange pekoe A superior grade of black tea from India or Ceylon with leaves slightly larger than **pekoe;** the name no longer refers to the flavor of the tea, but rather to leaf size.

orecchiette (It.) Eggless pasta in the shape of little ears; originally from Apulia, in Italy's heel, and usually made commercially; the traditional sauce for *orecchiette* is broccoli with anchovies and cheese.

oregano Wild **marjoram,** an herb especially popular in Italian cooking as well as Greek and Middle Eastern cooking; oregano is very similar to marjoram but more pungent; the Italian word is *origano,* the French *origan.*

Oregon grapes See **barberry.**

organic Refers to produce grown without artificial or chemical fertilizers or pesticides and therefore favored by the health movement.

orgeat (Fr.) A syrup or drink originally made from barley and later from almonds, flavored with orange flower water.

orientale, à l' (Fr.) Dishes seasoned with saffron or curry, sometimes in a garnish of tomatoes stuffed with rice.

Original-Abfüllung (Ger.) **Château-bottled.**

Orloff, veal See **veal Orloff.**

ormer See **abalone.**

ortolan (Fr.) A small bird, the European bunting, prized for its flavor; though once prolific in southern France, it is now nearly extinct; it is plucked and often boned but not drawn, and its entrails are considered delicious.

Orvieto A town in Umbria in central Italy whose white wine of the same name is light, pleasant, and popular.

orzo (It.) Rice-shaped pasta; the word actually means barley.

Oscar, veal See **veal Oscar.**

oseille (Fr.) Sorrel.

osso buco, ossobuco alla milanese (It.) Veal shanks or shin bones (literally "bone with a hole") slowly braised with onions, garlic, carrots, celery, tomatoes, stock, and white wine, and traditionally garnished with **gremolada** before serving; the morsels of marrow are removed with a special implement. In Milan, **risotto** accompanies the *oss bus,* as it is called in local dialect. The plural form is *ossi buchi.*

ost (Scand.) Cheese.

ostra (Sp.) Oyster; *ostion* is another kind of oyster, eaten cooked.

òstrica (It.) Oyster.

oursin (Fr.) **Sea urchin.**

ouzo (Gr.) A sweet anise-flavored liqueur from Greece.

ovos moles (Port.) Egg yolks and sugar mixed together and used as a sauce or filling; in Aveiro, the mixture is molded into fanciful shapes, cooked in rice water, and eaten sprinkled with cinnamon.

Oxford and Cambridge pudding (Brit.) Apricot tart masked with meringue.

Oxford sauce (Brit.) Virtually the same as **Cumberland sauce.**

oxidation When applied to wine, the process of exposing the wine (usually white) to the air. This generally causes it to darken, as well as robbing it of its freshness.

oxtail Tail of beef, excellent for stews and soups because of the gelatin rendered from the high proportion of bones; ox simply means steer or beef.

oyster A bivalve marine **mollusk** prized since ancient times and cultivated since the Romans; eaten raw or cooked (only until its edges curl) in preparations as various as **Hangtown fry, angels on horseback,** and *à la normande;* Marennes and Belon (French), Colchester and Whitstable (English), and Blue Point and Olympia (American) are choice varieties.

oyster mushroom An Oriental mushroom that grows both wild and cultivated and is available fresh, dried, and canned; the clusters, with gray oval caps and white stems, are sold in plastic pouches; the taste is peppery when raw, mild when cooked.

oyster plant See **salsify.**

oyster sauce (Chin.) See **li jiàng.**

oysters Rockefeller Oysters on the half shell, resting on a bed of rock salt, each topped with a spoonful of pureed seasoned spinach, quickly browned; originally from Antoine's in New Orleans and named for John D. Rockefeller; apparently first made with watercress rather than spinach.

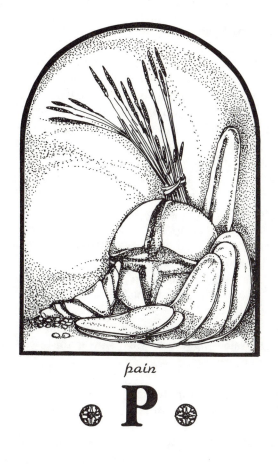

pain

❀ P ❀

paan (Ind.) Betel leaves, sometimes stuffed with spices and nuts, and used as a digestive.

pachadi (Ind.) Vegetables and yogurt with mustard seeds.

paella (Sp.) A dish of rice cooked with a variety of meats and fish (usually **chorizos,** chicken, rabbit, and shellfish) and an assortment of vegetables, including garlic, onions, peas, and tomatoes, seasoned with **saffron,** and served in the pan in which it is traditionally made; the exact ingredients vary widely according to region, season, and pocketbook.

pagello (It.) Red snapper.

paglia e fieno (It.) "Straw and hay" fettucine, the yellow and green colors coming from egg and spinach pasta dough; usually served in a cream sauce with ham or sausage, peas, and perhaps mushrooms.

paillarde de veau (Fr.) Grilled veal scallop.

paillettes (Fr.) Pastry straws.

pain (Fr.) Bread, loaf; *pain mollet* is soft bread; *pain grillé* is toast; *petit pain* is a roll; *pain perdu* is French toast as made in France, usually sweetened and spiced with cinnamon, so-called because it is made with stale bread; *pain de mie* is sandwich bread; *pain de Gênes* is Genoa cake, a rich almond pound cake.

pain à l'anglaise (Fr.) See **bread sauce.**

palacsinta (Hung.) **Crêpe;** the word in Austrian dialect is *Palatschinke.*

palak (Ind.) Spinach.

palate knife A flexible, wide-bladed knife without a sharp edge; used for spreading butter, icing, sandwich fillings, and other mixtures.

Palatinate See **Rheinpfalz.**

palm A large family of trees and shrubs, usually tropical, many of whose parts are edible: dates are its fruit, coconut its seed or nut, palm hearts its new buds or shoots, sago a starch from its trunk, and, in addition, palm oil and wine.

palmier (Fr.) A pastry made from strips of **pâte feuilletée** sprinkled with sugar, folded, sliced, and baked, which forms a palm-leaf shape as the pastry puffs out.

paloise (Fr.) Classic **béarnaise** sauce but with mint in place of tarragon.

palombe (Fr.) Wild pigeon or dove; in Spanish *palombacco* means squab or young pigeon.

palourde (Fr.) Clam.

pamplemousse (Fr.) Grapefruit.

panaché (Fr.) Mixed or multicolored; used to describe salad, fruit, or ice cream.

panade (Fr.) A peasant soup of water, stock, or milk thickened with bread; also a thick paste made with flour (see **roux**), breadcrumbs, or other starch, possibly thickened with eggs, and used to bind fish and meat **mousses** and **forcemeats;** from the Spanish word for bread, *pan.*

panais (Fr.) Parsnip.

panato (It.) Fried in breadcrumbs.

pancake A thin batter cake cooked on a griddle or pan and appearing in almost every cuisine the world over. See also **crêpe.**

pancetta (It.) Italian bacon that is rolled into a solid round.

pancit (Phil.) Pasta in the form of noodles, often stir-fried with chopped meats, shrimp, and vegetables, or in the form of dough-wrappers stuffed like **wontons.**

pan de Spagna (It.) Sponge cake, often soaked in liqueur and filled with jam or cream.

pandorato (It.) Bread dipped in an egg and milk batter and deep-fried; sometimes with a savory stuffing.

pandowdy A early American dessert, probably from New England, of sliced apples mixed with cider, brown sugar or molasses, spices, and butter, covered with biscuit dough, and baked.

pan-dressed   Refers to a whole fish that has been scaled and gutted, with head and fins removed; usually for sautéing or deep-frying.

pane   (It.)   Bread; *panino* is a roll or biscuit; in French *pané* means breadcrumbed; see also **panade, panure,** and **pain.**

panetière   (Fr.)   A cupboard with open latticework for storing bread; it is either suspended from the ceiling to keep away pests or set on a sideboard.

panettone   (It.)   A light yeast cake contining **sultana** raisins and candied lemon peel, baked in a cylindrical shape and eaten for breakfast; originally from Milan, *panettone* is traditional for Christmas.

panforte   (It.)   Fruit cake.

pan-fry   To sauté: to cook in a skillet in a small amount of fat, as opposed to **deep-frying.**

panna   (It.)   Cream; *panna montata* is whipped cream.

pannequet   (Fr.)   Small pancake or **crêpe** filled with a sweet or savory mixture and folded in quarters.

Pannerone   (It.)   An uncooked whole-milk cows' cheese from Lombardy, usually unsalted; the cheese is pale straw-colored with many holes, delicate and creamy in taste with a slight tang; it matures quickly; also called White **Gorgonzola** and *Gorgonzola Dolce,* rather misleadingly.

Pannhas   (Ger.)   A kind of mush made from **buckwheat** flour cooked in broth left over from cooking sausages; this Westphalian specialty, similar to Pennsylvania German **scrapple,** is a traditional part of the fall pig slaughter.

panucho   (Mex.)   A small **tortilla** puffed up, the pocket filled with a savory stuffing, then fried until crisp.

panure   (Fr.)   Golden breadcrumb crust.

panzanella   (It.)   A salad of vegetables and anchovies with stale bread soaked in water and squeezed dry, or perhaps fried in olive oil; from Tuscany.

panzarotti   (It.)   Pastry crescents stuffed with cheese and deep-fried.

papa   (Mex.)   Potato; also called *patata.*

papa dzules   (Mex.)   Literally "food for the lords," which the Mayans supposedly gave the Spaniards. This specialty from the Yucatán consists of **tortillas** filled with hard-boiled egg yolk, tomato sauce, pumpkin seed sauce, and green pumpkin seed oil.

papain   An enzyme derived from the **papaya** and used, diluted in sugar and salt, as a meat tenderizer. South American Indians have for centuries wrapped fresh papaya leaves around meat for the same purpose.

papaw, pawpaw   See **papaya.**

papaya   A tall tropical plant native to America; its large pear-shaped fruit has a thin skin that turns yellow when ripe, a smooth yellow or orange flesh, and many black seeds resembling peppercorns; the unripe papaya can be cooked as a vegetable like squash; the sweet ripe fruit is eaten in many ways, like melon, and even the leaves can be boiled like spinach; see also **papain.**

papillon   (Fr.)   A butterfly-shaped pastry cookie made from **feuilletage.**

papillote   (Fr.)   A paper frill used to garnish the end of the rib bone on chops and crown rib roasts; *en papillote* means an individual portion of fish, poultry, or meat that is wrapped in paper (usually parchment) with seasonings and liquid to moisten it, cooked in the oven, and served while still in the puffed-up paper, slit at table.

papos de anjo   (Port.)   Literally "angel's breasts"; small yellow egg cakes served with syrup.

pappardelle   (It.)   Long flat egg noodles, $\frac{5}{8}$ inch broad, cut with a crimped edge; they are the traditional accompaniment to hare cooked in a rich wine sauce; from Tuscany.

paprika   A condiment made from sweet red pepper, dried and powdered; widely used in Hungarian cooking and essential to **gulyás;** different types of paprika vary in strength.

paprikás csirke   (Hung.)   Chicken braised with onions and garlic, with plenty of **paprika** and sour cream; *paprikás,* a favorite Hungarian dish, is also made with meat and fish.

paquette   (Fr.)   Fully developed lobster roe about to be laid, turned from bright orange to dark greenish black—considered a great delicacy; *paquette* also means the female lobster carrying such roe.

paratha   (Ind.)   Flaky whole-wheat bread fried on a griddle.

parboil   See **blanch.**

pareve   (Jew.)   Food containing no meat or milk and therefore, by **kosher** law, suitable to be eaten with either.

parfait   (Fr.)   A **mousse**like dessert, originally a coffee cream, but now any fruit, nut, or flavored syrup into which whipped cream is folded, then chilled or frozen; in the United States a parfait is served in a tall narrow glass filled with ice cream, layered with sauce, with whipped cream on top.

Paris-Brest   (Fr.)   A pastry ring of **pâte à choux** topped with sliced almonds and filled with crème praliné (see **praline**) or **crème Chantilly** and fresh strawberries.

parisienne, pommes à la   (Fr.)   Potatoes cut into small ovals and sautéed in butter; there are various other *parisienne* preparations, including a white-wine reduction sauce with shallots.

Parker House roll   A yeast-bread roll folded into two halves before baking, named for the Parker House hotel in Boston, where the roll was first created in the nineteenth century.

Parmentier, Antoine-Augustin   (1737–1813)   A French pharmacist and agronomist who, when fed potatoes as a prisoner of war, realized their potential importance. Parmentier spent his life promoting the scorned tuber, eventually persuading Louis XVI to serve it at court. Parmentier's name is attached to many potato dishes.

Parmesan   See **Parmigiano Reggiano.**

parmesane, à la   (Fr.)   With grated Parmesan cheese; See **Parmigiano Reggiano.**

Parmigiano Reggiano   (It.)   A cooked, pressed, partially-skimmed cows' milk cheese shaped in large squat cylinders; protected by law, this very old and famous **grana** cheese comes from designated areas in northern Italy. Its rind is smooth and golden, its paste pale straw-colored, dense, and grainy, with tiny holes radiating from the center; sweet, mellow, and fragrant, it is eaten young as a table cheese or very old and sharp as a grating cheese.

parrilla   (Sp.)   Grill; *parrillada di pescado* is mixed seafood grill with lemon.

parsley   An herb known to the ancient Greeks and Romans for its medicinal properties but now used entirely for culinary purposes; it grows in several varieties, among them the curly-leaf, most popular in the U.S., and the more pungent flat-leaf, popular in Europe, especially in the Mediterranean where it originated.

parson's nose   See **pope's nose.**

partridge   A fall game bird with delicate flesh, cooked in various ways depending largely on age; a single bird serves one.

pasilla   (Mex.)   A long, thin, dark brown chili pepper, very hot and about 6 inches long.

paskha   (Russ.)   A traditional cake for Russian Orthodox Easter (*paskha* means Easter) made of cream cheese, dried fruits and nuts, and shaped in a high four-sided pyramid marked with the letters *XB* for "Christ is Risen"; usually served with **kulich.**

passata   (It.)   Puree.

passatelli in brodo   (It.)   Parmesan, eggs, and breadcrumbs mixed to a paste and pressed through a tool to form strands that are cooked and served in meat broth; from Romagna.

passer   (Fr.)   To strain through a sieve or tammy cloth.

passion fruit   A climbing vine or shrub, native to Brazil, whose unusual blossom is considered symbolic of Christ's passion; the egg-sized fruit turns deep purple with ripeness; its sweet yellow flesh is eaten raw with the seeds or squeezed and bottled for juice.

pasta   (It.)   Dough or paste, as well as the whole family of noodles; *pasta all'uovo* means egg pasta; *p. asciutta* means "dry" or plain pasta as opposed to *p. in brodo,* which is pasta cooked in soup; *p. frolla* means short pastry; *p. sfoglia* means puff pastry.

pasta asciutta   (It.)   "Dry" pasta; that is, pasta not served in a broth; *pasta asciutta* can be served stuffed or in a sauce.

pasta e fagioli (It.) A robust soup of pasta, white beans (some of which are pureed to thicken it), and salt pork.

pastel (Sp.) Pie, cake, pastry, **pâté**; a *pastelería* is a pastry shop.

pastèque (Fr.) Watermelon.

pasteurization The process of heating food high and long enough to kill microorganisms and prevent or slow down fermentation; used especially for milk; named after the French chemist Louis Pasteur (1822–95).

pasticcio (It.) A pie, either savory or sweet, but often of layered pasta with a savory filling; a *pasticcerìa* is a piece of pastry or pastry shop.

pastillage (Fr.) A mixture of sugar, water, and **gum tragacanth** that forms a paste that can be molded into fantastic shapes; though little used today, in centuries past it was used extensively for elaborate table ornamentation; **Carême** excelled in architectural *pastillage.*

pastina (It.) Small pasta for soup.

pastis (Fr.) An anise-flavored liqueur.

pastitsio (Gr.) Macaroni baked in a dish with ground meat, onion, tomato sauce, and cheese.

pastrami (Jew.) Beef, usually shoulder, first pickled in spices and then smoked; of Rumanian origin and now associated with Jewish cooking.

pastry bag A cone of paper or cloth with an open tip, sometimes fitted with a specially cut tip; soft smooth foods, such as whipped cream, icing, pureed potatoes, and **pâte à choux,** are forced through it to make even and decorative shapes.

pastry blender A simple kitchen tool—parallel stiff metal wires on a handle—for cutting fat into flour.

pastry cream See **crème patissière.**

pasty See **Cornish pasty.**

patata (It. and Sp.) Potato; *patate fritte* are fried potatoes; *p. lesse* are boiled potatoes; *p. stacciate* are mashed potatoes.

patate (Fr.) Sweet potato.

pâte (Fr.) Pastry, paste, pasta, dough, or batter; the word is often confused with **pâté.**

pâté (Fr.) A rich meat, poultry, game, seafood, or vegetable mixture or spread, strictly speaking cooked in pastry (*pâté en croûte*) rather than in an earthenware dish (*pâté en terrine*); *pâté de foie gras,* smooth, rich, and well seasoned, is a typical example; *pâté de compagne* has a coarse, crumbly texture. *Pâté* also means pastry, pie, pasty, or patty, but should not be confused with **pâte.**

pâte à choux (Fr.) Cream puff pastry; a simple paste made by stirring flour into boiling water and butter; eggs are then mixed in; upon cooking, the eggs puff up the dough, making a cavity, so the inside of the pastry is generally filled with flavored cream, as in *éclairs, profiteroles,* etc.; spelled both *pâte à chou* and *choux.*

pâte à croissant **Croissant** pastry dough.

pâte à foncer See **foncer.**

pâte brisée (Fr.) Pie dough, short pastry.

pâte d'amandes (Fr.) Almond paste, **marzipan.**

pâte feuilletée (Fr.) Flaky or puff pastry; it is made by enclosing butter within the **détrempe** or elastic dough and then folding and turning it many times to produce *mille feuille,* a "thousand leaves" or thin layers; during baking the steam from the melted butter pushes the layers up to make the delicate puff of pastry.

pâte levée (Fr.) Raised or leavened dough.

pâte sucrée (Fr.) Sweet pastry for pie dough and pastry shells, very high in fat (butter for best flavor) and low in moisture to form a crumbly base that will not become soggy when filled.

patis (Phil.) Fermented fish sauce, salty and pungent.

pâtissier (Fr.) A pastry chef or cook; a *pâtisserie* is a piece of pastry or a pastry shop.

pâtissière, crème See **crème pâtissière.**

pato, pata (Sp.) Duck.

paton (Fr.) One recipe or "pad" of **pâte feuilletée,** of optimal size for handling.

patty pan A variety of round summer squash with a scalloped edge, usually white, sometimes yellow.

Pauillac A wine-producing town in the **Haut-Médoc** of Bordeaux, where some of the greatest vineyards lie, including Châteaux **Lafite, Latour,** and **Mouton-Rothschild;** wines labeled simply *Pauillac,* while not among their class, can be very fine indeed.

paupiette (Fr.) A thin slice or scallop of meat filled with savory stuffing, rolled up, and braised; see also **meat birds** or **olivette** and **scallop.**

pavé (Fr.) A dish such as a savory **mousse** or **pâté** chilled in a square mold and garnished; a square cake, often sponge, spread with buttercream and garnished; the name means paving stone and designates a square or rectangular shape.

pavo (Sp.) Turkey.

payasam (Ind.) A pudding of mung beans, peas, and coconut milk.

paysanne, à la (Fr.) "Peasant style": with vegetables—most often carrots, onions, and potatoes—and diced bacon.

peanut Not a true nut but the seed of a leguminous bush indigenous to South America and brought to North America as a result of the slave trade; highly nutritious, peanuts are a staple in Africa and an important crop in India and China.

pearl barley Hulled and polished **barley,** small and round like pearls, usually eaten in soups or like rice.

pecan The nut of a tall tree native to the Mississippi Valley and a member (with the walnut) of the hickory family; an important dessert nut in the U.S. but uncommon elsewhere; the name is of American Indian origin.

pêche Melba   (Fr.)   Skinned peaches poached in vanilla-flavored syrup, served on vanilla ice cream with raspberry puree; created by **Escoffier** for Dame Nellie Melba, the great Australian coloratura soprano.

pechuga de pollo   (Sp.)   Chicken breast.

Pecorino Romano   (It.)   A cooked and pressed whole-milk ewes' cheese, originally made outside Rome but now made mostly in Sardinia. This ancient **grana** cheese is round, white or very pale straw-yellow, and dense, with a yellow brown rind. Aged at least eight months, its flavor is sharp, salty, and intense. There are other types of *pecorino* (from *pecora,* meaning ewe), but this is the most famous and finest.

Pecorino Siciliano   (It.)   A hard uncooked cheese made from whole ewes' milk, with a flavor made more pungent by the addition of peppercorns; a **grana** cheese, it is often used for grating.

pectin   A jellylike substance found in certain fruits—especially apples, currants, quinces, and citrus—and other plants. Pectin causes fruit to set when it is cooked for a long time with sugar and acid in jelly-making.

Pedro Ximénez   A Spanish grape variety, said to be (but probably not) the **Riesling** grape brought from the Rhine Valley; **sherry, Montilla,** and **Málaga** wines are made from it.

Peking duck   See **Bei jīng kǎo yā.**

pekoe   A superior grade of black tea from India and Ceylon whose leaves are slightly smaller than that of **orange pekoe** and that brews dark, though not necessarily strong.

Pellkartoffeln   (Ger.)   Potatoes boiled in their skins.

pemmican   Preserved meat, often buffalo or venison, dried, pounded, mixed with melted fat and sometimes berries, and pressed into cakes; used by the American Indians and early settlers on expeditions as a high-energy convenience food.

penne   (It.)   Quill-shaped pasta; that is, tubes cut on the diagonal.

pepe nero   (It.)   Black pepper; red pepper is *pepe rosso.*

peperonata   (It.)   Sweet peppers, tomatoes, onions, and garlic cooked in olive oil and served cold; an Italian **pipérade.**

peperoncino   (It.)   A hot red chili pepper, fresh or dried.

peperoni   (It.)   Green or red sweet bell peppers; also an Italian sausage of pork and beef highly seasoned with hot red peppers.

pepino   (Sp.)   Cucumber.

pepita   (Sp.)   Fruit seed; in Mexican cooking this means pumpkin seed.

pepitoria, en   (Sp.)   A sauce, usually for chicken, of almonds, garlic, herbs, saffron, and wine; probably of Arab origin.

pepper (black)   The fruit of a vine native to India, which has been fermented and dried; white pepper, used in pale foods for aesthetic reasons only, has a milder taste because the black outer skin has been removed. This type of pepper is not related to the *Capsicum* family, to which **cayenne, paprika, chili,** and **sweet red** and **green bell peppers** belong.

pepper (chili or red)   See **chili.**

pepper (sweet bell)   A mild member of the fiery *Capsicum* family native to tropical America; the unripe green fruits turn red, yellow, and deep purple when mature.

pepperpot   A soup or stew made from tripe and highly seasoned, originally from Philadelphia and probably derived from the German **Pfeffer-pothast.** The West Indian version of pepperpot contains *cassareep* (**cassava** juice), meat, and seafood, as well as vegetables.

pera   (It. and Sp.)   Pear.

perch   The name given to various fresh- and saltwater fish, many of them unrelated.

perdrix   (Fr.)   Partridge; *perdreau* is a young partridge.

peregrinos   (Sp.)   Scallops.

Périgord, périgourdine   (Fr.)   A **demi-glace** sauce with truffle essence and chopped truffles; *à la périgourdine* means garnished with truffles—for which Périgord is famous—and sometimes **foie gras.**

Perilla   (Sp.)   A cows' milk cheese from Spain similar to **Tetilla;** firm in texture, mild in flavor.

periwinkle   A small sea snail popular among the French and British seashores but largely ignored on the American Atlantic coast.

perlant   (Fr.)   A wine that is slightly and naturally sparkling but not deliberately vinified so.

Perlwein   (Ger.)   A wine that is slightly sparkling and intentionally vinified so.

pernice   (It.)   Partridge; the Spanish word is *perdiz.*

Pernod   (Fr.)   An anise-flavored liqueur.

perry   Pear cider.

persil   (Fr.)   Parsley; *persillade* is chopped parsley—perhaps mixed with chopped garlic—added to a dish before serving; *persillé* means sprinkled with parsley and also designates top-quality beef marbled with fat.

persimmon   The fruit of a tree native to the U.S. and China, though the Chinese varieties are, through cultivation, sweeter and larger; the deep orange fruit ripens in mid to late fall but until then it is unpleasantly astringent; known as *kaki* to the rest of the world, we call it by its American Indian name.

pesca   (It.)   Peach (the plural is *pesche*); *pesca noce* is nectarine.

pescado   (Sp.)   Fish; *pescado a la sal* is whole fish baked in rock salt; *pescadilla* is a small fish.

pesce (It.) Fish; *p. persico* is perch; *p. spada* is swordfish; *p. San Pietro* is John Dory.

pesto (It.) A sauce from Genoa of crushed basil, garlic, pine nuts, and **Parmesan** or **Pecorino** in olive oil; it is a robust and addictive sauce for minestrone and pasta (which in Italy is invariably **trenette**).

Petersilie (Ger.) Parsley.

pétillant (Fr.) Effervescent, slightly sparkling wine; the French equivalent of **frizzante** (Italian) and **Perlwein** (German) and deliberately vinified so (unlike **perlant**).

petite marmite (Fr.) A clear consommé served from the earthenware **marmite** in which it is cooked; lean meat, marrow bones, a whole chicken, and vegetables flavor the broth, which is served with **croûtes** spread with marrow or sprinkled with grated cheese.

petit four (Fr.) A very small cake or cookie, often elaborately garnished; also a sweetmeat served at the end of a dinner (literally, "little oven").

petit pain See **pain.**

petit salé (Fr.) See **salé.**

Petit-Suisse (Fr.) A pasteurized cows' milk cheese, sometimes enriched with cream, made into a fresh, mild cheese shaped in small cylinders; it was invented by a Swiss cowherd and a farmer's wife in France in the nineteenth century.

Petit Syrah The name used in California for the **Syrah** grape.

pétrissage (Fr.) Kneading the dough.

petto (It.) Breast, chest, brisket; *petti di pollo* are chicken breasts.

pez espada (Sp.) Swordfish.

pezzo (It.) Piece, chunk.

Pfannkuchen (Ger.) Pancake.

Pfeffer (Ger.) Pepper.

Pfefferkuchen (Ger.) A spice cake, similar to gingerbread, originally from Nuremberg; a traditional Christmas dessert.

Pfefferpothast (Ger.) A stew of beef ribs and onions in gravy, liberally seasoned with pepper and lemon; from Westphalia.

Pfifferling (Ger.) **Chanterelle.**

Pfirsich (Ger.) Peach.

Pflaume (Ger.) Plum.

pheasant A fall game bird with colorful plumage whose flesh, properly hung, is relished at the table; though a bit smaller, hen pheasants are considered slightly plumper and more succulent than cocks; plenty of moisture must be provided to prevent the meat from drying out during cooking.

phool gobhi (Ind.) Cauliflower.

phyllo (Gr.) Very thin sheets of dough, made from flour and water, layered, and filled with savory or sweet foods; the word means "leaf," and *phyllo* is, in fact, similar to the French **mille-feuille.**

piacere, a (It.) Cooked "to please"; as you like it.

piaz (Ind.) Onion.

pib, pibil (Mex.) A pit used in the Yucatán for barbecuing that allows the meat to smoke partially while cooking.

picada (Mex.) See **sope.**

picadilla (Sp.) Ground, minced, or shredded meat.

piccalilli (Ind.) A vegetable pickle from East India prepared with vinegar, mustard, and other spices.

piccante (It.) Piquant, spicy, sharp; the Spanish word *picante* emphasizes hot, spicy flavor.

piccata (It.) Veal scallop.

pichón (Sp.) A squab bred for the table.

pickerel See **pike** and **walleye.**

Pickert (Ger.) Peasant bread of potato or wheat flour, from Westphalia.

Picón See **Cabrales.**

picpoul (Fr.) See **Folle Blanche.**

pí dàn (Chin.) Thousand-year-old eggs: duck eggs preserved in a clay casing made of ashes, lime, salt, and strong tea, rolled in rice husks, and buried for three months; the yolks turn greenish brown, the whites deep aubergine; also known as hundred-year-old eggs.

pièce montée (Fr.) An ornamental centerpiece of **pastillage,** often inedible and very elaborate, that usually adorned the table at important banquets in the past. **Carême**'s emphasis on *pièces montées* revealed his passion for architecture as well as for display.

piémontaise, à la (Fr.) A classic garnish of **risotto timbales** mixed with grated white truffles.

pierna de cordero (Sp.) Leg of lamb.

Piesport A village in the German **Moselle** Valley that produces many fine white wines that are fruity and delicate.

pigeonneau (Fr.) A young squab bred for the table.

pignoli (It.) **Pine nuts;** the French word is *pignons.*

pike A freshwater fish whose sweet white flesh is used in many fine dishes, such as the renowned **quenelles** *de brochet;* Izaak Walton called the pike "choicely good."

pilaf, pilav, pilaw (Mid. E.) Rice that is briefly sautéed in butter, then steamed in stock, and often served with meat, poultry, or shellfish, with seasonings mixed in; *pilaf,* spelled variously, is eaten throughout the entire Middle East with regional variations and includes **bulghur** prepared similarly.

pilot biscuit See **hardtack.**

Pilsener **Lager** beer; strictly speaking *Pilsener* is only the very fine beer brewed in Pilsen, Czechoslovakia, but the term is now used generally for any high-quality lager of the same style; pale golden and lower in alcohol and calories than ordinary American beer.

Pilz (Ger.) Mushroom.

piment doux (Fr.) Sweet pepper.

pimienta (Sp.) Black pepper; *pimiento* means capsicum red pepper, either sweet (*pimiento dulce*) or hot.

piña (Sp.) Pineapple, so named for its visual resemblance to the pine cone.

Pineau de la Loire A white grape variety, whose proper name is **Chenin Blanc,** that produces many of the best white wines of Touraine and Anjou as well as of Saumur and California.

Pineau des Charentes (Fr.) An **apéritif** wine made from new wine with Cognac added, then matured in oak; it is high in alcohol, sweet, and has a distinctive bouquet.

pine nut The seed of the pine tree that comes from the pine cone, a multiple fruit.

Pinkel (Ger.) A smoked sausage of groats, raw bacon, and onions.

Pinot A family of wine grapes including the Pinot Noir, the variety from which fine red Burgundy is made, Pinot Blanc, responsible for most French Champagne, possibly Pinot **Chardonnay,** as well as Pinot Gris and Pinot Meunier. The Tyrol, northern Italy, and California also have many vineyards planted with Pinot grapes.

pintade (Fr.) Guinea hen; a young chick is a *pintadeau;* the Spanish word is *pintada.*

pinto bean A variety of common bean, splotched a reddish color, used in many Latin American stewed dishes.

pinzimonio (It.) A dipping sauce of oil, salt, and pepper for raw vegetables.

pipérade (Fr.) Tomatoes cooked in olive oil with green bell peppers and onions, with lightly beaten eggs and sometimes ham or bacon added; this Basque specialty has many variations.

pipián (Mex.) A deep red sauce for chicken made of sesame and pumpkin seeds ground with spices and sometimes peanuts or almonds.

piquante (Fr.) A classic sauce of chopped shallots reduced with white wine and vinegar, **demi-glace** added, strained, then garnished with chopped gherkins, parsley, chervil, and tarragon.

piquín (Mex.) A dark green chili pepper, very small and very hot.

piri-piri (Port.) A sauce made from hot red chili peppers and olive oil.

piroshki (Russ.) Small turnovers or dumplings filled with a savory or sweet stuffing; *pirogi* are large pastries cut into servings; the spellings vary, the fillings are infinite.

Pischingertorte (Aus.) A torte made of round wafers filled with chocolate hazelnut cream, covered with chocolate icing.

pisèlli (It.) Peas; *piselli alla romana* are peas cooked with butter, onion, and ham.

pissaladière (Fr.) A pizzalike tart from Nice, made with anchovies, onions, black olives, and perhaps tomatoes arranged in a decorative pattern.

pissenlit (Fr.) Dandelion leaves; the French name alludes to the plant's diuretic capabilities; wild dandelion greens are best eaten before flowering or after frost.

pistachio A deciduous tree, native to Asia, cultivated since ancient times for its nuts; their delicate flavor and green color make them useful in savory and sweet dishes, especially **pâtés** and stuffings, ice cream, and pastries.

pisto (Sp.) A vegetable dish of chopped tomatoes, red or green peppers, zucchini, and onions stewed together, with many variations; this dish is associated with La Mancha.

pistou, soupe au (Fr.) A rich Provençal vegetable soup, made with white beans, **mange-touts,** and **vermicelli,** garnished with crushed basil and garlic in olive oil; *pistou* is the French version of **pesto.**

pita (Mid. E.) A flat white pocket bread.

Pithiviers (Fr.) A pastry dessert, named for the town where it originated, consisting of a large round of puff pastry filled with almond paste and traditionally decorated with a pinwheel or rosette pattern.

pizza (It.) Literally pie, but the word usually denotes an open-faced tart spread with all manner of savory foods; originally from southern Italy.

pizzaiolo (It.) Fresh tomato sauce with herbs and garlic, often served with meat dishes.

plaice A European member of the **flounder** family; its fine-textured and delicate white flesh is eaten fresh or sometimes smoked.

plancher (Fr.) To **plank.**

plank To bake or broil food, especially fish, on a board of hard wood that seasons the food on it—a technique learned by early settlers from the American Indians.

plantain A fruit closely related to the banana, but whose higher starch and lower sugar content make it suitable for savory cooking; a native of Central America, the plantain is usually larger than the banana but is sometimes short and fat, with green, deep red, or yellow skin.

plátano (Sp.) **Plantain.**

pletzlach (Jew.) Apricot or plum pastry squares, traditional for Passover.

Plinz (Aus.) Pancake, fritter.

plover A shore bird particularly valued in Europe for its delicious eggs; the lapwing and golden plover are favorite species.

pluck The heart, liver, and lungs of an animal.

plum duff (Brit.) A restrained version of **plum pudding** made with dried raisins or currants; the word "duff" comes from dough.

plum pudding (Brit.) A steamed or boiled dessert of various dried fruits (excluding plums) and suet, often flamed with brandy; traditional for Christmas.

plum sauce See **suan mei jiāng.**

pluvier (Fr.) Plover.

poach To cook food gently in liquid held below the boiling point.

poblano (Mex.) A large, dark green chili pepper, mild but varying in flavor; it is about 5 inches long, 3 inches wide, and triangular in shape; sometimes available canned; when ripened and dried it becomes the **ancho** chili.

pocher (Fr.) To **poach.**

pochouse, pauchouse (Fr.) See **matelote.**

podina (Ind.) Mint.

poêler (Fr.) To cook food with a little butter or other fat in a tightly closed pot; *poêle* means both frying pan and stove.

point, à (Fr.) Just right or to the perfect point; with reference to steak, *à point* means rare; with reference to fruit and cheese, it means at the peak of ripeness.

Point, Fernand (1897–1955) Magnanimous *chef-patron* of La Pyramide in Vienne, near Lyons; at this celebrated restaurant he trained many of the finest chefs of the next generation, ensuring the continuity of French cuisine; at the same time, because of his emphasis on simplicity, Point is often called the father of **nouvelle cuisine.**

poire (Fr.) Pear.

poireau (Fr.) Leek.

pois (Fr.) Pea; *pois cassés* are split peas; *pois chiches* are chick-peas; *petits pois* are spring peas; *petits pois princesse* are snow peas; *pois à la francaise* are peas braised with lettuce, spring onions, parsley, butter, a pinch of sugar, and a little water.

poisson (Fr.) Fish; a *poissonnier* is a fish chef in a large restaurant kitchen or a fishmonger.

poitrine de porc (Fr.) Pork belly; *poitrine* can mean chest, breast, or brisket.

poivrade (Fr.) A sauce, usually for game, of **mirepoix** cooked in butter with game trimmings, reduced with crushed peppercorns and herbs, moistened with the marinade and vinegar, **demi-glace** and game essence added, then strained and finished with butter.

poivre (Fr.) Pepper; *grain de poivrade* is peppercorn; *poivré* is pungent or spicy; *poivron* or *poivre de la Jamaïque* is allspice; see also **poivrade.**

Pökel (Ger.) Pickle.

pokeweed A leafy plant, usually considered a weed, that grows wild in the eastern U.S.; only the young leaves and shoots are edible, and they are cooked like spinach and asparagus.

polenta (It.) A cornmeal pudding eaten as a porridge or more often cooled, sliced, and fried, grilled, or baked with various other foods; polenta is a specialty of Venice and northeastern Italy, where natives hold it in special regard; Marcella Hazan has written that "to call polenta a cornmeal mush is a most indelicate use of language."

pollack A member of the cod family.

pollame (It.) Poultry.

pollo (It., Sp.) Chicken; in Italian, *pollo ruspante* means free-range chicken; *pollastrino* means spring chicken.

pollo a la chilindrón (Sp.) Chicken braised in a sauce of sweet red peppers, tomatoes, onions, and a little garlic and ham.

polonaise, à la (Fr.) "Polish style": vegetables, especially cauliflower or asparagus, cooked and sprinkled with chopped hard-boiled egg, breadcrumbs, parsley, and melted butter.

polpetta (It.) Meat patty, croquette; *polpettone* is meat loaf, *polpetta* is meatball.

polpo, polipo, polipetto (It.) Squid or octopus; in Spanish the word is *pulpo* or *pulpetto;* in French, *poulpe.*

Polsterzipfel (Aus.) A jam-filled turnover.

pomace The fruit pulp remaining after all of the juice has been pressed out; refers particularly to apple or grape pulp in the making of cider or wine.

pomegranate A small tree native to the Middle East with a golden red fruit whose interior chambers hold its many edible seeds embedded in pith; the crimson juice in the seed sacs is refreshingly acid and is used for various savory and sweet dishes, especially in the Middle East, as well as for **grenadine;** the curious formation of the fruit probably accounts for its part in many ancient religious fertility rites.

pomelo The largest member of the citrus family, native to Malaysia and similar to the grapefruit, with a thick coarse skin; it is fibrous and sweet, with a dry pulp; also called shaddock, after Captain Shaddock, an English ship commander who is said to have brought the seed from the East Indies to Barbados in 1696. Also spelled pummelo.

Pomerol A wine-producing area in Bordeaux, just northwest of **Saint-Emilion,** whose velvety wines have a fullness, warmth, and depth of flavor; *Château Pétrus* is the finest among them.

Pommard A **commune** in Burgundy between **Beaune** and **Volnay,** producing a quantity of red wine especially popular in the U.S. and England; the best, estate-bottled wines, are excellent, the lower range is less good than its reputation.

pomme (Fr.) Apple.

pomme de terre (Fr.) Potato (literally, "apple of the earth"); often abbreviated to *pomme,* especially for certain potato preparations, such as *pommes frites,* but not to be confused with apple; *pommes frites* are French fried potatoes, as are *pommes Pont-Neuf,* originally sold on the *Pont Neuf* over the Seine River in Paris.

pommes Anna (Fr.) A dish of layered potato slices baked with butter in a special casserole; brown and crisp on the outside, soft on the inside; see also **château potatoes.**

pommes paille (Fr.) Deep-fried potato "straws."

pomodoro (It.) Tomato (literally "golden apple"), so named because the first tomatoes in Europe, in the sixteenth century, were yellow.

pompano A silvery fish found off the southeastern U.S. coastline in the Atlantic Ocean and Gulf of Mexico; its rich white meat is a delicacy that can be cooked in many ways, often *en papillote* with shrimp and crab.

Pont-l'Evêque (Fr.) A soft, uncooked and unpressed cheese made from whole or partially skimmed raw cows' milk, from Normandy; this washed-rind cheese has a rich creamy texture and taste, a full aroma, and a square golden rind.

Pont-Neuf (Fr.) See **pomme de terre.**

poori (Ind.) Whole-wheat deep-fried puffy bread.

poor knights of Windsor (Brit.) Sliced bread soaked in sherry, dipped in egg batter, fried in butter, and served with sugar and cinnamon; a British version of French toast.

popcorn Certain varieties of corn with a high protein content and specific moisture content; with dry heat the corn kernel explodes, and the endosperm swells into the light and crisp snack we know as popcorn.

pope's nose The tail piece of a bird; also known as parson's nose.

popone (It.) Melon.

popover A puffed-up hollow muffin made from an eggy batter very much like that of **Yorkshire pudding,** baked in muffin tins, and served with butter; American in origin.

poppy seed The dried seed of the poppy plant, much used in breads and pastry as well as in Middle Eastern and Indian cooking.

porchetta (It.) Roast suckling pig; the Spanish is *porcella.*

porcino (It.) A wild mushroom, the French *cèpe* or **boletus.**

porgy A saltwater fish related to the **bream;** bony but with delicate moist flesh, the porgy is best barbecued or fried.

porridge A cereal or grain, usually oatmeal, cooked in water or milk to a thick puddinglike consistency; it may or may not be flavored with salt, sugar, butter, and various other ingredients.

pòrro (It.) Leek.

port A sweet fortified dessert wine from Portugal's upper Douro Valley, shipped from Oporto (hence the name); brandy is added to partially fermented grape juice, arresting fermentation and producing a strong, sweet wine that is then matured. *Vintage port* is wine from exceptional years that is unblended, bottled young (usually in England), and then aged for at least a dozen years. *Tawny port* is blended with wine from several years, aged in oak in Oporto to give it a rounder flavor and softer color, then bottled and shipped ready for sale. *Ruby port* is kept in wood for a shorter time to retain its color and can be blended or not, either in Oporto or England. *White port* is made similarly but from white grapes.

porter   (Brit.)   A very dark and strongly flavored **lager** beer in which malt is toasted before brewing; porter is usually higher in alcohol than lager beer.

porterhouse   A superior cut of beef from the **short loin** next to the **T-bone,** with a large portion of the **filet mignon** and **strip loin.**

porto, au   (Fr.)   A classic French sauce of **demi-glace** and **port;** when *à l'anglaise* it is a reduction of port, orange and lemon juice and zest, shallots, and thyme, strained and mixed with veal stock.

Port-Salut   (Fr.)   An uncooked, pressed, pasteurized cows' milk cheese, originally made on a small scale by Trappist monks, using unpasteurized milk (this type of cheese is now called *Entrammes*), but now factory-produced; similar to its cousin **Saint-Paulin.**

portugaise   (Fr.)   A classic sauce of chopped onions cooked in butter or oil, with chopped tomatoes, tomato sauce, meat glaze, garlic, and chopped parsley; the garnish *à la portugaise* is stuffed tomatoes with **château potatoes** and *portugaise* sauce.

posset   (Brit.)   An old-fashioned punch made of milk, eggs, wine or ale, lemon juice, spices, and sugar, with whipped cream folded in; a remedy for colds as far back as the Middle Ages, posset is akin to **syllabub** or our latter-day **eggnog.**

postre   (Sp.)   Dessert.

potage   (Fr.)   Soup, especially a thickened vegetable soup, but not as hearty as **soupe;** the Spanish word *potaje* means a thick soup or stew.

potage Saint-Cloud   (Fr.)   A soup of green peas and lettuce pureed; served with **croutons.**

potato flour   Flour ground from cooked potatoes, used in thickening gravies and soups and in breads, where it keeps the crumb moister than wheat flour.

pot-au-feu   (Fr.)   Meat and vegetables cooked together in water; the resulting broth is served first, followed by the meat and vegetables as the main course; this classic provincial dish can contain several different meats.

pot de crème   (Fr.)   A small, individual covered cup that holds custard, mousse, and similar desserts; the top keeps a skin from forming on custards.

potée   (Fr.)   Originally any food cooked in an earthenware pot, now usually a thick soup of pork and vegetables—often potatoes and cabbage.

potiron (Fr.) Pumpkin.

pot liquor, potlikker The broth remaining after greens and vegetables have been cooked; it is nutritious and an essential part of southern Black cooking, usually served with cornbread or **corn pone.**

potpie Meat or poultry and perhaps vegetables, cut up and baked with gravy in a deep dish covered with pie crust; American in origin and ranging in quality from the ridiculous to the sublime.

pot roasting A method of braising food (usually large cuts of meat) slowly in a tightly covered pot; the food is browned in a little fat and cooked with some stock or other liquid and vegetables over low heat until tender.

potted shrimps (Brit.) Small shrimps shelled, warmed in **clarified butter,** seasoned with mace or nutmeg, and preserved in the butter for a few days; served as an hors d'oeuvre with brown bread.

Pouilly-Fuissé A popular white wine from southern Burgundy, just west of **Mâcon,** made from the **Chardonnay** grape; it is dry, clean, fresh, and fruity, with a lovely bouquet.

Pouilly Fumé (Fr.) A white wine produced from the **Sauvignon Blanc** grape in the village of Pouilly-sur-Loire: dry, pale, fresh, with a slightly "smoky" *(fumé)* quality; similar to its neighbor **Sancerre** but no relation to **Pouilly-Fuissé.**

poularde (Fr.) A fat hen or chicken—a "roaster"—over four pounds in weight.

poule-au-pot (Fr.) **Pot-au-feu** including a sausage-stuffed chicken, made famous by Henri IV's perhaps apocryphal remark that he wanted every household in France to have *poule-au-pot* on Sunday; the chicken is a plump hen, even though *poule* means stewing chicken.

poulet (Fr.) A young spring chicken—a "fryer" or "broiler"—weighing up to about four pounds; *poule* means a stewing chicken, one that is too old for other treatment; *poulet d'Inde* is a turkey.

Pouligny-Saint-Pierre (Fr.) A goats' milk cheese, uncooked and unpressed, from Berry; soft, crumbly, and pyramid-shaped.

poultry All domestic fowl, excluding game birds.

pound cake Cake traditionally made with one pound each of flour, butter, sugar, and eggs.

pourriture noble (Fr.) **Noble rot.**

pousse (Fr.) Rise, as in a first rise for yeast pastry.

poussin (Fr.) A very young chicken.

Powidl (Aus.) A special plum preserve used for pastries and puddings.

pozole (Mex.) A thick soup, almost a stew, made of pork, hominy, and large white dried *cacahuazintle* corn kernels, and served with a hot chili sauce.

praline Almonds, or in America often pecans, in a caramel syrup or coating; in French cooking, praline is usually crushed and added to confections; named after the seventeenth-century French *maréchal* du Plessis-Praslin, duc de Choiseul, whose chef created this preparation; the adjective is *praliné.*

prawn   A crustacean similar to the shrimp, strictly speaking, but the term is used loosely for any large shrimp.

Preiselbeer   (Ger.)   A red berry similar to the cranberry.

Premier Cru   (Fr.)   For **Burgundy** wine, the next to highest classification of vineyards, usually including the name of the vineyard's commune as well as the name of the vineyard itself. For *Premier Cru* wines from **Bordeaux,** see **classed growth.**

pre-salé   (Fr.)   Lamb and mutton from coastal Normandy that graze on saltmarsh meadows (hence the name), giving their flesh a special salty flavor much prized.

pressure cooker   A covered pot that, because it is under pressure, can cook food above the boiling point, saving time and energy. Pressure cookers are suitable for any food cooked by moist heat, such as soup, stock, stew, pudding, and preserves, but generally not for meat. A safety valve keeps the cooker from exploding in case of malfunction.

pretzel   A crisp savory kind of biscuit made from a flour and water paste that is formed into a rope and twisted into a knot, sprinkled with coarse salt, and baked; the pretzel is associated with German cooking but goes back to the Romans; the name may come from the Latin word for bracelet.

prezzemolo   (It.)   Parsley, which in Italy is the flat-leafed variety.

prickly pear   An edible cactus, native to Mexico, with a spiny exterior and soft interior flesh, eaten fresh or sometimes cooked; the fruit is shaped like a pear and tastes rather sweet and mild; also called Indian fig.

primavera, alla   (It.)   Literally, "spring style"; dishes so garnished, especially pasta, include raw or blanched spring vegetables—the Italian version of **à la printanière.**

prime   Top-quality beef graded by the U.S. Department of Agriculture— the top 10 percent of beef cattle, available mostly in restaurants and special retail outlets, but not generally sold in markets.

primeur   (Fr.)   Early or forced fruit or vegetables; also first or new wine, as in *Beaujolais Nouveau.*

princesse, à la   (Fr.)   A classic garnish of asparagus tips with sliced truffles in cream sauce; also artichoke bottoms stuffed with asparagus tips, served with **noisette** potatoes.

pringar   (Sp.)   To baste.

printanière, à la   (Fr.)   Literally "spring style"; garnished with spring vegetables; the classic garnish consists of new carrots, turnips cut into olive shapes, peas, small green beans, and asparagus tips.

processed cheese   Cheese produced by means of a technique developed in the early twentieth century: green and aged cheeses, often of different varieties and qualities, are finely ground and blended. Emulsifiers are mixed in before the cheese is pasteurized to arrest ripening, and it is packaged in plastic while still hot. Certain kinds of acid, salt, preservatives, coloring, spices, water, and other additives may also be used.

profiteroles   (Fr.)   Small puffs of **choux** paste often filled with whipped cream or **crème patissière** and piled high in a dish with chocolate sauce poured over; or as an hors d'oeuvre, stuffed with something savory or flavored with cheese.

prosciutto   (It.)   Fresh ham cured by salting and air-drying but not generally by smoking; the name implies that it is *crudo,* or uncooked, although *prosciutto cotto* (cooked) is also made; ham from Parma, where pigs are fed the **Parmigiano** whey, is especially fine and somewhat sweet in flavor.

provençal   (Fr.)   From **Provence;** the classic sauce consists of chopped tomatoes sautéed in olive oil with garlic, parsley, and a pinch of sugar; the garnish *à la provençale* is small tomatoes with stuffed mushrooms and parsley.

Provence   A region in southeastern France on the Mediterranean; garlic and olive oil are the basis of its pungent cuisine, and the region abounds with herbs, vegetables, and seafood, not unlike its neighbor, Italy.

Provolone   (It.)   A cooked and kneaded spun-curd cheese made from cows' milk, originally from southern Italy; Provolone is made in many versions, shapes, and sizes, and is matured either briefly or up to two years; when two to three months old, its color and flavor are buttery and pale; it becomes more pungent when aged and is used then for grating.

prugna   (It.)   Plum; *pruna* and *prugna secca* both mean prune.

prune   (Fr.)   Plum; *pruneau* means prune.

puchero   (Sp.)   Pot; *puchero de gallina* is a special dish of braised stuffed chicken with a sauce of chicken livers; in the Mexican Yucatán, *puchero* is a hot pot including various meats, vegetables, legumes, and even fruit, with the broth served first, followed by the solids.

pudding   A vague culinary term which in Britain usually means dessert, but can also mean a savory dish, because of its derivation from *boudin,* meaning sausage.

pudim flan   (Port.)   The Portuguese version of caramel custard, richer and thicker than the Spanish.

puerco   (Sp.)   Pig, pork.

puerro   (Sp.)   Leek.

Puffer   (Ger.)   Pancake, fritter.

puff pastry   See **pâte feuilletée.**

puit d'amour   (Fr.)   Literally, "wishing well": a small round pastry filled with pastry cream, jelly, or fruit.

Puligny-Montrachet   A village in the Burgundian **Côte de Beaune** which, with its neighbor Chassagne-Montrachet, produces excellent dry white wine, almost all from the **Chardonnay** grape.

pullao   (Ind.)   **Pilaf.**

pullet   A young hen under one year old.

pulse   The edible seeds, often dried, of leguminous plants such as peas, beans, lentils, and chick-peas; respected by the ancients and virtually all cultures since for their nutritional importance.

Pultost   (Nor.)   A cooked cows' milk cheese, soft and rindless, often flavored with caraway and eaten year-round.

pumpernickel   A dark, coarse-textured, slightly sour bread made from unbolted **rye** flour; originally from Westphalia, Germany.

puree   (Fr.)   Food that is mashed, very finely chopped, or pushed through a sieve to achieve a smooth consistency.

puri   (Ind.)   Puffed, light, whole-wheat bread that is deep-fried in vegetable oil; from northern and central India.

purslane   A once-popular herb with small fleshy leaves, now considered a weed except by the French, who eat it fresh in salad and boiled or sautéed like spinach; in its native India it is used more widely.

Puter   (Ger.)   Turkey.

pyramide   (Fr.)   The generic name for **chèvre,** or fresh goats' milk cheese, uncooked and unpressed, shaped in a small truncated pyramid; this type of cheese is very white, soft, crumbly, and delicate in flavor, becoming sharper if allowed to mature; it is sometimes covered with vegetable ash to keep it from drying out.

quail

Q

quadrucci (It.) "Little squares" of egg pasta for chicken or meat broth.

quaglia (It.) Quail.

quahog A hard-shelled North Atlantic clam found off the New England coast; appropriate for many preparations, the very large ones with heavy shells are particularly good for chowder.

quail A small migratory game bird (two or three per serving) relished for its delicious flavor; there are many varieties the world over, but since wild quail are becoming scarce, those that we eat today are mostly farm-bred; the meat is cooked without hanging.

Quark (Ger.) A soft, runny, acid-curd cows' milk cheese made from skimmed or partially skimmed milk; *Quark* is a type of cottage cheese and is eaten with fruit or salad or used in cooking; originally Central European and also spelled *Quarg* or *Kvarg;* known as *Topfen* in Austria and widely used in such pastries as *Topfen Schnitten* and *Topfen Strudel.*

Quartirolo (It.) A soft, uncooked, pressed, whole-milk cows' cheese from Lombardy, similar to **Taleggio** but cured in caves where it acquires a mushroomy flavor; square, with a thin washed rind, the paste is smooth, pale, and creamy; still made by traditional small-scale farmhouse methods.

quasi de veau bourgeoise (Fr.) Veal chump or hind end braised in a casserole with pork, calf's foot, and vegetables.

quatre-épices (Fr.) A mixture of finely ground ginger, clove, nutmeg, and white pepper; a descendant of the elaborate spice mixtures used to flavor savory and sweet food in the Middle Ages.

quatre-quarts (Fr.) A classic pound cake, made of "four quarters"; that is, equal parts of egg, butter, flour, and sugar.

queen of puddings (Brit.) A breadcrumb and custard pudding base baked with strawberry jam covering, then topped with meringue and lightly browned in the oven.

Queensland nut See **macadamia nut.**

queijo (Port.) Cheese.

quenelle (Fr.) A light dumpling made of seafood, chicken, game, or veal forcemeat bound with eggs; although *quenelles* were once quite large, nowadays they are usually small ovals, like light **mousselines,** poached in simmering water or broth and served with a creamy or buttery sauce.

quesadilla (Mex.) A **tortilla** turnover filled with a savory stuffing and toasted or fried.

queso (Sp.) Cheese; *queso blanco* is the fresh, smooth, rindless cows' milk cheese made throughout Latin America; it is an acid-curd cheese made from whole or partially skimmed milk, pressed, salted, and eaten fresh with fruit or matured for two or three months.

quetsch A variety of plum made into tarts and other confections but best known for the clear colorless **eau de vie** or liqueur distilled from it in Alsace.

queue de boeuf (Fr.) **Oxtail.**

quiche (Fr.) An open custard tart, usually savory, from Alsace and Lorraine; in the United States it has come to mean *quiche Lorraine,* which is filled with eggs, cream, bacon, and (more recently) **Gruyère,** but the variations are infinite; from the German word *Kuchen.*

quick bread Any bread or muffin made with a quick-acting leavening agent, usually **baking powder** or **baking soda.**

quince A tree indigenous to Persia, whose fruit may be the golden apple of antiquity; popular throughout the temperate world until the last century or so, especially for pies and preserves, it is now largely ignored except in the Middle East; long, slow cooking and generous amounts of sugar bring out the quince's mellow flavor and golden color.

Quitte (Ger.) Quince; *Quittengelee* is quince marmalade.

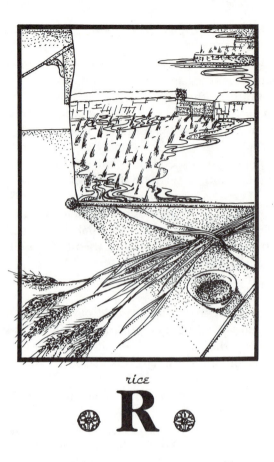

rice

• R •

rabadi (Ind.) Thickened, reduced milk.

rábano (Sp.) Radish.

rabattage (Fr.) Deflating the dough in yeast pastry-making.

rabbit A small member of the hare family, both wild and domesticated, whose flesh can vary in flavor depending on its age and diet; leaner and sweeter than chicken, rabbit is cooked in similar ways.

rabbit, Welsh See **Welsh rarebit.**

râble de lièvre (Fr.) **Saddle** of hare.

Rachel (Fr.) Garnished with bone **marrow** and accompanied by **bordelaise** sauce; for **tournedos.**

racine (Fr.) Root vegetable.

rack A cut of lamb or veal from the rib section, with tender and flavorful meat; can be kept whole, cut into seven rib chops, or made into crown roast.

racking Drawing off clear wine from one barrel or vat to another, leaving the sediment.

Raclette (Switz.) From the verb *racler,* "to scrape"; half a large wheel of cows' milk cheese is placed near the fire, melting the rich, buttery cheese, which is scraped onto a plate and eaten with boiled potatoes *en chemise,* pickled onions, and gherkins. A specialty of the Valais region of the Swiss Alps; see also **walliser.**

radicchio (It.) A type of chicory with red or pinkish leaves, used for garnishing or for salad, whose root can also be delicious. In the U.S., Verona chicory has recently enjoyed a vogue; in Italy there are other types as well, and they are often cooked.

radis (Fr.) Radish.

rafano (It.) Horseradish.

raffinade (Fr. and Ger.) Refined sugar.

rafraîchir (Fr.) To "refresh" boiling vegetables by plunging them into cold water to halt cooking and retain color; to chill.

ragoût (Fr.) A stew of meat, poultry, or fish, which may contain vegetables; a *ragoût* literally "restores the appetite."

Ragoût fin (Ger.) A delicate combination of organ meats such as sweetbreads and brains, cooked with mushrooms in a winy cream sauce; often served in a puff pastry shell.

ragù Bolognese (It.) A meat sauce from Bologna and not a stew or **ragoût** as commonly thought; often used for pasta. Ground beef and sometimes pork and ham are sautéed in butter and oil with chopped vegetables and simmered with milk, white wine, and tomatoes. Pasta *alla bolognese* designates this sauce.

Ragusano (It.) A spun-curd cows' milk cheese from Sicily, cooked, kneaded, and sometimes smoked; rectangular in shape; delicate and sliceable table cheeses are matured for three months, firm, sharp grating cheeses up to twelve months.

Rahm (Ger.) Cream.

raidir (Fr.) To sear.

raie (Fr.) Skate.

raifort (Fr.) Horseradish.

Rainwater A general term for a very pale dry **Madeira** developed by an American in the early nineteenth century.

raisin (Fr.) Grape; *raisin sec* is raisin; *raisin de Corinthe* is **currant.**

raita (Ind.) Vegetables, raw or cooked, or sometimes fruits, mixed with yogurt.

rajas (Mex.) **Poblano** or other chili strips, fried with onions and sometimes potatoes or tomatoes.

rajma (Ind.) Red kidney beans.

rallado (Sp.) Grated.

ramen (Jap.) Chinese soup noodles.

ramequin (Fr.) A small flameproof dish; the English term is ramekin; also a small cheese tart.

ramp   A wild leek—an Appalachian spring delicacy—that looks like a scallion but tastes stronger.

rampion   A plant, cultivated or wild (but rarely eaten nowadays), whose leaves are eaten like spinach and whose roots, also either raw or cooked, taste like **salsify.**

ranchero   (Sp.)   Country style; *salsa ranchera* combines tomatoes, **serrano** chilies, garlic, and onion into a hot and spicy sauce known best in **huevos rancheros** but also served with meat.

rapa   (It.)   Turnip.

rape   A type of turnip whose seeds yield an oil used for salad and frying (mostly in India and the Mediterranean) and for blending in margarine; it is sometimes called *colza.* The young leaves and shoots can be braised as a vegetable but are mostly used for fodder; in southern Italy, where rape is called *broccolirab,* the tender leaves and stems are best appreciated, especially as a robust accompaniment to **orecchiette.**

rapé   (Sp.)   Monkfish, angler.

râper   (Fr.)   To grate, especially cheese; the adjective is *râpé.*

rarebit   See **Welsh rarebit.**

rasher   (Brit.)   A slice of bacon or ham.

ratafia   A liqueur flavored by infusion with the kernels of certain fruits, such as peaches and apricots; a favorite homemade Victorian cordial. In Britain the word also means **macaroon.**

ratatouille   (Fr.)   A vegetable stew or sauté from Provence of diced eggplant, tomatoes, zucchini, green peppers, onions, and garlic all cooked in olive oil; there are many variations, and it can be eaten hot or cold.

räuchern   (Ger.)   To smoke.

Rauenthal   A village in the German **Rheingau** that produces perhaps the best Rhine wines: fruity, elegant, with a characteristic spiciness.

ravanèllo   (It.)   Radish.

rave   (Fr.)   Turnip or other root vegetable.

ravigote   (Fr.)   A classic cold sauce of **vinaigrette** with capers, chopped onions, and herbs; as a classic sauce served hot, it is a reduction of white wine and vinegar with **velouté,** shallot butter, and herbs.

ravioli   (It.)   Small pasta squares filled with spinach, **ricotta,** and herbs rather than meat; see also **agnolotti.**

raw   Uncooked, fresh; in reference to milk products, the word means unpasteurized.

ray   See **skate.**

raya   (Sp.)   Skate.

Reblochon   (Fr.)   An uncooked, lightly pressed cows' milk cheese made in the Haute-Savoie and across the Italian border. Originally made with the undeclared second milking (concealed from the owner after his quota had been collected), while the milk was still warm, it is a rich, soft, and delicately fruity cheese shaped in a disc and with a golden rind.

recette (Fr.) Recipe.

rechauffé (Fr.) Food that is reheated or made with leftovers.

récolte (Fr.) Harvest, crop, vintage.

red beans and rice A Louisiana specialty of red beans (sometimes kidney beans) and rice, cooked with ham hock; there are many variations. Louis Armstrong signed his letters, "Red beans and ricely yours."

redeye gravy Ham gravy made with ice water or even coffee and perhaps a little brown sugar; served in the South for breakfast with **grits** and biscuits.

red flannel hash Cooked beets fried with bacon, potatoes, and onions, and often served with corn bread; rustic American fare.

red herring Herring salted strongly to a deep red color.

red mullet See **mullet.**

red snapper A saltwater fish from the Gulf of Mexico, usually marketed at about five pounds but sometimes much larger; there are many types of snapper, but the rosy red snapper, with white, succulent, sweet meat, is a choice delicacy cooked in many ways, often stuffed whole.

reduce To boil down a liquid to thicken its consistency and concentrate its flavor, as in a reduction sauce. **Escoffier** was the first chef to thicken sauces by reduction rather than with flour or other starch.

réduire (Fr.) To reduce.

Réforme, à la (Fr.) Lamb chops breadcrumbed, fried, and garnished with **julienne** of ham, truffles, carrots, and hard-boiled egg whites, with a **poivrade** sauce; created by **Alexis Soyer** for the Reform Club in London.

refried beans Cooked pinto beans, mashed and fried with garlic, often for a **tortilla** filling; of Mexican-American origin. See also **frijoles.**

régence, à la (Fr.) Garnished with **quenelles, truffles, foie gras,** and cockscombs if for sweetbreads or chicken, or with oysters and roe if for fish—a classic garnish.

Regensburgerwurst (Ger.) A short, fat sausage of pork and beef.

Reh (Ger.) Venison; *Rehrücken* is saddle of venison and also an oblong chocolate cake garnished with almonds.

reiben (Ger.) To grate or rub; a *Reibschale* is a mortar.

reine, à la (Fr.) Garnished with chicken in some form; named after Louis XVI's queen.

Reis (Ger.) Rice.

relâcher (Fr.) To thin a sauce or puree with liquid; literally, to relax or loosen.

relevé (Fr.) Highly seasoned.

religieuse (Fr.) Resembling a nun's habit—hence the name—this pastry is a small cream puff atop a large one, each filled with **crème pâtissière,** glazed, and decorated with buttercream.

relleno (Sp.) Stuffing, stuffed.

rémol (Sp.) **Brill.**

remolacha (Sp.) Beet.

rémoulade (Fr.) **Mayonnaise** seasoned with mustard, anchovy essence, chopped gherkins, capers, parsley, chervil, and tarragon—a classic sauce.

remuage (Fr.) In making Champagne, the daily shaking and turning of the bottles, nearly upside down, to bring the sediment down to the cork before the *dégorgement.*

Renaissance, à la (Fr.) Various spring vegetables arranged separately around a large roast—a classic garnish.

render To melt fat, thus clarifying the drippings to use in cooking or flavoring.

rennet The stomach lining of an unweaned calf, kid, or lamb, containing rennin and other enzymes that coagulate milk; in cheesemaking, rennet extracts are used to curdle milk. There are also vegetable rennets with the same property.

renverser (Fr.) To unmold or turn out onto a serving dish.

repollo (Sp.) Cabbage.

repos (Fr.) A rest, as for the resting of dough in pastry-making.

resserrer (Fr.) To "tighten" or pull a sauce together by thickening it.

Rettich (Ger.) Radish.

revenir (Fr.) To brown, as for meat (*faire revenir*).

Rheingau A white-wine district in Germany where the Rhine flows east-west for twenty miles between Mainz and Rüdesheim; the southern-facing slopes produce the finest German wines, mostly **Rieslings,** which are separately entered.

Rheinpfalz A wine-producing region in Germany, also known as the Palatinate, west of the Rhine and northeast of Alsace-Lorraine; the vineyards are on the slopes of the Harz mountains.

Rhine A major river flowing northwest to the North Sea through West Germany; along her slopes and those of her tributaries, especially the Nahe and the Moselle, most German wine is produced; spelled *Rhein* in German.

Rhône A major river flowing west from Switzerland through Lake Geneva and south through France into the Mediterranean; along her slopes many wine grapes are grown, most notably those grown in France between Lyons and the sea, for Rhône wines.

rhubarb Native to southeastern Russia, this leafy vegetable is cultivated for its thick reddish stalks, which are used in pies and compotes and occasionally in savory sauces. The leaves are poisonous, but the astringent stalks are made palatable for "fruit" desserts with lots of sugar and cooking.

rib   A section of beef from the top forequarter comprising the most tender steak and roast cuts, including the **Delmonico, rib-eye,** rib steak, and **rib roast.**

ribes   (It.)   Gooseberry, currant.

rib-eye steak   A cut of beef from the **rib** section, virtually the same as a **Delmonico** except that the rib-eye has been further trimmed of fat.

ribollita   (It.)   A hearty soup of white beans, vegetables, bread, cheese, and olive oil, from Florence; usually served reheated, hence the name.

rib roast   A cut of beef from the forequarter, between the **chuck** and **loin;** this seven-rib cut is often divided into three parts, the first cut of which, partially boned, becomes the "prime ribs" of a standing rib roast.

rice   To force cooked fruits or vegetables, especially potatoes, through an instrument with small perforations in it, so that the food resembles grains of rice; the tool is called a ricer.

rice   A grain native to India and probably the world's most important food crop, especially in Asia where it has been cultivated for millennia. The thousands of varieties divide into long-grained rice, which separates into distinct kernels when cooked, and short-grained rice, which is higher in starch, wetter, and stickier when cooked. In the milling process, removal of the hull produces *brown rice.* Removal of the bran and most of the germ produces *unpolished rice.* To reduce spoilage, removal of the outer aleurone layer produces *polished rice,* which is then coated with a thin layer of vitamins (which should not be rinsed off). *Converted rice* has been steamed and dried before milling for higher nutritional content and easier processing. "Instant" rice grains have been partially cooked and split open. See also **wild rice.**

rice wine   Distilled from fermented rice and made in many varieties, qualities, and strengths, rice wine is far less common in China than it used to be. **Saké, sherry,** Scotch whisky, or dry **vermouth** can be substituted for rice wine in cooking.

Richelieu, à la   (Fr.)   Garnished with stuffed tomatoes and mushrooms, braised lettuce, **château potatoes,** and veal stock—a classic garnish for meat.

ricotta   (It.)   Strictly speaking not a cheese, ricotta is made from the leftover whey from other cheeses, either ewes' or cows' milk, and is sometimes enriched with milk or cream. As the whey is heated, the cloudy top layer is skimmed off and drained to make the cheese. Bland, slightly sweet, and dry, ricotta is eaten fresh or cooked in pasta dishes and sweet desserts.

Riesling   A superlative white-wine grape variety probably native to the Rhine Valley, where it has been cultivated since the Romans; the grape has been transplanted to many other countries where it continues to distinguish itself. It is fortunately subject to **noble rot.**

rigaglie   (It.)   Giblets.

rigatoni   (It.)   Fat-ribbed macaroni, commercially made.

rigodon   (Fr.)   A **brioche** custard tart filled with bacon, ham, nuts, or pureed fruit, served either warm or cold; a specialty of Burgundy.

rijstaffel   (Neth.)   Literally "rice table," this is the elaborate colonial Dutch version of the Indonesian rice table, with dozens of side dishes. The various offerings in the buffet include meat and seafood dishes, savory fried and steamed foods, **satés,** sauces, vegetable salads, rice, fruit, and chili dishes—hot and cool, spicy and bland—in great profusion.

rillettes   (Fr.)   Pork cubed and cooked with its fat and herbs, then pounded in a mortar and potted; goose and rabbit are sometimes prepared similarly. *Rillauds* and *rillons* are the same but are not pounded.

Rind   (Ger.)   Beef; *Rinderbraten* is roast beef, *Rinderbrust* is brisket of beef, *Rindertalg* is beef suet, *Rindswurst* is beef sausage.

riñones   (Sp.)   Kidneys.

Rioja   A wine region in northern Spain where light, dry, and refined red wines and more ordinary white wines are made.

ripièno   (It.)   Stuffed or filled; stuffing.

Ripp   (Ger.)   Rib; *Rippenbraten* is roast loin, *Rippenspeer* is ribs of pork, *Rippenstück* is a chop.

ris   (Scand.)   Rice.

ris de veau   (Fr.)   Veal sweetbreads; *ris d'agneau* are lamb sweetbreads.

riso   (It.)   Rice; *risi e bisi* is a very thick soup of rice and spring peas cooked in broth with onion, parsley, and **Parmesan**—a Venetian specialty.

risotto   (It.)   Rice cooked in butter with a little chopped onion to which stock is gradually added as it is absorbed; all manner of savory foods can be added; **Arborio rice** gives the proper texture, tender and creamy but never sticky.

risotto milanese   (It.)   **Risotto** flavored with **saffron;** a classic accompaniment to **osso buco.**

rissoler   (Fr.)   To brown in hot fat; *rissolé* refers to food, such as potatoes, that has been fried thus; a *rissole* is a puff-pastry turnover or fritter that is stuffed, often with ground meat, and deep-fried.

riz   (Fr.)   Rice.

riz à l'impératrice   (Fr.)   Rice pudding flavored with vanilla, crystallized fruit soaked in **Kirsch,** and custard cream.

roast   To cook food by baking it in hot dry air, either in an oven or on or near a fire or hot stones; by extension, the noun *roast* is a large piece of meat that has been roasted.

Robert   (Fr.)   A classic sauce of sautéed onions reduced with white wine and vinegar, **demi-glace** added, and finished with mustard.

Robiola   (It.)   A soft, uncooked, and unpressed cheese from northern Italy; in Lombardy, cows' milk is used and the cheeses are shaped in rectangles, while in Piedmont either ewes' or goats' milk is used, perhaps mixed with cows', and the cheeses are shaped in discs. *Robiola* is named for its reddish thin rind; the interior paste is smooth and even.

robusta   A type of coffee bean, hardy, prolific, and high in caffeine, but with a flavor inferior to **arabica;** used mostly for commercial blends and instant coffee.

Rock Cornish game hen   A crossbreed of a Plymouth hen and a cock from Cornwall which, when fresh, can be deliciously succulent.

rocket   An aromatic salad herb much loved by the Italians but usually disdained by Anglo-Saxons for its peppery, piquant taste (at least until the new California cuisine made it fashionable); also called *arugula, rugola,* and *misticanza,* but not to be confused with a poisonous weed also called rocket.

rockfish   A large family of saltwater fish in the Pacific, sometimes mistakenly called red snapper or rock cod; the firm, lean, delicate flesh is versatile and is especially appreciated by the Chinese.

rodaballo   (Sp.)   Turbot.

roe   Fish or shellfish eggs, ranging from the humble cod all the way to **beluga caviar;** the male **milt** is sometimes, rather euphemistically, called soft roe.

roebuck   Male roe deer; venison.

Roggenbrot   (Ger.)   Rye bread.

roghan josh   (Ind.)   Spiced lamb braised in yogurt and cream; from Kashmir.

rognons   (Fr.)   Kidneys; *rognonnade de veau* is saddle of veal with kidneys attached. In Italian the word is *rognoni.*

rognures   (Fr.)   Trimmings, especially in making **pâte feuilletée,** useful for certain kinds of pastry; also called *demi-feuilletage.*

roh   (Ger.)   Raw; *Rohkost* means raw vegetables or **crudités.**

Rohwurst   (Ger.)   Sausage cured and smoked by the butcher, eaten uncooked.

rolé   (It.)   A slice of meat stuffed and rolled; *rollatini* are small rolls; in Spanish the word is *rollo.*

rollmop   See **herring rollmop.**

roly-poly pudding   (Brit.)   A nursery pudding of suet or biscuit-dough crust, spread with jam, rolled up, and baked or steamed.

romaine lettuce   A variety of lettuce with long, thick central stems and narrow, green leaves; also called cos lettuce.

Romanée-Conti   An exceedingly fine, rare, and celebrated red Burgundy wine from the **Côte d'Or,** made from the **Pinot Noir** grape.

Romano   See **Pecorino Romano.**

Romanoff, strawberries   See **strawberries Romanoff.**

romarin   (Fr.)   Rosemary.

Roncal   (Sp.)   A ewes' milk cheese from the Navalle Valley in Spain, similar to **Manchego** but smaller and harder; the texture is close-grained, the flavor pungent.

Roquefort   (Fr.)   An ancient and celebrated blue cheese made from the milk of Larzac sheep; the curd from the raw, uncooked milk is molded, salted, and inoculated with *Penicillium roqueforti,* then matured for three months in limestone caves in the southwestern town of Roquefort-sur-Soulzon, whose fissures naturally provide the proper humidity and ventilation. The six-pound round cheeses have a thin orange rind, an ivory paste with blue green veining (*persillage*), and a salty and sharp but still creamy taste that is unique.

roquette   (Fr.)   **Rocket.**

rosbif   (Fr.)   Roast beef.

rosé   (Fr.)   Wine made from black grapes with some of the skins included during fermentation, thus producing its characteristic color; rosé is best drunk young and served well chilled. The Italian word for rosé is *rosato.*

rose hips   The fruit of certain roses, which turn red with ripeness; used for making syrup and jelly; high in vitamin C.

rosemary   A shrub native to the Mediterranean, whose needlelike leaves are used dried and fresh as an herb, especially with pork, lamb, veal, and game. Its name means "dew of the sea," although often mistakenly thought to mean "rose of the Virgin Mary." To the ancient Egyptians it symbolized death, to the Greeks and Romans it also meant love.

Rosenkohl   (Ger.)   Brussels sprouts.

rosewater   An extract distilled from water steeped with rose petals, which impart their essential oil; this extract is used as a flavoring in the Middle East, the Balkans, and India.

Rosine   (Ger.)   Raisin.

rosmarino   (It.)   **Rosemary.**

Rossini   (Fr.)   A classic garnish of **foie gras,** sliced truffles, and **demi-glace,** usually for **tournedos;** named after the composer and gastronome Gioacchino Rossini (1792–1868).

Rostbraten (Ger.) In northern Germany, roast beef; in Bavaria and Austria, a thin steak quickly cooked with onions and gravy.

Rostbratwurst (Ger.) Ham sausage seasoned with caraway and nutmeg, roasted over a wood fire.

Rösti (Switz.) Potatoes grated and fried in a pancake.

roti (Ind.) Bread.

rôti (Fr.) Roasted, a roast; a *rôtisserie* is a broiling device with a motorized spit for roasting large pieces of meat and birds; a *rôtisseur* is the cook responsible for roasting in a large kitchen.

Rotwein (Ger.) Red wine.

rouelle (Fr.) A round slice of meat.

rouennaise (Fr.) **Bordelaise** sauce with a reduction of red wine and shallots, finished with pureed raw duck livers—a classic sauce.

rouget (Fr.) Red mullet.

rouille (Fr.) A spicy red pepper and garlic **mayonnaise** from Provence, served with fish soups.

roulade (Fr.) A rolled slice of meat or piece of fish filled with a savory stuffing; the term can also mean a sheet of sponge cake or the like spread with a suitable filling, rolled up, and perhaps garnished.

Roulade (Ger.) Stuffed rolled beef.

rouleau (Fr.) Rolling pin.

round A cut of beef from the hindquarter, comprising the hind leg; the top and bottom round, eye of round, and top sirloin (sirloin tip) are lean subdivisions that can be further cut into steaks or left whole and braised or roasted.

roux (Fr.) A mixture of flour and butter or other fat, usually in equal proportions, cooked together slowly and used to thicken sauces and soups. A white *roux* is heated long enough to cook the flour but not color it and is used for **béchamel** and **velouté** sauces; a blond *roux* is allowed to color slightly during cooking; a brown *roux,* which may use a clarified fat other than butter, is cooked slowly for a long time so that it acquires a mellow brown shade to color the sauces it thickens. The word *roux* means reddish or reddish brown.

rowanberry The fruit of the mountain ash, which ripens in the fall. The berries are used to make a bright red, tart jelly often served with lamb, venison, and other game; in Alsace an **eau de vie** is made from the berries.

royale (Fr.) Unsweetened custard, possibly flavored, cooked in a mold and then cut into decorative shapes; used to garnish clear soups.

royale, charlotte See **charlotte.**

royal icing Icing used for pastry-writing, decorating, and glazing Christmas or wedding cakes; made from confectioners' sugar, egg white, and a little lemon juice.

royan (Fr.) Fresh sardine.

Rübe (Ger.) Turnip, **rape;** *Weisserübe* is turnip, *Roterübe* is beet, *Gelberübe* is carrot.

ruchetta (It.) **Rocket.**

Rücken (Ger.) Saddle.

rucola (It.) **Rocket.**

Rüdesheim A small town on the western end of the **Rheingau,** opposite the mouth of the Nahe, on whose steep slopes excellent **Riesling** wines are produced.

rue An herb used by the ancients for medicinal puposes but now used only as a flavoring for **grappa.**

rugola (It.) **Rocket.**

Rührei (Ger.) Scrambled eggs.

rump A cut of beef from the **round,** usually braised or roasted; unboned, it is a standing rump roast, while boned, it is a rolled rump roast.

ruote (It.) Wheel-shaped pasta.

rusk Bread sliced and baked again slowly until crisp and golden brown, such as **zwieback.**

russe, à la (Fr.) Food served sequentially course by course, hot from the kitchen, as opposed to all of the dishes for a service being laid out on the table in a large and elaborate display (*service à la francaise*); this Russian style of service gradually overtook the older French style in the early nineteenth century and survives today, greatly simplified.

russe, charlotte (Fr.) See **charlotte.**

rustica, alla (It.) A spaghetti sauce of anchovies, garlic, oregano, and **Pecorino** cheese.

rutabaga A yellow or Swedish turnip; a swede.

rye A grain native to central Asia and invaluable because of its hardiness in poor soils, in cool climates, and at high altitudes; it has long been the favored flour of northern and eastern Europe. Because it does not form **gluten** well, rye and wheat flours are often mixed together for bread. In the U.S. it is also used to make whiskey and for fodder. See also **pumpernickel.**

ryōri (Jap.) Food, cooking.

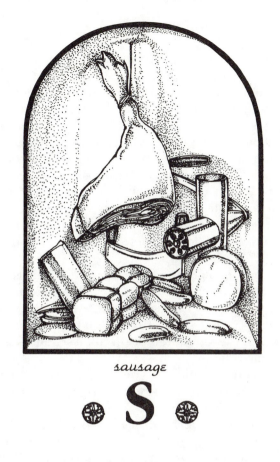

sausage

❖ S ❖

saag (Ind.) Greens or spinach.

Saankäse (Switz.) A cooked, pressed, hard cheese made from cows' milk from two successive milkings; it is made into large orange discs, aged up to five years, and prized as a dessert or grating cheese for its mellow fragrant flavor.

Saar A German tributary of the **Moselle** River whose vineyards produce white wine that is legally Moselle but with an austere quality of its own.

saba (Jap.) Mackerel.

sabayon (Fr.) The French version of **zabaglione,** in which various wines or liqueurs can be substituted for **Marsala.**

sablé (Fr.) Shortbread from Normandy whose high sugar and butter content account for its "sandy" texture; shaped into various forms and thicknesses; *pâte sablée* is similar to **pâte sucrée.**

sabzi (Ind.) Vegetables, sometimes stir-fried.

saccharin A noncaloric sugar substitute, far sweeter than sugar, discovered over a century ago and now suspected to be a carcinogenic agent.

Sachertorte (Ger.) A rich chocolate cake containing many eggs, a layer of apricot jam, and chocolate icing. Created by Franz Sacher (of the Sacher Hotel in Vienna) for Prince Metternich in 1832.

sack The Elizabethan English word for **sherry.**

sacristain (Fr.) A strip of **pâte feuilletée** sprinkled with cheese or chopped almonds and sugar, twisted into a spiral, and baked; so named for its resemblance to a corkscrew (the *sacristain* is responsible, among other things, for uncorking the communion wine).

saddle A cut of meat extending along the hindquarters from the end of the ribs to the legs on both sides.

safflower A thistlelike plant, also called Mexican saffron, whose seeds yield oil and whose flowers yield an orange dye; the oil is light in flavor and high in polyunsaturates.

saffron The deep orange dried stigmas of a particular crocus, which must be gathered by hand, hence the spice's exorbitant price; since ancient times and in many cultures it has been used as a medicine, aphrodisiac, dye, and spice; it colors and flavors such classic dishes as **risotto milanese, paella, bouillabaisse,** and **kulich.**

Saft (Ger.) Juice, syrup, gravy.

sage A perennial herb with gray green leaves, used since ancient times for medicinal and culinary purposes; it is used especially, though with discretion, in cooking pork and goose.

Sage Derby (Brit.) A **Derby** cheese flavored and marbled with sage; aged nine months or more, it is flaky and mild and considered one of England's most distinctive cheeses; also called *Derby Sage.*

sago A starch extracted from the stem of an Asian palm tree and used for thickening puddings and occasionally soups; similar to **tapioca,** sago is formed into pearl-like beads.

Sahne (Ger.) Cream; *Sahnenkäse* means cream cheese; *Sahnenkuchen* is a cream tart or cake.

saignant (Fr.) Rare, as in meat; literally, "bleeding."

saigneux (Fr.) Neck of veal or lamb.

Sailland, Edmond See **Curnonsky.**

Saint-Cloud, potage See **potage Saint-Cloud.**

Sainte-Maure (Fr.) A goats' milk cheese, uncooked and unpressed, from the town of the same name in Touraine, also Poitou; cured for three weeks, the cheese is log-shaped with a white soft smooth paste and a white bloomy rind.

Saint-Émilion A small town in the Dordogne Valley of Bordeaux celebrated for its many fine red wines, especially the rich full châteaux wines. Saint-Emilion is also the varietal name of the **Trebbiano** grape in Cognac.

Saint-Estèphe A wine **commune** at the northern tip of the **Haut-Médoc** producing solid, full-bodied, robust wines, less delicate than some of its neighbors; aside from its **classed growths,** its *crus bourgeois* are also excellent.

Saint George's agaric   A wild field mushroom, found in Europe in spring and autumn.

Saint-Germain   (Fr.)   With fresh peas; *potage Saint-Germain* is a thick puree of fresh peas.

Saint-Honoré, gâteau   See **gâteau Saint-Honoré.**

Saint-Jacques   (Fr.)   See **coquille Saint-Jacques.**

Saint John's bread   See **carob.**

Saint-Julien   A wine **commune** in the **Haut-Médoc** of Bordeaux, just south of **Pauillac,** overlooking the Gironde River; its red wines are of consistently fine quality, well-balanced and smooth.

Saint-Malo   (Fr.)   A classic white sauce for fish, flavored with mustard, shallots, and anchovy essence.

Saint-Marcellin   (Fr.)   An uncooked and unpressed cheese from the Isère Valley, made in farmhouses from goats' milk and in factories from mixed milk; ripened for two weeks, it is disc-shaped with a smooth paste and a delicate bloomy rind.

Saint-Nectaire   (Fr.)   An unpasteurized cows' milk cheese, uncooked and pressed, from the Auvergne; the flat rounds are cured up to two months for a dark pinkish rind and a creamy smooth interior, with good melting properties.

Saint-Paulin   (Fr.)   An uncooked, pressed cows' milk cheese made from whole pasteurized milk; it is large and round, with a smooth yellow rind and an even mild paste; a descendant of *Port-du-Salut* and similar to **Port-Salut,** *Saint-Paulin* is widely made.

Saint-Pierre   (Fr.)   **John Dory.**

saisir   (Fr.)   To sear.

sakana   (Jap.)   Fish.

saké   (Jap.)   Rice wine, sweet or dry, usually drunk warm in small cups and also used for cooking; *sake* (without the accent mark) means salmon.

salamander   A gas oven with a top element for quickly glazing or browning dishes, used in restaurant kitchens.

salambo   (Fr.)   An oval **choux pastry** filled with kirsch-flavored **crème pâtissière** and glazed with caramel.

salami   (It.)   A sausage, infinitely variable in ingredients, seasoning, shape, and method, and long made in many countries other than Italy. Salami is usually made of pork meat and fat, sometimes with beef, veal, or other meats, fairly highly seasoned, and cured as long as six months; its name derives from its being salted.

Salbei   (Ger.)   Sage.

salchicha   (Sp.)   Sausage.

salé   (Fr.)   Salted or pickled; *petit salé* means salt pork; *salaison* means salting; the Italian word for salt is *sale* (no accent mark), the Spanish *sal.*

Salisbury steak   A patty of lean beef broiled and seasoned; devised by the nineteenth-century dietician Dr. James H. Salisbury to avoid supposedly unhealthy fermentation in the digestive tract.

Sally Lunn   A light, sweet bun or bread supposedly named after the woman who first sold them in Bath, England, in the late eighteenth century.

salmagundi   (Brit.)   A mixed dish, really a *salade* **composée,** including greens, chopped meats, hard-boiled eggs, pickles, anchovies, onions, and perhaps other vegetables, all carefully arranged and dressed.

salmi   A stew made from leftover or partially roasted feathered game, in a wine sauce; also spelled *salmis.*

salmon   A noble fish that is spawned in fresh water before migrating to the sea, returning several years later to its original upstream waters to spawn, thus completing its life cycle. Salmon meat ranges from very pale to deep orange red, depending on species and habitat. In the United States, the king or chinook salmon is largest; the coho salmon is smaller and paler-fleshed; the sockeye turns deep red before spawning and is considered choice for canning. The northern Pacific and Atlantic Oceans provide feeding grounds for marine salmon, in addition to landlocked salmon. The firm, rich, flavorful meat—before spawning—lends itself to varied culinary preparations, simple or elaborate; cured salmon is a great delicacy; the specific types are separately entered.

salmonette   (Sp.)   Red mullet.

salmon trout   See **sea trout.**

salpicão   (Port.)   Smoked ham roll.

salpicon   (Fr.)   One or more ingredients cooked separately, cut into fine dice, and bound with a sauce; often used as a filling or garnish, like **mirepoix; allumettes** cut across into small cubes make *salpicon.*

salsa   (It. and Sp.)   Sauce; this is also the general name for hot sauces in Mexican-American cooking; see also **sugo.**

salsa Mexicana cruda   (Mex.)   Literally "fresh Mexican sauce," made of tomatoes, onions, and chilies (preferably **serranos**), chopped and mixed together with water; much used in Mexican cooking, with regional variations.

salsify   A plant whose long white tapered root is eaten boiled or sautéed; also called oyster plant, its resemblance in flavor to oyster requires a vivid imagination; scorzonera, with its black-skinned root, is very similar.

saltare   (It.)   To sauté, literally "to jump."

saltimbocca   (It.)   Veal scallop with a sage leaf and a thin slice of **pro-**

sciutto laid on top, braised in butter and **Marsala** or white wine; this dish, whose name means "jump in the mouth," comes from Rome.

saltpeter, saltpetre   Potassium nitrate; used in small quantities to preserve meat, saltpeter gives flavor and imparts a red color.

salvia (It.) Sage.

Salz (Ger.) Salt; *Salzgebäck* is a salty biscuit, cracker, or pretzel.

sambal (Ind.) A very hot and spicy side dish, often a sauce, several of which accompany the main dish.

sambar (Ind.) Vegetables and lentils stewed with **tamarind** and spices.

samosa (Ind.) A pyramid-shaped savory pastry filled with vegetables or meat spiced with curry or chilies; from India and Pakistan.

samphire   A plant that grows wild along the rocky Mediterranean and European coastline; its crisp leaves are eaten fresh in salads, cooked as a vegetable, and pickled; also called sea fennel and *herbe de Saint Pierre* (its name is a corruption of the latter).

Samsø (Den.) A whole-milk cows' cheese from the island of Samsø; cooked and pressed, the large, round, firm cheese is golden yellow with scattered holes and a nutty, mild, but not bland taste; widely used in Denmark.

sanbusak (Mid. E.) A tartlet of minced meat with pine nuts, onions, and cinnamon in a thin yeast dough.

Sancerre   A town perched on a hill overlooking the Loire Valley in central France; its white wine is agreeably fresh and flinty, not unlike the **Pouilly-Fumé** produced nearby, also from the **Sauvignon Blanc** grape.

San Gioveto   A very good Italian red-wine grape planted widely in Tuscany; vinified especially for **Chianti.**

sangria (Sp.) Red wine, a little brandy, soda water, sugar, and sliced orange or lemon and other fruit; a cool refreshing drink for warm weather.

sangue, al (It.) Rare, as for steak.

San Pedro (Sp.) **John Dory.**

San Simon   A cows' milk cheese from northwest Spain, semihard, rather bland, pear-shaped, and often smoked.

Saône   A tributary of the Rhône River, joining it at Lyons, France, where the **Beaujolais** is said to be the third river.

sapsago See **Schabzieger.**

saracen corn See **buckwheat.**

Sarah Bernhardt (Fr.) With puree of **foie gras.**

sardine   A young herring, pilchard, or sprat varying widely in species and treatment; usually brined, cooked, and canned in oil, but excellent cooked fresh.

sashimi (Jap.) Literally "fresh slice," this really means raw fish expertly sliced according to the particular variety and served with garnishes, condiments, and sauces.

saté   (Indon.)   Pieces of meat or seafood marinated in a spicy sauce, skewered, and grilled; usually served with a peanut sauce; also spelled *satay.*

sauce   From the Latin word meaning salted, sauce includes all liquid seasonings for food and a few that are not liquid; **Carême** organized the many French sauces into families with four mother sauces: **espagnole, velouté, allemande,** and **béchamel,** with emulsified sauces, such as **mayonnaise,** forming the fifth group. *Saucier* means the chef responsible for sauces.

saucisse   (Fr.)   Fresh sausage; *saucisson* is a cured sausage, usually large; see also **salami.**

Sauerbraten   (Ger.)   Top round of beef marinated in red wine and vinegar, beer, or buttermilk, then braised, and sometimes served with dried fruit and nuts or other spicy or fruity accompaniments; *sauer* means sour.

Sauerkraut   (Ger.)   Shredded white cabbage pickled in brine and flavored with juniper berries—a classic accompaniment to a wide variety of German dishes.

sauge   (Fr.)   **Sage.**

saumon   (Fr.)   Salmon.

Saumur   A French town and wine region on the south bank of the Loire River producing a variety of wines, including sparkling wines.

saunf   (Ind.)   Fennel, anise.

sauter   (Fr.)   To cook food quickly in butter or other hot fat, stirring to brown it evenly; *sauter* means literally "to jump"; a *sauté* is a dish that has been cooked thus; a *sauteuse* is a shallow sauté pan with sloping sides; a *sautoir* is a shallow pan with straight sides.

Sauternes   A French village south of Bordeaux whose five surrounding townships produce the white dessert wine of the same name. Sauternes grapes are late-harvested for their high sugar content and **noble rot,** resulting in a very sweet but natural wine: fruity, intense, buttery, golden, and long-lived. Sauterne (without the final *s*) is altogether unconnected—a meaningless California term for white wine.

sauvage   (Fr.)   Wild, uncultivated, undomesticated.

Sauvignon Blanc   An excellent white-wine varietal grape, widely planted in **Graves, Sauternes** (with the **Semillon** grape), in the **Loire** Valley (where it is known as *Blanc Fumé*), and in California.

savarin   (Fr.)   A ring-shaped **baba** filled variously with **crème Chantilly, crème pâtissière,** or fresh fruit; this pastry is named after **Brillat-Savarin.**

Savoie, biscuit de   See **biscuit de Savoie.**

savory Food that is not sweet; in Britain, where it is spelled *savoury,* it is the last dinner course after pudding, consisting of sharply flavored salty dishes intended to cleanse the palate for port—a custom favored by Victorian and Edwardian gentlemen. Savory is also an herb in the mint family known since Roman times and used traditionally with beans, meat, and poultry.

savoyarde, pommes à la (Fr.) Potatoes cooked **à la dauphinoise,** but with **bouillon** instead of milk; *savoyarde* generally means with cheese and potatoes.

saya-éndō (Jap.) Snow pea.

Sbrinz (Switz.) A whole-milk cows' cheese made immediately after milking, cooked, and pressed; it is an ancient cheese, originally Swiss but now made elsewhere. Hard, grainy, and yellow, Sbrinz is aged six to twelve months or longer and mostly used as a flavorful grating or cooking cheese or slivered into curls to accompany wine.

scald To heat a liquid, usually milk, to just below the boiling point, when small bubbles form around the edge. For vegetables and fruit, to scald means to **blanch.**

scallion A young, undeveloped onion, sometimes called spring onion or green onion.

scallop A **mollusk** with an edible adductor muscle; in Europe, the pink roe is also eaten; also, a **collop** or **escalope** of meat—a thin slice possibly flattened by pounding.

scaloppina di vitello (It.) Veal scallop, properly cut across the grain from a single muscle, top round, so that there are no separations.

Scamorza (It.) A whole-milk cows' cheese, sometimes mixed with ewes' milk; this spun-curd cheese is similar to **Mozzarella** but firmer; the cheeses are tied in pairs with string or raffia, hence their name, which means "beheaded" in southern Italian dialect.

scampi (It.) Saltwater crayfish found in the Adriatic and a favorite dish in Venice; pale in color and quite large, similar to the **Dublin Bay prawn, langoustine,** and **Norway lobster.**

scarola (It.) Escarole.

Schabzieger (Switz.) A skimmed-milk cows' cheese, uncooked but hard, sometimes called sapsago in the U.S.; it is flavored with blue melilot clover to give it a pungent flavor and green color and is shaped in truncated cones.

Scharzhofberg A vineyard on a steep slope in Wiltingen on the **Saar,** whose **Rieslings** yield a very fine white wine with bouquet, depth, freshness, and austerity.

Schaum (Ger.) Froth, foam, mousse; *Schaumrollen* are puff-pastry rolls filled with whipped cream; a *Schaumschlager* is a whisk or beater; *Schaumwein* is sparkling wine or Champagne.

Scheibe (Ger.) Slice.

Schiava A very fine red-wine grape extensively planted in the northern Italian Adige; also used as an eating grape.

Schinken (Ger.) Ham.

Schlächter (Ger.) Butcher; a *Schlachtplatte* is a plate of various cold meats and sausages.

Schlag, mit (Ger.) With cream; *Schlagobers* and *Schlagsahne* both mean whipped cream.

Schlegel (Ger.) Drumstick.

Schlesisches Himmelreich (Ger.) Salted pork belly and dried fruits stewed together and served with dumplings; literally, "Silesian heaven."

Schmalz (Ger.) Melted fat, grease, or lard; *Schmalzgebackenes* means food fried in lard or fat. In Yiddish, the word means rendered chicken fat.

Schmand (Ger.) Sour cream.

Schnapps (Ger.) A German version of **akvavit.**

Schnitte (Ger.) A cut or slice, chop or steak; *Schnittlauch* means chive.

schnitz, apple See **apple schnitz.**

Schnitzel (Ger.) A cutlet, slice, scallop, chop, steak; see also **Wiener Schnitzel.**

Schokolade (Ger.) Chocolate.

Schrotbrot (Ger.) Whole-wheat bread.

Schulter (Ger.) Shoulder.

Schwamm (Ger.) Mushroom.

Schwärtelbraten (Ger.) Roast leg of pork cooked with sauerkraut and dumplings and served with a sour cream sauce; from Silesia.

Schwartzwalder Kirschtorte (Ger.) A rich chocolate cake made with cherries, Kirschwasser, and whipped cream on an almond pastry base; from the **Black Forest.**

Schwarzfisch (Ger.) Carp.

Schwarzsauer (Ger.) A stew of goose giblets and blood stewed with dried apples, prunes, and pears.

Schwarzwald (Ger.) **Black Forest.**

Schwein (Ger.) Pork; *Schweinebauch* means pork belly; *Schweinbraten* means roast pork, a very popular dish cooked variously according to region.

scone (Scot.) A traditional cake of white flour, sometimes mixed with whole-wheat flour, oatmeal, or barley, and combined with buttermilk and baking powder; the batter is usually shaped into a round and quartered or dropped onto a greased girdle (griddle) and turned; pronounced "skawn."

score To make cuts, usually parallel, in the surface of food to help it cook evenly.

scorzonera See **salsify.**

Scotch broth   (Scot.)   Vegetable soup made with lamb and barley.

Scotch woodcock   (Brit.)   A **savory** of creamy scrambled eggs on toast with anchovies.

scrapple   Pork scraps, including meat, offal, and fat, boiled together, chopped, seasoned, and thickened with buckwheat and cornmeal; this Pennsylvania German specialty is derived from the Westphalian **Pannhas.**

scrod   A marketing term for young **cod** under $2\frac{1}{2}$ pounds; schrod (spelled with an *h*), indicates that the fish is young haddock.

scungilli   (It.)   See **whelk.**

sea bass   See **black sea bass.**

sea cucumber   See **hǎi shēn.**

sea fennel   See **samphire.**

seafood   Edible saltwater fish or shellfish.

sea kale   A perennial vegetable of the mustard family that grows cultivated and wild, especially on the coasts of England, France, and northern Europe; the tender stalks are white and delicate and are cooked like asparagus.

sea moss   See **dulse.**

sear   To cook the surface of food, especially meat, over intense high heat, in order to brown the exterior; searing does not "seal in" the juices, as is commonly thought, but it does affect flavor.

sea slug   See **hǎi shēn.**

sea trout   A brown **trout** in its marine cycle, from Atlantic waters; also called the salmon trout (but no relation to seatrout), its succulent pink flesh comes from its diet of crustaceans.

seatrout   See **weakfish.**

sea urchin   A spiny marine creature; the French relish it most cut in half, the pink or orange roe scooped out and eaten raw with a little lemon juice—a delicacy also eaten in Japan, where it is called *uni.*

seaweed   Marine vegetation, dried and processed, appreciated for its texture, flavor, and high nutritional value, especially in the Orient. Different kinds of seaweed, separately entered, are made into gelatin, used in making soup stock and for wrapping **sushi,** drunk like tea, or simply eaten as a vegetable.

sec   (Fr.)   A wine term meaning dry, as opposed to sweet; the exception is in describing Champagne, where *sec* has come to mean sweet; the feminine is *sèche.* The Italian word is *secco,* the Spanish *seco.*

sedano   (It.)   Celery.

sediment   The solid deposit that a wine naturally leaves in the bottle as it ages. In bottles of red wine, especially big or old ones, the sediment should be allowed to settle and then left behind when the wine is **decanted;** in white wines, the clear crystals are tasteless and harmless cream of tartar.

Seezunge (Ger.) Sole.

sel (Fr.) Salt.

selchen (Ger.) To smoke or cure; *Selchfleisch* is smoked meat, often pork loin.

self-rising flour White flour to which baking powder (and salt) has already been added for convenience; used, especially in Britain, for making cakes, biscuits, and other baked goods; not appropriate for doughs that use yeast or eggs as leavening or that do not rise at all.

selle (Fr.) Saddle.

Sellerie (Ger.) Celery.

Seltzer water Naturally effervescent mineral water, or water made to resemble it, from the German village of Selters near Wiesbaden.

sem (Ind.) Green beans.

semifreddo (It.) A chilled or frozen mousselike dessert, including cream, custard, cake, and fruit; the Spanish version is *semifrío.*

semilla (Sp.) Seed.

Semillon An exceptional white grape variety extensively planted in southwestern France and Australia, also grown in California. Often combined with **Sauvignon Blanc,** it is used for **Sauternes** and **Graves.** Like the Riesling grape, it is subject, fortunately, to **noble rot.**

Semmel (Ger.) Breakfast roll; a *Semmelkloss* is a bread dumpling.

semolina The coarsely milled endosperm of wheat or other flour, from which the bran and germ have been removed; **durum** semolina, made from a special kind of hard wheat, is excellent for (commercial) pasta because it has few loose starch granules to soften the dough; other types of semolina are good for **gnocchi** and **couscous.**

Senf (Ger.) Mustard.

Sercial A type of **Madeira,** pale and dry; an excellent apéritif wine comparable to a **fino** sherry, named after the white grape variety.

Serra (Port.) A ewes' milk cheese, sometimes combined with goats' milk, from the mountainous region of Portugal called *Serra da Estrela;* the disc-shaped cheese is creamy white with a runny center and yellow rind, but with aging becomes pungent, hard, and crumbly.

serrano (Mex.) A very hot green chili pepper, about $1\frac{1}{2}$ inches long and $\frac{1}{2}$ inch wide; usually cooked fresh but also available pickled and canned.

serviette (Fr.) Napkin; food served in a folded napkin is *à la serviette.*

sesame A plant native to Indonesia and East Africa and known to the ancient Egyptians, Greeks, and Romans; in Middle Eastern cooking sesame seeds are used raw, either for oil or **tahini,** while in Far Eastern cooking they are first roasted, yielding a darker, stronger taste, and used mostly for flavoring, rather than frying.

sesos (Sp.) Brains.

seviche (Sp.) Raw fish or shellfish marinated in citrus juice (usually lime) and seasonings but not cooked by heat; also spelled *cebiche* and often confused with **escabeche.**

Seville orange A bitter orange with a thin skin; the skin is used widely in making **marmalade.**

sfogliata (It.) Puff pastry.

sgombro (It.) Mackerel.

shabu-shabu (Jap.) Meat and vegetables cooked at table in stock, served with a seasoned sesame sauce; not unlike **sukiyaki.**

shad A member of the **herring** family; though there are numerous species, American shad alone is *Alosa sapidissima*—"shad most delicious." This fish migrates up rivers on the eastern coast of the United States for spawning, a welcome harbinger each spring. Shad flesh has a distinctive, rich, sweet flavor, and removing the rows of tiny bones increases the pleasure of eating it. The roe is a great delicacy, poached, broiled, or sautéed to enhance its nutty flavor, often complemented with bacon and lemon.

shaddock See **pomelo.**

shallot A variety of the onion family whose bulbs form small clusters; the French favor its subtle, delicate taste and often use it in their cooking.

shandy (Brit.) Beer mixed with lemonade—a refreshing summer drink; shandygaff is beer with ginger beer.

shao (Chin.) Braising.

sharbat (Ind.) A fruit punch or flavored drink, from which the word **sherbet** is derived.

shark Although prolific and similar to **swordfish** in flavor and texture, shark (especially mako and dogfish) is not particularly popular in the United States, probably because of its voracious reputation; its dense, delicate flesh takes well to baking, broiling, and marinating.

shark's fin (Chin.) See **yú chì.**

she-crab soup A springtime soup from South Carolina, made with the meat and roe from female blue crabs, mixed with cream and flavored with Worcestershire sauce and sherry.

shellfish Any kind of seafood with a shell, including **mollusks** and **crustaceans.**

shell steak A cut of beef from the **strip loin;** a boneless and tender steak.

shepherd's pie (Brit.) Cooked meat, cubed or ground, in a gravy and covered with a layer of mashed potatoes.

shepherd's purse A wild green in the mustard family, eaten in Europe.

sherbet A frozen dessert much like **water ice,** made with sweetened fruit juice or puree or another flavoring, such as coffee or liqueur, but including beaten egg white or **Italian meringue** to keep ice crystals from forming during freezing; *sorbet* is the French word for sherbet.

sherry A fortified blended wine, strictly speaking from a specified area around the city of Jerez in southern Spain, from whose name the anglicized word "sherry" comes. The young wine, from several grape varieties, is kept in oak casks where it is **fortified,** worked on by **flor** yeasts, blended in **soleras,** and perhaps sweetened and colored with a dose of reserve sherry into several different categories such as **fino, amontillado,** and **oloroso.** In California and other countries the term sherry is used more loosely.

shiitake (Jap.) An Oriental mushroom, dark brown with an earthy flavor, available both fresh and dried; cultivated widely in the Orient and now also in the United States; the woody stem is usually discarded; sometimes called golden oak mushroom in the U.S.

shimofuri (Jap.) To blanch.

shio (Jap.) Salt.

ship biscuit See **hardtack.**

shirataki (Jap.) Translucent noodles made from **konnyaku.**

shirred eggs Eggs cooked in a shallow dish, either on the stove or in the oven, perhaps with a sauce.

shiru, shirumono (Jap.) Soup of all kinds, including thick and thin (*suimono* means thin soup).

shōga (Jap.) Fresh ginger root.

shoofly pie A pie with a molasses and brown sugar filling, of Pennsylvania German origin; supposedly so sweet that you have to shoo away the flies.

shortbread (Scot.) A rich pastry made from butter, flour, and sugar mixed together, shaped in round tins, and baked until golden; traditional in Scotland for New Year's Day.

shortening Any fat, usually butter, lard, or vegetable fat, used in baking; shortening lends its name to rich pastries such as **shortbread,** shortcake, shortcrust, and shortening bread.

short loin A cut of beef from the hindquarter, between the **rib** and **sirloin,** comprising the **porterhouse, T-bone,** and **club steak.**

shorva (Ind.) Soup.

shōya (Jap.) **Soy sauce.**

shred To cut into narrow strips.

shrimp A small decapod crustacean of many species, usually marine— a miniature version of the **lobster;** the family includes the tiny shrimp from cold northern waters, the rock shrimp off the warmer southeastern American coastlines, and the saltwater **crayfish.** Commercially marketed shrimp are sorted—and priced—by size and usually flash-frozen on board immediately after they are caught, either peeled or not, raw or cooked; when thawed, shrimp should have a resilient texture and fresh smell. Shrimp are cooked in innumerable ways around the world from earthy peasant dishes to *haute cuisine* creations.

shrub   A fruit drink, sometimes alcoholic—a distant relative of the fruit **sherbet.**

shuàn yáng ròu   (Chin.)   Mongolian hot pot: various pieces of seafood, poultry, and meat cooked individually in a communal pot of simmering stock that is placed in the middle of the table; it is served with sauces, and the rich stock is consumed afterward; a kind of Chinese **fondue.**

sild, sill   (Scand.)   Herring.

silverside   (Brit.)   A cut of beef from the crown of the **rump.**

simmer   To cook food in liquid just below the boiling point.

Simmons, Amelia   The author of *American Cookery,* published in Hartford, Connecticut, in 1796; it was the first cookbook written by an American for Americans using native produce and methods.

Simon, André Louis   (1877–1970)   A French-born wine connoisseur and gastronome who spent his adult life in London writing about his enthusiasms; he also formed a book collection of considerable distinction and founded the Wine and Food Society.

singer   (Fr.)   To sprinkle or dust, as with flour or sugar.

Single Gloucester   (Brit.)   A nearly extinct cheese made from part skimmed and part whole milk of the rare Gloucester breed (now being revived); half as large as **Double Gloucester** and milder in taste.

sippet   A small piece of bread to dip in soup; a **croûte.**

sirloin   A cut of beef from the hindquarter, between the **short loin** and **round.**

sirloin tip   See **round.**

sirop à trente   (Fr.)   See **heavy syrup.**

skate   A diamond-shaped relative of the **shark,** often very large, with edible wings that are usually skinned and trimmed before cooking; skate is most often poached, fried, or sautéed, and in classic French cuisine, served with **beurre noir;** also called ray.

skim   To remove the top layer from a liquid, as cream from milk or scum from stock.

skim milk, skimmed milk   Milk with nearly all of its cream removed by centrifugal force, leaving .5 percent butterfat; low-fat milk, slightly richer, contains 1 percent butterfat. The skimming also removes vitamins A, D, E, and K, so these nutrients are usually added.

slivovitz   Plum brandy from Eastern Europe, dry and slightly bitter.

sloe   The fruit of the blackthorn—a wild European plum, small, dark, and astringent; used for flavoring sloe gin and, when touched by frost, for preserves.

slump   A dessert of cooked fruit baked with a dumplinglike top, served with cream; popular in eighteenth- and nineteenth-century America. Louisa May Alcott named her home in Concord, Massachusetts, "Apple Slump."

smelt A small silvery fish, called sparling in Britain, that migrates between fresh- and saltwater unless landlocked; eaten whole or gutted, most often floured and fried.

smetana (Russ.) Sour cream.

smitane (Fr.) A classic sauce of chopped onions sautéed in butter, sour cream added, cooked, strained, and flavored with lemon.

Smithfield ham Ham from Virginia hogs fattened on peanuts. It is cured, salted, smoked, and aged, but not cooked; from the town of the same name.

smoke To cure meat over burning wood chips by means of the steady low heat and chemical components in smoke; there are many variations of this prehistoric technique, often used in combination with salt curing.

smörgåsbord (Swed.) A profusely varied buffet of open sandwiches, pickled fish, meats, vegetables, eggs, and salads served in Scandinavian countries as hors d'oeuvres or as the meal itself.

smørrebrød (Den.) Literally "buttered bread," an open-faced sandwich made with all kinds of fish, meat, and vegetable fillings with various sauces, artfully presented.

smothered Braised; in southern cooking, meat—often chicken—that is cooked in a closed pot with a gravy or sauce.

snail A land-dwelling gastropod **mollusk** appreciated by gastronomes since the Romans; usually canned already prepared for the table, *escargots* (in French) are often served *à la bourguignonne*—fattened on Burgundian grape leaves and bathed in a rich garlic and parsley butter sauce—as well as in other ways.

snap bean String bean.

snow eggs Meringue shaped like eggs with spoons, poached in sweetened milk, drained, and served with custard sauce made from the milk; a classic dessert known in French as *oeufs à la neige.*

snow peas Peas that are undeveloped and have thin, flat pods; bred to be eaten whole, as their French name *mange-tout* ("eat-all") implies; much used in Chinese cookery.

Soave An Italian white wine produced around Verona, dry, pale, fresh, and clean. This wine, which is sold in distinctive tall green bottles, is best drunk young.

soba (Jap.) Buckwheat noodle.

sockeye salmon See **salmon.**

soda See **baking soda.**

sodium bicarbonate See **baking soda.**

soffrito (It.) See **battuto** and **sofrito.**

sofrito (Sp.) A mixture of chopped vegetables—tomatoes, onions, garlic, and other herbs—cooked together in olive oil, perhaps with diced sweet peppers, ham, and **chorizo,** or other flavorings; the *sofrito,* which can be made ahead, is a base for many sauces and stews. The Italian *soffrito,* made from cooking the **battuto,** is essentially the same thing.

soft-ball stage Sugar syrup that has reached a temperature of 234–239°F. (113–115°C.) and that forms a soft ball between the fingertips when immersed in cold water.

soft-crack stage Sugar syrup that has reached a temperature of 270–290°F. (135–140°C.) and that forms brittle threads between the fingertips when immersed in cold water.

soft-shell crab A blue crab caught while molting, when its new shell is so thin that it is edible.

sògliola (It.) Sole.

sole A flatfish family that includes the flounder and many other varieties (see under **flounder**); Dover sole is the common sole of European waters, whose white and delicate but firm flesh has inspired many culinary creations. Although there are few true soles in the U.S., many types of flounder are called sole to make them more marketable.

solera (Sp.) The method by which **sherry** and other fortified wines are blended and matured to achieve consistency.

sole Véronique (Fr.) Sole poached in white wine and served with **velouté** sauce, garnished with skinned and seeded white grapes.

solyanka (Russ.) Boiled freshwater fish with cucumbers, onions, olives, vinegar, sour cream, and dill; also made with meat.

sommelier (Fr.) Wine steward, wine waiter.

Sonoma A California wine-producing county just north of San Francisco and east of the Napa Valley; various wines are grown here, especially reds.

sonth (Ind.) Dried ground ginger.

sooji (Ind.) Semolina, farina.

sookha dar (Ind.) Coriander seeds.

sopa (Sp.) Soup.

sopari (Ind.) Betel nut.

sope (Mex.) A small round of **tortilla** dough cooked and filled with a savory stuffing; *sopes* can be eaten as a first course or appetizer. Also called *garnacha* or *picada.*

sorbet (Fr.) **Sherbet.**

sorghum A grain similar to **millet** and used in Asia and Africa for porridge, flour, beer, and molasses, but in the United States mostly for forage; it is a drought-resistant staple crop in East Africa, where it originated, and in Asia; an African bread called *durra,* flat because sorghum has no **gluten,** is made from a variety of the grain.

sorrel   A leafy green plant similar to spinach, whose name, derived from the German word for "sour," is appropriate; especially popular in France, this lemony-tasting green is used in salads or cooked for purees, soups, and sauces, often to complement fish; of the many varieties, wild sorrel is highest in oxalic acid and is sometimes called lemon grass.

Sosse   (Ger.)   Sauce.

Soubise   (Fr.)   Chopped onions sautéed in butter with **béchamel** and strained; *Soubise* can also be a puree of onions and rice finished with butter and cream—a classic sauce.

Souchong   A black tea from India or Ceylon with large, coarse leaves that make a pale but pungent brew; Lapsang Souchong is a variety with a smoky, dark taste.

soufflé   (Fr.)   A sweet or savory pudding made with a white sauce, basic flavoring ingredients, egg yolks, and beaten whites, which cause it to puff up during baking; *soufflé* means blown or puffed up.

soupe   (Fr.)   A hearty and robust peasant soup, usually based on vegetables; not to be confused with **consommé** or **potage.**

sourdough   Dough for various baked goods, especially bread, leavened with a fermented starter culture kept from a previous baking rather than with fresh yeast.

sous chef   (Fr.)   Second chef; literally, "under chef."

soused   Pickled in brine or vinegar; usually used to describe fish.

soutirage   (Fr.)   **Racking.**

souvlakia   (Gr.)   Meat marinated in olive oil, lemon juice, and herbs, then skewered and grilled.

soybean   A bean extremely important to Asia for its nutritive value (very high in minerals and protein) and for its uses in various forms (fresh, dry, sprouted, and processed in innumerable ways). The seeds yield **soy milk,** flour, and oil (highly unsaturated), all of which can be processed into many useful products. See also **tōfu.**

soybean curd   See **tōfu.**

Soyer, Alexis (1809–1858)   A French chef who gained renown in England through his food served at the Reform Club in London, his books, and his philanthropic efforts in Ireland and the Crimea. He introduced the gas oven, a great improvement over coal.

soy milk   A nutritious vegetable product made from dried **soybeans** which are soaked in water, crushed, and boiled; various other products, such as soy cheese, made when a coagulant forms curds and whey from the milk, come from soy milk.

soy sauce   A condiment widely used in Chinese and Japanese cooking (where it is known as *shōya*), made from naturally fermented soybeans and flour; some commercial brands, however, are chemically fermented and contain additives that attempt to make up for lost color, flavor, and body; Chinese soy sauce (**jiāng yóu**) comes in light, medium, and dark grades, depending on their use; Japanese soy sauce is lighter, sweeter, and less salty than Chinese soy sauce. (Note: some types of soy sauce are separately entered.)

spaghettini (It.) Thin spaghetti.

spanakopita (Gr.) Spinach pie wrapped in **phyllo** dough.

Spanferkel (Ger.) Suckling pig.

Spanische Windtorte (Aus.) A meringue shell—not unlike the French **vacherin**—elaborately decorated with swirls, filled with berries, and served with whipped cream.

spareribs A cut of pork from the breast section, usually broiled.

Spargel (Ger.) Asparagus; the white blanched asparagus are favored in Germany, rather than the green, and in spring much is made of their season.

sparling See **smelt.**

spätlese (Ger.) A wine term meaning late-picked—after the regular harvest, when these riper grapes will yield a bigger, sweeter, natural wine (which is also more expensive).

Spätzle (Ger.) Noodle or dumpling from Swabia, small and handmade, usually pressed through a colander.

Speck (Ger.) Bacon, lard.

spelt A type of wheat eaten as food in ancient times but now used mostly as livestock fodder.

Spencer steak See **Delmonico.**

spèzie (It.) Spices.

spezzatino (It.) Stew; literally, "cut into little pieces."

Spickgans (Ger.) Smoked goose, usually the breast—a great delicacy.

spiedo (It.) Spit for roasting meat; *spiedino* means skewer or brochette.

Spiegelei (Ger.) Fried egg.

Spiess (Ger.) Skewer; *Spiessbraten* is meat roasted on a spit.

split pea A pea of several varieties, generally green or yellow, that is dried and hulled; mostly used for soup and, in Britain, for "pease" pudding or porridge.

sponge cake A cake whose texture is lightened with separately beaten egg whites but little or no shortening; it contains some sugar and flour but no leavening other than eggs.

spoom See **spuma.**

spoon bread A moist and unsweetened southern American dish made from stoneground white cornmeal and eggs, eaten at various meals; although called "bread," the consistency of spoon bread is more like that of pudding; also called batter bread.

spotted dick, spotted dog (Brit.) A steamed suet pudding with raisins—a traditional nursery food.

sprat See **brisling.**

Springerle (Ger.) Cookies, pale yellow and anise-flavored, sometimes molded into very large and elaborate figures; traditional for Christmas and originally from Swabia.

spring-form pan A cake pan whose bottom is removed by means of a spring or hinge, rather than by inverting the cake.

spring onion See **scallion.**

spring roll See **chūn juǎn.**

spritzig (Ger.) Sparkling, effervescent, as for wine.

sprout A dried bean that, with proper moisture and warmth, germinates; mung, alfalfa, and soybeans are favorite varieties for sprouting, and they can be eaten raw or lightly cooked.

spuma (It.) A fruit or water ice with **Italian meringue** folded in halfway through the freezing process, as in a **sherbet.** *Spuma* means foam, froth, or mousse. *Spumone* is a mousselike ice cream lightened with whipped cream or beaten egg whites.

spumante (It.) Sparkling, as for wine.

squab A young pigeon about to leave the nest. Squabs are full-grown at about four weeks but still unfledged; most squabs are domesticated and their meat is tender, all dark, but not gamy.

squid A marine **mollusk** with a long body and ten arms, highly nutritious and with little waste; most appreciated by Mediterranean and Oriental cultures; squid can be cut into diamonds or rings or stuffed whole to be cooked in various ways, sometimes in sauces flavored and colored with its own ink.

Stachelbeere (Ger.) Gooseberry.

Stampfkartoffeln (Ger.) Mashed potatoes.

Stange (Ger.) Stick; *Stangen* and *Stangerl* are stick-shaped pastries, sweet or savory; *Stangenspargel* means asparagus spears.

star anise, Chinese anise (Chin.) See **ba jiao.**

star fruit See **carambola.**

steak and kidney pudding (Brit.) Beef and kidney pieces, perhaps flavored with onions, mushrooms, and oysters, steamed in a suet crust (or baked for steak and kidney pie).

steam To cook by steam heat, thus preserving most of the food's nutrients; food can be steamed over boiling water or, wrapped in leaves, foil, or other protection, directly in hot coals or boiling water.

steep To soak or infuse in liquid.

Steinberg A famous old vineyard in the **Rheingau,** located in the *Kloster Eberbach* monastery and created in the twelfth century by the same Cistercian monk who established the *Clos de Vougeot* in Burgundy; its several wines have exceptional body, power, and depth.

Steinbutt (Ger.) Turbot.

Steinpilz (Ger.) *Cèpe* or **boletus** mushroom.

stew To cook food slowly in a small amount of liquid at low heat in a closed container in order to make the food—usually meat—tender and allow the flavors to mingle.

Stilton (Brit.)   An uncooked cows' milk cheese injected with the *Penicillium roqueforti* mold and aged for about six months to make one of the world's great blue cheeses. Stilton is made in Derbyshire, Nottinghamshire, and Leicestershire in large cylinders with a brownish crust. The paste is creamy with a variable blue green veining, moist and slightly crumbly, but not dry or salty. There is also a White Stilton.

stir-fry (Chin.)   To cook quickly in a small amount of very hot fat, constantly stirring, to give the food a crisp yet tender texture; a method much used in Chinese cooking with the **wok.**

stock   Broth in which meat, game, poultry, fish, or vegetables have been cooked; stock is usually seasoned, strained, degreased, concentrated, and used as the foundation for soups and sauces—what the French call *fond de cuisine;* meat stock usually contains gelatin, from veal and other bones, and can be white or brown.

Stollen (Ger.)   Fruit bread filled with various dried fruits, shaped in a long loaf, and sprinkled with confectioners' sugar; traditional for Christmas and associated with Dresden.

stone crab   A variety of **crab** found off the southeastern Atlantic and Gulf coastlines, especially Florida, with very fine meat mostly from the claws; sold already cooked.

Stör (Ger.)   Sturgeon.

stout (Brit.)   Ale whose malt has been toasted before brewing to produce darker color, stronger flavor, and higher alcoholic content.

stoved (Scot.)   Simmered on top of the stove, as in **étouffer.**

Stracchino (It.)   An uncooked, unpressed cows' milk cheese, originally unpasteurized but now generally pasteurized, from Lombardy; this fresh, rindless cheese is buttery, smooth, and delicate. *Stracchino di Gorgonzola* is the original name of **Gorgonzola.** *Stracchino* cheeses were originally made with milk from cows still tired—*stracche* in the Lombardian dialect—from their long descent from the Alps.

stracciatella (It.)   Light chicken or beef stock thickened with a paste of egg, cheese, and **semolina.**

stracòtto (It.)   Pot roast or braised meat.

strasbourgeoise, à la (Fr.)   Garnished with sauerkraut, small pieces of bacon, and sautéed slices of goose liver—a classic garnish.

strawberries Romanoff (Fr.)   Strawberries macerated in orange-flavored liqueur and garnished with **crème Chantilly.**

straw mushroom   A wild mushroom cultivated in the Orient on rice straw and available in the west either canned or dried; it is small with a long thin stem and conical tan cap.

Streusel (Ger.) A sprinkling, as of sugar or breadcrumbs; *Streuselkuchen* is a yeast cake topped with a cinnamon-sugar crumble.

striped bass A western Atlantic fish that migrates from the sea to spawn in freshwater streams in autumn; its size varies greatly, but smaller fish taste better; the flesh of the striped bass is white, flaky, and firm, with a delicate flavor, making it a popular table fish that is very versatile in cooking.

strip loin A cut of beef from the top of the **short loin,** tender and boneless, often cut into steaks.

Strudel (Ger.) Very thin pastry sheets with a sweet or savory filling, rolled up and baked; from Bavaria.

Stück (Ger.) Piece, portion.

stufa (It.) Stove; *stufato* means stew.

sturgeon A marine fish that spawns in rivers, sometimes growing to great age and size; its flesh is white, rich, firm, and tight in texture—almost like meat—taking well to smoking or pickling; the roe, of course, is a great delicacy.

su (Jap.) Rice vinegar.

suan mei jiāng (Chin.) Duck sauce, a Cantonese dipping sauce (literally, "plum sauce") traditionally served with duck or goose and used more widely in American-Chinese cooking; it is a thick sweet-and-sour sauce made of plums, apricots, vinegar, and sugar.

subric (Fr.) A small ball of vegetable or other food, fried.

succotash A dish of dried beans and corn derived from the Naragansett Indians' *msickquatash.* Early versions included poultry and meat as well as other vegetables, and succotash today need not be reduced to lima beans and corn kernels.

sucker See **buffalo fish.**

sucre (Fr.) Sugar; *sucre filé* is spun sugar.

suédoise (Fr.) Cold "Swedish" sauce of **mayonnaise** flavored with apple puree and grated horseradish—a classic sauce.

suet Solid lumps of fat around the loins and kidneys of beef, lamb, and other animals, used for making pastry, puddings, and tallow.

sugarcane A tall grass of South Pacific origin from which raw sugar was first extracted in India around 500 B.C. To refine the sucrose, the ten-to-twelve-month-old stalks are cut and pressed for their juice which is then clarified, reduced, spun (to separate the sugar crystals from the **molasses** and other impurities), washed, and uniformly crystallized.

sugaring See **chaptalization.**

sugo (It.) Sauce; *sugo de carne* is gravy. When speaking of pasta sauce, *sugo* rather than **salsa** is the correct term. The plural is *sughi.*

suimono (Jap.) Clear soup.

sukiyaki (Jap.) Thinly sliced beef and a variety of vegetables cooked in a pot with suet at the table, seasoned, and served with ceremony; a relatively recent dish in Japanese cuisine.

sulphiting   The addition of sulphur to **must** in order to delay or prevent fermentation—not necessarily an abuse in wine-making.

sultana   A golden raisin made from sweet, white, seedless grapes originally grown in Smyrna, Turkey and named after the Turkish sultan; see also **currant.**

Sülz   (Ger.)   Aspic or meat in aspic, such as **head cheese.**

summer pudding   (Brit.)   Fresh raspberries and red currants stewed together gently, sweetened, pressed in a bread-lined bowl overnight, then turned out and served with cream; the result, though from humble origins, is exquisite.

sǔn   (Chin.)   Bamboo shoots.

sunflower   A large heliotropic flower whose seeds are roasted and eaten like nuts and whose oil, extracted from the seeds, is light in flavor and polyunsaturated.

sunomono   (Jap.)   Green beans.

superfine sugar   Very fine sugar crystals that dissolve quickly in liquid.

suprême de volaille   (Fr.)   The breast and wing fillet of a young chicken or other bird, lightly floured and sautéed in butter. *Sauce suprême* is a reduced chicken **velouté** with cream.

surimi   (Jap.)   Imitation crab meat made from pollock or other fish; it is processed in sheets, rolled up, and colored to resemble crab legs; sometimes called seafood legs or other euphemisms.

sushi   (Jap.)   Vinegared rice formed into fingers or rounds, seasoned with **wasabi** or other spices, perhaps rolled in seaweed, and garnished with raw seafood or fish and sometimes a vegetable; in Japan, *sushi* is eaten as a meal; in the United States, it is also eaten as an appetizer.

süsse   (Ger.)   Sweet; *süsse Speisen* are sweet dishes or desserts.

Suzette, crêpes   See **crêpes Suzette.**

sweat   To cook in a little fat over very low heat in a covered pot, so that the food exudes some of its juice without browning; used especially with vegetables.

swede   (Brit.)   A rutabaga or Swedish turnip.

sweet bean sauce   (Chin.)   See **tien mien jiàng.**

sweet bell pepper   See **pepper (sweet bell).**

sweetbreads   The thymus gland of a calf, sheep, or pig, located in the throat and chest of young animals. Veal sweetbreads are considered the best, pork inferior; the chest or heart sweetbread is larger and therefore the better of the pair. Sweetbreads are highly perishable and should be used quickly. They are soaked in **acidulated water** to whiten the tissue, **blanched** to firm them, and the membranes are trimmed before further cooking.

sweet cicely See **cicely.**

sweet marjoram See **marjoram.**

sweet potato A root vegetable indigenous to Central America and brought by Columbus to the Old World; high in sugar, nutrients, and calories, it is often confused with the **yam,** especially in the U.S.; the sweet potato has a reddish skin, a texture like the regular potato, and an affinity for similar preparations.

Swiss cheese American-made (or foreign-made) **Emmental.**

Swiss roll (Brit.) Jelly roll.

swordfish A large marine fish whose dense white meat is marketed in steaks or chunks; because of its expense, mako **shark** is sometimes substituted; excellent for baking or broiling.

syllabub (Brit.) An old-fashioned drink made of rich milk or whipped cream with wine, beer, or cider, and flavored with sugar and spices; variously spelled; similar to **posset** and **eggnog.**

Sylvaner A very good white-wine grape, more productive but less distinguished than the **Riesling;** extensively cultivated in Germany, Austria, Alsace, and also grown in Switzerland, the Italian Tirol, California, and Chile.

Syrah A distinguished red-wine grape variety yielding a long-lived, deep-red wine; used for **Hermitage** and (with others) **Châteauneuf-du-Pape;** grown in the Rhône area as well as in California, Australia, and South Africa.

syrup, heavy See **heavy syrup.**

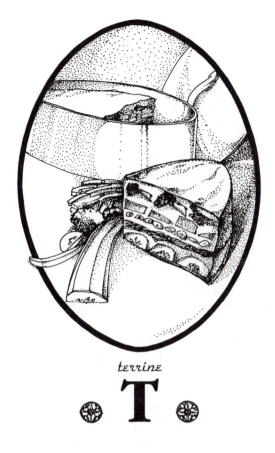

terrine

T

Tabasco   A fiery hot commercial sauce made of red chili peppers, vinegar, and salt, aged in oak barrels and bottled; made since the Civil War in **Cajun** Louisiana.

tabbouleh   (Leb.)   **Bulghur** mixed with chopped tomatoes, onion, mint, parsley, olive oil, and lemon juice, eaten as a salad with lettuce leaves.

tacchino   (It.)   Turkey.

Tâche, La   A small vineyard in the **Vosne-Romanée** that produces an outstanding red Burgundy: rich, velvety, and full-bodied.

taco   (Mex.)   A **tortilla** filled with shredded meat and sauce, rolled or folded, and sometimes fried; the word literally means "snack."

Tafelspitz   (Aus.)   Top round of beef boiled and accompanied with root vegetables, horseradish, and sauces—from Vienna.

taffy   Candy made from sugar or molasses cooked down, usually with butter, nuts, and other flavorings. American taffy, especially saltwater taffy, tends to be soft and chewy, while British taffy (called *toffee*) is brittle.

tagliatelle   (It.)   Long thin flat strips of egg pasta; this is the Florentine

185

and northern name for **fettucine**, slightly wider and flatter. **Ragù bolognese** is the classic sauce for *tagliatelle.*

tagliolini, tagliarini (It.) Very thin noodles, but not as thin as **capelli d'angelo**; often used in soups.

tahini (Mid. E.) A paste of crushed raw sesame seeds used as the basis of many Arab dishes such as **halvah, hummus,** and **baba ghanoush;** spelled variously.

takenoko (Jap.) Bamboo shoots.

tala (Ind.) Deep-fried.

Taleggio (It.) An uncooked, unpressed, whole, unpasteurized cows' milk cheese from Lombardy; made in squares with an orange rind and a delicate buttery paste. There is also a cooked-curd variety made from pasteurized milk, with a gray rind. *Taleggio* is a **stracchino** cheese.

Talleyrand (Fr.) A classic garnish of macaroni mixed with butter and cheese, truffle **julienne,** and diced **foie gras**—for sweetbreads and poultry.

tamago (Jap.) Egg.

tamale (Mex.) Corn dough (*tamal*) made with lard, filled with a savory stuffing, wrapped up in a piece of corn husk, and steamed; the filling can be savory or sweet; *tamales* are traditionally for holidays and special occasions, and their history is ancient.

tamari (Jap.) Dark, thick sauce, similar to **soy sauce,** also made from soybeans; used primarily as a dipping sauce or in a basting sauce.

tamarind The pod or fruit of a large tropical tree native to India; when fresh, its pulp is white, crisp, and sweet-sour, but when dried it turns brown and very sour; in Indian cooking it is used in curries, chutneys, pickling fish, sauces, and refreshing drinks.

tamatar (Ind.) Tomato.

tamis (Fr.) Sieve, sifter, strainer; the Spanish word is *tamiz. Tamiser* in French means to strain through a sieve or tammy cloth.

tampon (Fr.) A bed of rice or vegetables.

tandoor (Ind.) A clay oven, usually recessed in the ground; *tandoori,* the food roasted in it at high temperatures, is first marinated in yogurt and spices.

tāng (Chin.) Soup.

tangelo A hybrid citrus fruit—a cross between a grapefruit and a tangerine; there are several varieties, Minneola considered by many to be the best of them; see also **ugli fruit.**

tannin A chemical compound in the stems and seeds of grapes that imparts a characteristic astringency and puckery quality to wine; tannin is pronounced in young red wines, especially good claret, but gives them longevity.

tansy   An herb with a rather bitter flavor, once popular in England but now largely ignored; a tansy pudding used to be traditional for Easter.

tapas   (Sp.)   Appetizers served in Spanish bars with cocktails, in great variety and profusion.

tapenade   (Fr.)   A puree of capers, anchovies, black olives, garlic, and perhaps tuna and other foods, thinned to a paste with olive oil; from **Provence.**

tapioca   A starch extracted from the tuberous root of the **cassava** or manioc plant, native to tropical and subtropical America where Indians once ate it as a bread. Tapioca, almost pure starch—easily digestible and nutritious—is made into flour and "pearls," which are used for thickening soups and for puddings. It has become a staple in India and Indochina.

taramasalata   (Gr.)   Pink fish roe, usually gray mullet or carp, pureed with bread that has been moistened with a little milk, olive oil, lemon juice, and garlic; served with crusty bread.

taro   A tropical and subtropical plant valuable for its spinachlike leaves, asparaguslike stalks, and potatolike root. Its high starch content makes it an important staple in Polynesia, Africa, and Asia. In the Caribbean, its leaves are made into a spicy stew called **callaloo.**

tarragon   An herb in the daisy family used widely in French cooking; it is an essential in the **bouquet garni,** in **béarnaise** sauce, and chicken *à l'estragon,* and is one of the **fines herbes.**

tart   A sweet or savory pie, usually with no top crust; a **flan.** A tartlet is a small individual tart.

tartare   (Fr.)   *Sauce tartare* is mayonnaise with hard-boiled egg yolks and garnished with finely chopped onions and chives; *boeuf à la tartare* is chopped lean beef served with capers, chopped onions, and parsley, with a raw egg.

tarte, tartelette   (Fr.)   Tart, tartlet; *tartine* means a slice of bread spread with butter or jam, also a small tart. The Spanish words are *tarta* and *tartaleta.*

tarte des demoiselles Tatin   (Fr.)   An apple tart devised by the Tatin sisters in their restaurant near Orléans, baked upside down; the bottom of the pan is buttered and strewn with sugar, covered with sliced apples, then topped with a pastry crust; during baking the sugar on the bottom caramelizes, and the finished tarte is turned out and served.

tartufo   (It.)   Truffle.

tasse   (Fr., Ger.)   Cup; the Spanish word is *taza.*

Tatin, tarte des demoiselles   See **tarte des demoiselles Tatin.**

Tavel   A **rosé** wine from the Rhône Valley near Avignon—flavorful, strong, and celebrated.

T-bone steak   A cut of beef from the **loin,** very similar to the **porterhouse,** but containing less of the fillet.

té   (Sp., It.)   Tea; the German word is *Tee.*

tejolate   See **molcajete.**

tel   (Ind.)   Oil.

tempura   (Jap.)   Seafood and vegetables dredged in a light batter and quickly deep-fried in oil; served with a dipping sauce called *tentsuyu.*

tenderloin   A cut of meat, especially beef, from the hindquarter, consisting of one long, slender, and very tender muscle running through the **loin** section ending at the ribs; it is divided into **filet mignon, chateaubriand,** and **tournedos** for roasts or steaks.

tentsuyu   See **tempura.**

teri   (Jap.)   Glaze; *teriyaki* is poultry, fish, or meat marinated in a sweet soy-sauce preparation and grilled over charcoal so that the marinade forms a glaze.

Terlano   A well-known and excellent white wine from the Italian Tirol, in the Alto Adige Valley; dry, fruity, rounded, and soft.

ternera   (Sp.)   Veal.

terrapin   An edible water turtle that lives in fresh or brackish water; see **turtle.**

terrine   (Fr.)   A mixture of meat, game, poultry, or vegetables and seasonings, cooked in a dish lined with bacon or pork; the dish was originally earthenware, hence its name; see also **pâté.**

tête d'aloyau   (Fr.)   Rump steak.

tête de veau   (Fr.)   Calf's head; in Italian, *testa di vitello.*

Tetilla   (Sp.)   A Spanish cheese usually made from ewes' or goats' milk— soft, creamy, and bland.

thé   (Fr.)   Tea.

thon   (Fr.)   Tuna.

thousand-year-old eggs   (Chin.)   See **pí dàn.**

thyme   An herb of Mediterranean origin (and in many varieties) that is an essential part of the **bouquet garni;** besides its many culinary applications, it has been used since ancient times for medicinal purposes.

Tia Maria   A liqueur flavored with Blue Mountain coffee extract and spices; from Jamaica.

tian   (Fr.)   A shallow casserole or, by extension, food baked in it— usually an aromatic **gratin** of chopped vegetables, perhaps with some leftover meat or seafood; from Provence.

tiède   (Fr.)   Lukewarm; tepid; at room temperature.

tien mien jiàng   (Chin.)   A thick, sweet, and salty paste made from fermented red beans, flour, salt, and water; used for flavoring sauces and marinades and as a dipping sauce, especially in northern China.

til   (Ind.)   **Sesame** seeds.

tilefish   A western Atlantic fish with firm but delicate lean flesh, usually cut into fillets or steaks; very versatile in cooking.

Tilsit   (Ger.)   A cooked, unpressed cheese made from raw or pasteurized cows' milk; oblong or cylindrical, it has a thin yellow rind and straw-colored paste with holes; the acidulated taste becomes more pronounced with age, and the cheese is sometimes flavored with caraway seeds; now made in several central European countries.

timbale   (Fr.)   A drum-shaped mold, usually metal, or the food prepared in such a mold, including rice, diced vegetables, or fish **mousseline;** also a high, round, covered pastry case, usually decorated, or the food in such a case.

timo   (It.)   Thyme.

tipsy parson or pudding   (Brit.)   An old-fashioned English dessert pudding of sponge cake soaked with spirits and covered with custard or whipped cream; not unlike a **trifle.**

tirage   (Fr.)   "Drawing off" wine from the cask.

tire-bouchon   (Fr.)   Corkscrew.

tiropita   (Gr.)   A cheese pie wrapped in **phyllo** dough.

tisane   Herbal tea.

toad-in-the-hole   (Brit.)   Meat, usually sausage, baked in batter.

tocino   (Sp.)   Bacon; *tocino de cielo,* literally "bacon from heaven," is a thick caramel custard dessert (not made with bacon, however).

toffee   (Brit.)   See **taffy.**

tōfu   (Jap.)   Bean curd, white, soft, and easily digestible; in one form or another it is eaten throughout the Orient and valued for its healthful properties: it is high in protein, low in calories, and free of cholesterol. *Tōfu* is made from dried soybeans processed into a "milk" that is coagulated like cheese; the molded *tōfu* curds are kept fresh in water. Of the many types, *momen* ("cotton") is the most common fresh *tōfu* in the United States as well as in Japan; *kinu* ("silk") has a finer texture; *yakidōfu* has been lightly broiled. Chinese bean curd (*dòu fu*) is drier and firmer than Japanese.

tōgarashi   (Jap.)   Red hot chili peppers, fresh or dried.

Tokay   A famous wine from the town of the same name in northeastern Hungary, made with some proportion of grapes with the **"noble rot"** in varying grades and ranging in sugar and alcoholic content; the best and rarest Tokay has an incomparable rich, buttery, peach-caramel flavor. Tokay is also the name of an Alsatian grape, totally unrelated.

Toma   (It.)   An uncooked whole or partly skimmed cows' milk cheese, sometimes mixed with ewes' or goats' milk, made in the Alps near the French Haute-Savoie and Swiss borders; shaped in discs, it ripens quickly to a pale supple paste or can be matured to a dense, pungent cheese. See also **Tomme.**

tomalley   The liver of the lobster, colored olive green—a special delicacy.

tomate verde, tomatillo   (Mex.)   A Mexican green tomato, small and pungent; not an unripe red tomato (**jitomate**); used as the basis of an important Mexican **salsa,** with **serrano** peppers, garlic, and coriander, all chopped together, either fresh or cooked.

tomber à glace   (Fr.)   To reduce liquid to a glaze.

Tomino   (It.)   An uncooked, unpressed cows' milk cheese, usually pasteurized and sometimes enriched, from the Italian Alps; this rindless cheese ripens quickly to a delicate, fresh flavor and a soft, smooth paste, making it an excellent dessert cheese. See also **Tomme** and **Toma.**

Tomme de Savoie   (Fr.)   An uncooked, pressed cows' milk cheese from the French Alps, with an Italian version across the border; made in 8-inch discs with a light brown rind, a pale yellow paste, and a nutty lactic flavor. *Tomme* means cheese in the Savoy dialect, and there are many varieties of it there, made from cows', goats', or ewes' milk. See also **Toma** and **Tomino.**

Tomme Vaudoise   (Switz.)   An uncooked, soft cheese made from whole or sometimes partly skimmed milk in the Swiss Alps; round or oblong, it has a thin, delicately molded white rind and a smooth, buttery, aromatic interior.

tonkatsu   (Jap.)   Pork marinated in a spicy sauce, dipped in egg and breadcrumbs, and fried.

tonno   (It.)   Tuna.

Topf   (Ger.)   Pot; stew or casserole.

Topfen   (Aus.)   See **Quark.**

topinambour   (Fr.)   **Jerusalem artichoke;** the Italian spelling is *topinambur.*

top round   See **round.**

top sirloin   See **round.**

toriniku   (Jap.)   Chicken meat.

torrone   (It.)   **Nougat.**

torsk   (Nor. and Swed.)   Cod.

torta   (It. and Sp.)   In Italian, tart, pie, or cake. In Spanish, cake, loaf, or roll of bread. In Mexico, the word can also mean a savory pudding of **tortillas** stacked like **chilaquiles.**

Torte   (Ger.)   Tart, round cake, flan; *Tortenbäcker* is a pastry cook.

tortellini   (It.)   Small rounds of egg pasta stuffed, folded, and wrapped around the finger; almost the same as **cappelletti** but round instead of square.

tortilla   (Sp. and Mex.)   In Spain the word means omelet; in Mexico *tortilla* means a thin, flat, unraised pancake made of dried cornmeal flour, salt, and water—from the Aztec cuisine. The Mexican term for omelet is *tortilla de huevos.*

tortoni   Ice cream topped with chopped almonds or **macaroons;** Italian-American in origin and often called *biscuit tortoni.*

tortue   (Fr.)   Turtle; *sauce tortue* is **demi-glace** with tomato puree, herbs, truffle essence, and **Madeira;** *à la tortue* means calf's head garnished with veal **quenelles,** mushrooms, olives, gherkins, calf's tongue, and brains, with *sauce tortue.*

Toscanello   (It.)   A cooked, semihard ewes' milk cheese from Tuscany and Sardinia, made in six-pound cylinders; it has a brownish yellow rind and a pale dense paste and is aged three to four months to develop a mild or piquant taste.

tostada   (Sp. and Mex.)   Toast; in Mexico this means a **tortilla** fried flat and then topped with all kinds of garnishes, sometimes stacked high.

tostaditas   (Mex.)   See **totopos.**

totopos   (Mex.)   **Tortillas** cut into six to eight smaller triangles, fried crisp, and served with dips or as a garnish.

toulousaine, à la   (Fr.)   Garnished with chicken **quenelles,** sweetbreads, mushroom caps, cockscombs and kidneys, and truffle slices arranged separately, with **allemande** sauce—a classic garnish.

tourage   (Fr.)   Repeated turns of the dough—rolling and folding—in the making of **pâte feuilletée.**

tourin   (Fr.)   Onion soup made with milk instead of meat stock (as in *soupe à l'oignon*), thickened with egg yolks and cream, and sometimes served with grated cheese; from southwest France.

tourné   (Fr.)   A vegetable that is "turned" or shaped with a knife, as with potatoes and mushrooms; also, food that has gone bad or a sauce that has separated.

tournedos   (Fr.)   Thick slices from the middle of the beef fillet, sautéed or grilled.

tourte   (Fr.)   Tart or pie, usually round and savory; a *tourtière* is a pie dish or flan case.

toute-épice   (Fr.)   **Allspice.**

tragacanth   See **gum.**

Traminer   A white-wine grape family to which the **Gewürztraminer** belongs.

trancher   (Fr.)   To carve, slice; a *tranche* is a slice, chop, or steak. The Italian word is *trancia.*

Trappiste   (Fr.)   A cheese made all over the world by Trappist monks—**Port-Salut** being the best known of this type—all of them with slight variations. The round cheese is semihard, with a soft rind and a dense, smooth paste with small holes.

Traub(e)   (Ger.)   Grape; bunch of grapes.

travailler   (Fr.)   To beat; to stir in order to blend or smooth.

treacle   (Brit.)   A syrup similar to molasses but slightly sweeter; used in making puddings, tarts, and other desserts; either golden or black.

Trebbiano   A white-wine grape much used in Italy (for White **Chianti, Soave,** etc.) and also grown in southern France and California, where it is called *Ugni Blanc.*

tree ear   (Chin.)   See **yún ĕr.**

trenette   (It.)   Flat pasta similar to **fettucine;** traditional pasta for **pesto.**

triflach   (Jew.)   **Farfel** lightened with extra eggs.

trifle   (Brit.)   A dessert pudding of sponge cake or biscuits soaked with sherry or other liquor, topped with custard and whipped cream, usually garnished with sliced fruit or jam.

triglia   (It.)   Red mullet, a Mediterranean fish.

trigo   (Sp.)   Wheat.

tripe   The first and second stomachs of ruminants (plain and honeycomb tripe, respectively); *tripe à la mode de Caen* (see **Caen**), requiring the laborious preparation of beef tripe, is the classic dish.

triple sec   (Fr.)   A clear, colorless orange-flavored liqueur, such as **Cointreau** and **Curaçao.**

Trockenbeerenauslese   (Ger.)   A very sweet wine made from raisined (nearly dry) grapes left on the vine and individually chosen from bunches—the most selective and expensive German wine produced.

Troja   An Italian red-wine grape, productive and widely grown for its deep color and full body; used for blending.

trota   (It.)   Trout.

trotter   The foot of an animal, especially a pig or sheep.

trout   A game fish, primarily freshwater and related to **salmon,** with fine-textured flesh high in fat content, usually white but sometimes pink (see **sea trout**). With very small scales, a simple bone structure, and succulent flesh, it is adaptable to many culinary uses. Brook, brown, lake, rainbow, **sea trout,** and **char** are a few of the many varieties.

trouvillaise, à la   (Fr.)   Shrimp, mussels, and mushroom caps with shrimp sauce—a classic garnish.

trucha   (Sp.)   River trout.

truffle   The fruiting body of a black or white fungus which grows underground, unlike other mushrooms. The dense truffle, rough, round, and with interior veining, grows in symbiosis with certain trees, especially oak, and only in particular soils and climates. Trained dogs, goats, and sows, who find the scent of truffles similar to that of boars' saliva in mating season, sniff them out. Their exquisite aroma makes their exorbitant price worthwhile. The best black truffles, increasingly rare, come from Périgord, France; white truffles come from Alba, in northern Italy. Chocolate truffles are chocolate buttercream balls rolled in cocoa, crushed almonds, or chocolate shavings to resemble real truffles.

truite au bleu   See **bleu, au.**

truss   To tie poultry or game with string in order to hold its shape during cooking, to ensure even cooking, and to improve its appearance; the particular method of trussing depends on the animal, its size, and the cooking method used.

Trut-hahn (m.), **Trut-henne** (f.) (Ger.)   Tom turkey or hen.

tsukemono (Jap.) Pickled food.

tube pan   A ring-shaped cake pan traditionally used for rich cakes, since the hollow center can be filled and the extensive surface coated with syrup or icing.

tuile (Fr.)   A crisp cookie, sometimes made with crushed almonds, that is placed on a rolling pin immediately after baking so that it curves and becomes shaped like a "tile" (hence its name).

tulipe (Fr.)   A crisp, thin, cookielike dough ruffled while still warm from the oven into a flower shape to hold dessert berries, ices, etc.

tuna   A large saltwater fish with rich meat varying in color and oiliness from one species to another and also from one part of a fish to another; albacore is high-quality tuna with white meat; other species yield darker flesh, **bonito** being the darkest; tuna is often brined before cooking to lighten the color. Much of the commercial catch is canned, solid ("fancy"), chunks, and flakes being the three styles, packed either in oil or water. Baking, broiling, braising, marinating, and smoking are good cooking methods for tuna; the Japanese hold it in special regard for its use in **sashimi.**

tuna (Mex.) Prickly pear.

Tunke (Ger.)   Sauce, gravy.

tunny (Brit.) Tuna.

turban   Food, often cooked in a ring mold, served in a circle; used primarily for seafood or poultry dishes.

turbinado sugar   Partially refined sugar, light brown in color, similar to **demerara.**

turbot   An eastern Atlantic **flounder** with delicate white flesh that rivals the Dover **sole** in culinary preparations.

turmeric   A spice obtained from the dried and powdered rhizome of an Indian plant, whose bitter flavor and ochre color contribute to curries; in the Middle Ages its color made it a substitute for **saffron,** and even today turmeric is used as a dye for cloth and dairy products such as **margarine.**

turnover   A pastry square or round filled with a sweet or savory stuffing, folded in half to enclose the stuffing, and baked; the turnover appears in many cultures.

turrón (Sp.)   A chewy candy made of toasted almonds, honey, egg whites, and sometimes other ingredients; from Alicante and traditional for Christmas.

turtle   Land and water turtles are both edible, but the aquatic green and diamondback are especially valued for their flesh, mainly in soups and braised dishes; the expense and difficulty of preparing turtle meat and also conservation measures designed to protect the species' diminishing numbers have made turtle recipes far less fashionable than in the past. A terrapin is an edible water turtle that lives in fresh or brackish coastal water; tortoise generally means a land turtle.

Tuscany   The region around Florence, Italy, producing **Chianti** and other red table wines. The Tuscan style of cooking is relatively simple, featuring olive oil, herbs, **cannelloni,** beans, game, and bread, rather than pasta (except for hare with **pappardelle**).

tutti-frutti   (It.)   Mixed fruits (literally "all fruits") chopped and preserved in syrup, usually with brandy.

Tybo   (Den.)   A cooked cows' milk cheese similar to **Samsø**; brick-shaped, supple-textured, with fairly large holes, Tybo is straw-colored on the inside with a yellow rind; its taste is mild and slightly acidulated.

tyrolienne, à la   (Fr.)   Fried onion rings and tomatoes *concassées*—a classic garnish.

tzimmes   (Jew.)   A casserole of **brisket of beef** with carrots, prunes or other dried fruit, and syrup, topped with potatoes and dumplings; traditional for Rosh Hashanah.

uccèllo

◦ U ◦

---

uccèllo   (It.)   Bird; *uccèlli scappati* (literally "escaped birds") are veal birds skewered with bacon and sage; *uccelletti* or *uccellini* are small birds, usually skewered and roasted whole; see also **meat birds**.

uchepos   (Mex.)   Fresh corn **tamales** from Michoacán.

udon   (Jap.)   Wheat noodle.

ugli fruit   A hybrid cross between a grapefruit and tangerine, not to be confused with the Minneola, Orlando, and Seminole **tangelos;** grown in Jamaica where it is called *boogli,* it has a yellowish green, thick, coarse skin and sweet orange flesh.

Ugni Blanc   See **Trebbiano**.

umé   (Jap.)   Plum (actually a kind of apricot); *umeboshi* are pickled plums; *umeshu* is plum wine.

umido, in   (It.)   Stewed.

unagi   (Jap.)   Eel.

uovo   (It.)   Egg; *tuorlo d'uovo* is the yolk, *bianco d'uovo* the white;

uovo affogato is a poached egg, *uovo molletto* is a soft-boiled egg, *uovo al burro* is a fried egg, and *uovo sode* is a hard-boiled egg.

usu-kuchi shōya (Jap.) Light soy sauce, clearer, thinner, and saltier than dark soy sauce (**koi-kuchi shōya**).

uva (Sp.) Grape; *uva espina* is gooseberry; *uva passa* or *secca* is raisin.

vanilla

V

vacherin (Fr.) A meringue shell made of a solid disc of meringue and separate rings stacked on the circumference to form a container; the baked *vacherin* shell is decorated with piped scrolls, then filled with ice cream, **crème Chantilly,** berries, or other fruit.

Vacherin Mont-d'Or (Switz. and Fr.) A whole-milk cows' cheese, uncooked and unpressed, from the Alps; the disc-shaped cheese has a soft, creamy, rich texture with small holes and a delicate, buttery, sweet flavor. Other types of this winter cheese are *Vacherin des Beauges* and *Vacherin Fribourgeois,* and they are all often banded with spruce bark, which imparts its subtly resinous flavor.

Valdepeñas Red and white table wines from La Mancha, south of Madrid, a very large quantity of which is produced; officially called *Vino Manchego;* the red is especially light, pleasant, best drunk young, and inexpensive.

Valencia A seaport and region in eastern Spain notable for its rice and seafood, both of which grace **paella** *valenciana.* The Valencia orange, sweet, thin-skinned, and nearly seedless, is an excellent juice or dessert orange.

197

valenciano (Mex.) A chili pepper similar to the **güero.**

valencienne, à la (Fr.) A classic garnish of rice **pilaf** and sweet red peppers with a tomato-flavored sauce.

Valois (Fr.) A **béarnaise** sauce with meat glaze.

Valpolicella A red wine produced in northern Italy, northwest of Verona, in five townships. The wine is soft, light, dry, and fragrant, best drunk young; it has been called the **Beaujolais** of Italy.

Valtellina A wine-producing region in northern Italy, near Switzerland, where the **Nebbiolo** grape yields some of the country's best wine; dark, robust, and long-lived.

vanilla The fruit pod of a climbing orchid indigenous to Central America, which is picked immature, then cured in a long process. The pod and interior seeds are used to flavor desserts, and the pod can be dried and used again, immersed in vodka or sugar, which it permeates with its aroma; the synthetic vanillin is an inferior substitute.

vanner (Fr.) To stir a sauce until cool, ensuring smoothness and preventing a skin from forming.

vapeur (Fr.) Steam.

varietal wine Wine made from a particular grape, such as **Cabernet Sauvignon, Riesling,** or **Nebbiolo,** which in part gives the wine its character; depending on the location, the wine is not necessarily made entirely from the varietal.

variety meat Edible meat other than skeletal muscle, especially organs; see **offal.**

Västerbottenost (Swed.) A pasteurized cows' milk cheese in which the curd is scalded, pressed, and matured for eight months. The rind of this cylindrical cheese is hard, with a wax covering; the paste is firm, with small holes, and the taste is pungent.

veal The meat of young beef; milk-fed veal, lean and pale pink to white in color, comes from animals under three months of age; grass-fed veal (sometimes called calf or baby beef), rosy pink with cream-colored fat, is under five months of age.

veal Orloff (Fr.) Saddle of veal (or sometimes lamb) braised and carved in slices. Each slice is coated with **Soubise** and **duxelles,** the slices are placed back together, and the whole is masked with **béchamel,** and garnished with asparagus tips; from classic *haute cuisine.*

veal Oscar Veal cutlets sautéed and garnished with asparagus tips, crab legs or crayfish tails, and sauce **béarnaise.**

veau (Fr.) Veal.

vellutata (It.) A soup thickened with egg yolk, like the French **velouté.**

velouté (Fr.) "Velvet" white sauce based on a white **roux** with white stock, either fish, chicken, veal, or vegetable; this basic classic sauce is similar to **béchamel** but uses stock rather than milk. A soup *velouté* is a puree combined with *velouté* and finished with cream and egg yolks.

vénitienne, à la (Fr.) Fish fillets poached in white wine, served in a reduction sauce flavored with shallots, tarragon, chervil, and a little vinegar, and garnished with **croûtons** in the shape of a heart.

venison Deer meat; the word used to mean any furred game.

ventre (Fr.) Belly, breast.

verbena See **lemon verbena.**

Verdelho A type of **Madeira,** now quite rare, fairly dry and not unlike a **Sercial;** the name is from a grape variety.

verdura (It. and Sp.) Vegetable; the Italian plural is *verdure,* the Spanish *verduras;* in French *verdure* means greenery or foliage.

verjuice The juice of unripened grapes or possibly other fruit, not necessarily fermented; in the Middle Ages sour flavorings such as verjuice and vinegar were used a great deal in cooking.

vermicelli (It.) Very thin pasta—literally "little worms"—often used for soups and puddings.

vermouth A white apéritif wine, fortified and flavored with herbs and spices, including wormwood flower (*Wermut* in German, hence its name); French vermouth is dry and pale, Italian vermouth sweet and amber.

Véronique, sole See **sole Véronique.**

verte, mayonnaise See **mayonnaise verte.**

vert-pré (Fr.) A garnish for grilled meats of straw potatoes, watercress, and beurre **maître d'hôtel;** also chicken or fish masked with **mayonnaise verte;** literally, "green meadow."

vessie (Fr.) Pig's bladder; *poularde en vessie* is a famous old dish from Lyons of stuffed chicken poached in a pig's bladder.

Vezzena (It.) A hard cows' milk cheese made in the Italian Alps from partially skimmed milk; it is a scalded-curd cheese, aged six months to a year, depending upon whether it is to be used as a table or grating cheese.

viande (Fr.) Meat.

Vichy, carrots à la See **carrots à la Vichy.**

vichyssoise Cream of potato and leek soup, served chilled and garnished with chives; the creation of Louis Diat, chef of the Ritz-Carlton in New York, and named for his native French city.

Victoria (Fr.) Lobster sauce with diced lobster and truffles, for fish; also a classic meat garnish of tomatoes stuffed with **duxelles** and artichoke quarters sautéed in butter, the pan deglazed with veal stock and port or Madeira; also various cakes.

viennoise, à la (Fr.) "Viennese style"—coated with egg and bread-crumbs, fried, and garnished with sliced lemon, capers, olives, chopped parsley, and hard-boiled egg yolks and whites (separately); a classic garnish, used especially for veal and chicken cutlets or fish fillets.

Vierlander Poularde (Ger.) Chickens bred in the Vierlande district near Hamburg, known for their fine quality.

vigneron (Fr.) Winegrower; *à la vigneronne* means with wine, brandy, grapes, or grape leaves.

Villalón (Sp.) A fresh ewes' milk cheese, originally from the Spanish Old Castile near Portugal; white, even-textured, sharp-flavored and salty; cylindrical in shape.

Villeroi, Villeroy (Fr.) A **velouté** sauce well reduced with truffle and ham essence.

vinaigrette (Fr.) A basic sauce or dressing of oil and vinegar, usually in a proportion of three to one, with salt and pepper and perhaps some chopped herbs.

vindaloo (Ind.) A spicy dish from Goa, highly seasoned with vinegar, garlic, and curry; usually made with rich meat.

vin du pays (Fr.) Local wine of a specific region, usually not well known or shipped elsewhere.

vine leaves Young grape leaves blanched and used to wrap small birds and savory mixtures such as **dolmas;** the leaves both flavor and encase their stuffing and keep it from drying out.

vinho verde (Port.) "Green" young wine produced in northern Portugal, often very enjoyable and occasionally sparkling.

vin nature (Fr.) Unsweetened French wine—a term used loosely.

vin ordinaire (Fr.) Common table wine of unknown origin but specific alcoholic content.

vintage The grape harvest of a particular year and the wine made from it.

violet A plant whose flowers are crystallized as a dessert garnish; the fresh flowers and young leaves can be used in salads.

Virginia ham See **Smithfield ham.**

Viroflay, à la (Fr.) A classic garnish of spinach balls, quartered artichoke hearts, **château potatoes,** and veal stock; also means "with spinach."

vitello (It.) Veal; *vitello tonnato* is braised veal marinated in tuna sauce flavored with anchovies, capers, and mayonnaise and served cold—a classic dish.

volaille (Fr.) Poultry, fowl, or chicken.

vol-au-vent (Fr.) Puff pastry cases, literally "flight of the wind"; either large or small round shells with a cap, used to hold savory or sweet fillings; the small shells are sometimes called *bouchées à la reine.*

Vollrads, Schloss A celebrated vineyard in the German **Rheingau** next to *Schloss* **Johannisberg** and with its own medieval castle; the wide-ranging and numerous wines produced there, despite the complicated labeling, all reveal the vineyard's breeding and charm.

Volnay   A village in the French **Côte de Beaune,** between **Pommard** and **Meursault,** producing excellent and renowned red Burgundy wine; it is soft, delicate, and refined, with a long aftertaste.

vongola   (It.)   Clam.

Vorspeisen   (Ger.)   Appetizers, hors d'oeuvre.

Vosne-Romanée   A wine-producing **commune** in Burgundy with some extraordinarily fine red wines that possess exceptional bouquet, balance, and breeding.

Vouvray   A white wine of the Touraine region of the Loire Valley made from the **Chenin Blanc** grape; *Vouvray* can vary greatly in character from dry, fruity, and tart, to rich, sweet, and golden, or even effervescent or sparkling. For a white wine it is extraordinarily long-lived.

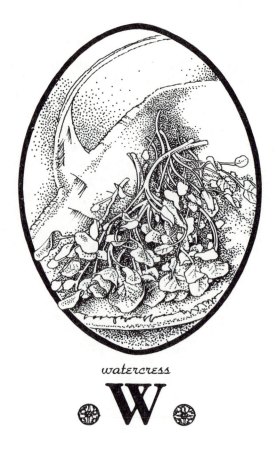

watercress

W

Wachenheim A wine-producing town in the German **Rheinpfalz**; its fine white wines are mostly from the **Sylvaner** and **Riesling** grapes.

waffle A crisp, thin cake made from a pancakelike batter and baked inside a special double-sided and hinged iron, giving it its thin honeycombed surface; waffles, whose history reaches far back, are eaten with sweet or savory toppings.

Wähen (Switz.) Large open tarts filled with vegetables, cheese, or fruit.

wakegi (Jap.) Scallionlike onion.

Waldmeister (Ger.) Woodruff.

Waldorf salad Chopped apples, celery, and walnuts in mayonnaise; created by Oscar Tschirky of the Waldorf-Astoria in New York before the turn of the century, although the walnuts were added later.

Walewska, à la (Fr.) Garnished with sliced **langoustine** and truffles and glazed with **Mornay** sauce with langoustine butter; a classic sauce named after the son of Napoléon's Polish mistress.

walleye, walleyed pike Actually a member of the **perch** family, this excellent freshwater fish, with firm, white, fine-textured flesh, lives in large North American lakes.

walliser (Switz.) A generic term for **Raclette** cheese.

Walnuss (Ger.) Walnut.

walnut A tree indigenous to Asia, Europe, and North America, whose nuts have been favored since ancient times. The nut meats are eaten plain, pickled, or used in sweet and savory dishes; their oil is much esteemed for its distinctive flavor; their husks are even made into a liqueur called *brou.* In several European languages the word for walnut is also the generic name for nut, showing its dominance.

wasabi (Jap.) A plant, often called Japanese horseradish, whose root is used as a spice for raw fish dishes; it comes fresh, powdered, and as a paste, and is very hot in flavor and green in color.

washed rind cheese A cheese whose rind is washed with water, brine, beer, wine, or another liquid during ripening. The purpose is to prevent the growth of certain bacterial cultures but encourage that of others and to keep the cheese from drying out.

Washington, à la (Fr.) A classic garnish of corn with cream sauce.

wassail A spiced punch, traditionally some kind of beer, drunk on festive occasions, very often Christmas; the word, of Scandinavian derivation, means "to your health."

water chestnut The fruit of a long-stemmed water plant that grows inside irregularly shaped thorns beneath the floating leaves. The starchy fruit has a crisp texture and delicate taste not unlike boiled chestnuts and can be used in many ways. It grows all over the world but is little appreciated outside the Orient.

watercress A plant growing in shallow streams, whose crisp, deep green leaves are used as an herb, a salad green, and a garnish; a member of the mustard family, its flavor is characteristically peppery and slightly pungent.

water ice A frozen dessert of syrup and fruit juice or puree, usually with a little lemon juice or other flavoring such as coffee or liqueur; the ice is frozen smooth but without the addition of egg white, as in a sherbet; see also **sherbet, granita,** and **spuma.**

waterzooï (Bel.) A traditional Flemish stew, probably originating in Ghent (*à la gantoise*), made with either fish or chicken. The fish version probably came first, with perch, eel, carp, pike, and possibly other varieties of fish, cooked in white wine with herbs; in the other version chicken is poached in stock with onions, leeks, celery, and carrots, flavored with lemon juice, and finished with egg yolks and cream.

weakfish Also known as seatrout (but not to be confused with **sea trout**), this member of the **drum** family is no trout at all—nor is it weak; this marine fish has lean, sweet, delicate flesh that is versatile in cooking.

Wehlen A small town on the Moselle River whose wines have become the best of the Mittel-Mosel; *Sonnenuhr*—a sundial painted on a slate outcropping in the steep vineyard slope—is the name given to the best of these fine wines.

Weinbeere (Ger.) Grape; *Weintraube* means a bunch of grapes.

Weinberg (Ger.) Vineyard.

Weissbier (Ger.) Light frothy summer beer ("white beer") from Bavaria, served with a slice of lemon.

Weisswurst (Ger.) A small delicate sausage stuffed with veal, flavored with wine and parsley; a specialty of Munich, it is eaten for breakfast with sweet mustard.

Weizen (Ger.) Wheat.

Wellington, beef See **beef Wellington.**

Welsh rarebit (Brit.) Pronounced "rabbit," this **savory** consists of hard Cheddar-type cheese melted with beer or milk and seasonings, poured over toast, and briefly grilled.

Wensleydale (Brit.) An uncooked, pressed cows' milk cheese made in both white and blue styles. The white, made in eight-pound flat discs and aged three to four weeks, is white, flaky, moist, and mellow, properly not yellow or sour. The blue, aged four to six months, is similar to **Stilton,** but less veined and smoother, sweeter, and nuttier.

Westminster The export name for **Lymeswold** cheese.

Westphalian ham (Ger.) Called *Westfalischer Schinken* in German, this ham is made from acorn-fed pigs, and is believed by many to rival **prosciutto, Bayonne,** and **Smithfield** hams in quality. The meat is lightly smoked, cured, but not cooked, and served in paper-thin slices with **pumpernickel** bread.

wheat A grain of great importance because of its ability, when combined with yeast and water, to form leavened bread; the **gluten** thus developed stretches to contain the expanding air bubbles. The higher the proportion of protein to starch in the kernel, the more gluten. There are many types of wheat flour, subject to climate and season as well as variety, but in general soft spring wheat (low in gluten) is good for pastry, cakes, pies, biscuits, and cookies. Hard winter wheat (high in gluten) is good for bread. **Durum semolina** (also high in gluten) is good for pasta.

whelk A gastropod **mollusk** similar to the **periwinkle,** appreciated in Europe, especially in Italy as *scungilli.*

whey The watery liquid which, after coagulation, separates from the curds in the cheesemaking process; whey contains albumin, lactose, and other nutrients and can be used to make **ricotta** or **Gjetost** cheeses.

whitebait Herring and sprat fry, plentiful in the Thames and Garonne Rivers and along the North Sea coast; the tiny fish are usually dipped in batter and deep-fried without being cleaned.

white butter sauce   See **beurre blanc.**

white chocolate   Cocoa butter, milk solids, and sugar; contains no cocoa solids and is therefore, strictly speaking, not chocolate at all.

whitefish   A small freshwater fish, mainly North American, related to **trout** and **salmon,** with delicate white meat that tastes best in winter and is often smoked (see **cisco**); the roe is used as a **caviar** substitute.

white sauce   Béchamel or velouté sauce, both made from **roux,** or any of their descendants.

whortleberry   See **bilberry.**

Wiener Schnitzel   (Ger.)   Literally "Viennese cutlet," veal scallops coated with layers of flour, beaten egg, and breadcrumbs, then fried in butter or lard and served without a sauce, usually with a slice of lemon; sometimes spelled as one word.

Wienerwurst   (Ger.)   **Frankfurter** sausage.

Wild   (Ger.)   Game.

Wildgeflügel   (Ger.)   Feathered game.

wild rice   A grass native to the Great Lakes region of North America and a distant cousin of common **rice.** It is now planted and harvested commercially rather than gathered in canoes, but is still prohibitively expensive for most consumers. A staple Indian food due to its high protein and carbohydrate value, wild rice is parched, hulled, and polished before cooking.

Wiltingen   A famous town on the **Saar** River near Trier, Germany, whose steep vineyards planted with **Riesling** grapes produce superb wines in good years.

Windbeutel   (Ger.)   Cream puff.

winkle   See **periwinkle.**

wintergreen   A creeping evergreen, native to the American northeast, with deep green, round leaves and red berries; the aromatic leaves are used as a flavoring.

winter melon   A melon with hard, smooth, or furrowed skin and white to pale green or orange flesh; lacking the perfumed aroma and separation layer in the stem of the **muskmelon,** the winter melon can be harvested into frost and allowed to travel as long as a month on the way to market. Honeydew, Casaba, Cranshaw (or Crenshaw), Santa Claus, and Canary melons fall into this category.

Wirsing   (Ger.)   Savoy cabbage.

witloof   See **Belgian endive.**

wok   (Chin.)   A round-bottomed metal cooking pan with sloping sides that provide the large cooking surface suitable for most Chinese methods of cooking: stir-frying, deep-frying, steaming, smoking, and (with the top on) braising and poaching. Special ring trivets or flat-bottomed *woks* can adapt the utensil to western electric stoves.

wonton   (Chin.)   See **hún tún.**

wood ear   See **yún ěr.**

woodruff   A perennial herb found in forests and sometimes used as a groundcover in shady gardens; its leaves, dried or fresh, are used to flavor teas, drinks, and punches, while its delicate flowers, which bloom in May, impart their scent to **May wine.**

Worcestershire sauce   A highly seasoned commercial sauce, made by Lea & Perrins of Worcester, England, for 150 years and used widely as a savory condiment; the recipe, of Indian origin, includes soy sauce, vinegar, molasses, anchovies, onion, chilies and other spices, and lime and tamarind juices; the sauce is fermented and cured before bottling.

wormwood   An herb once used as a medicine against intestinal worms, hence its name; the toxic leaf gives **absinthe** its potency and anise flavor, while the more delicate flower imparts its taste (and its name) to **vermouth.**

wu hsiang fun   (Chin.)   Seasoning used in Chinese cuisine, a variable mixture of star anise, fennel seeds, Sichuan peppercorns, clove, cinnamon, and nutmeg; five-spice powder.

Wurst   (Ger.)   Sausage; a *Würstchen* is a little sausage.

Würz   (Ger.)   Spice or seasoning; *Würzfleisch* is a special beef stew with sour-cream sauce, usually accompanied by dumplings or potatoes.

xérès

❀ X ❀

xató (Sp.) A winter salad from Catalonia of **Belgian endive** with red
  chili peppers, almonds, garlic, oil, and vinegar.

xérès (Fr.) **Sherry.**

xia (Chin.) Shrimp.

xiāng cài (Chin.) Coriander.

xiè (Chin.) Crab.

x-ni-pec (Mex.) A Yucatecan version of **salsa Mexicana cruda,** made
  with juice of the Seville orange.

xoconostle (Mex.) Green **prickly pear.**

Yule log

Y

yā (Chin.) Duck.

yakhni (Ind.) Meat broth.

yaki (Jap.) To grill or broil; *yakimono* means grilled food; *yakitori* is chicken pieces and vegetables skewered, marinated in a spicy sauce, and grilled.

yam A tuberous vegetable whose high starch content has enabled it to serve as a valuable food source for millennia, especially in tropical and subtropical regions; it has white or yellow flesh and brown skin and is often confused with the sweet potato, especially in the U.S., where a variety of sweet potato is mistakenly called yam.

yàn cài (Chin.) The nest of cliff-dwelling birds, considered a great delicacy in Chinese cuisine. The dried nests, either white or black, are soaked in water to restore their gelatinous texture and used to garnish soups at banquets and special occasions; very expensive, especially the white ones.

yaourt, yahourt (Fr.) Yogurt.

yard-long beans See **Chinese beans**.

208

yarrow   A plant native to England whose fine lacy leaves are used as an herb or for tea.

yasai   (Jap.)   Vegetables.

yeast   A microscopic, naturally occurring fungus that induces fermentation, thus initiating the chemical process that makes bread, cheese, wine, and beer. The many types of yeast, mainly fresh, dry, and brewer's, convert starch into gas and alcohol. **Baking powder** is a recent chemical alternative for leavening bread.

yemas de San Leandro   (Sp.)   Egg-yolk threads poured into hot syrup and twisted into sweets—a confection of Moorish origin made by the nuns of San Leandro in Seville.

yemitas de mi bisabuela   (Mex.)   Egg yolks, sherry, and syrup formed into balls and rolled in cinnamon sugar.

yen wo   (Chin.)   See **yàn cài.**

yogurt, yoghurt, yoghourt   Milk that has been fermented with a lactic culture, turning it slightly acid and custardlike in texture; although health claims for yogurt have been exaggerated, it is useful for its cooking and keeping properties; yogurt originated in the Balkans where it is still much used in cooking.

Yorkshire pudding   (Brit.)   A batter of milk, eggs, and flour, originally baked under a roast beef on an open spit or rack to catch the drippings, puffing up in the process; the pudding is cut into squares for serving. Yorkshire sauce is port wine sauce with red currant jelly, garnished with julienne of orange zest—a classic sauce.

Yquem, Château d'   A very great white dessert wine, awarded the unique *Grand Premier Cru* of **Sauternes** in the 1855 classification; it is very sweet, fruity, and luscious; made from grapes with the **noble rot,** it is exorbitant in price.

yú chì   (Chin.)   Shark's fin; a nutritious delicacy in Chinese cuisine which, after considerable soaking and preparation, is savored for its gelatinous texture; an expensive specialty reserved for banquets and special occasions.

Yule log   (Brit.)   See **bûche de Noël.**

yún ěr   (Chin.)   An irregularly-shaped fungus that grows on logs, used in Chinese cooking for its interesting texture; yellow, brown, or black on one side and white on the other, the dried fungus expands greatly with soaking before cooking; also called tree ear, wood ear, and other names.

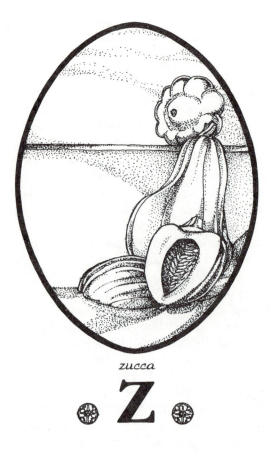

zucca

● Z ●

zabaglione (It.) A dessert custard in which egg yolks, flavored with **Marsala** and sugar, are beaten over simmering water until they foam up into a frothy mass; also spelled *zabaione*; the French version is **sabayon.**

zafferone (It.) **Saffron.**

zakuski (Russ.) Russian hors d'oeuvre starting with caviar and running the whole gamut; traditionally accompanied with vodka. However modest or grand the circumstances, the main meal of the day and any party always begin with *zakuski,* a tradition that goes back a thousand years to Scandinavia.

zampone (It.) A highly seasoned pork sausage encased in the skin of a pig's foot; from Modena.

zanahoria (Sp.) Carrot.

zarda (Ind.) Sweet rice **pilaf** flavored with saffron and other spices, nuts, and raisins.

zarzamora (Sp.) Blackberry.

zarzuela (Sp.) A seafood stew, varying widely, in a piquant sauce flavored with wine or liqueur, all arranged spectacularly; the word means operetta and implies that the dish is a fantastic mixture.

Zeltingen A wine-producing town in the central Moselle Valley producing a large quantity of fine wine, all estate-bottled **Riesling.**

zènzero (It.) Ginger.

zest The outer colored skin of citrus fruits where the essential oils are concentrated. The French word is *zeste,* not to be confused with *ziste,* the white pith beneath the outer colored layer of skin.

zhá (Chin.) To deep-fry.

zhēng (Chin.) To steam.

zhī má yóu (Chin.) Chinese sesame oil, which is darker in color and stronger in flavor than western sesame oil; used more for seasoning sauces than for cooking.

zhú (Chin.) Pork; *zhú rou* means pork meat.

Zigeuner Art (Ger.) Gypsy style; *Zigeunerspies,* an Austrian specialty, is skewered cubes of meat, peppers, and onions grilled over an open fire.

zik de venado (Mex.) Venison cooked in a **pib,** then shredded and served with onions, Seville oranges, hot chili peppers, and **cilantro;** from the Yucatán.

Zinfandel A red-wine grape variety of uncertain origin but widely planted in California; its style ranges considerably from light and fruity, almost like a **Beaujolais,** to deep, strong, and intense.

zingara, à la (Fr.) Gypsy style—a classic garnish of julienne of ham, tongue, mushrooms, and truffles in a **demi-glace** flavored with tomato puree, **Madeira,** and tarragon essence; *zìngara* is the Italian word for gypsy woman.

ziti (It.) Large tube pasta cut into segments.

Zitrone (Ger.) Lemon.

zucca (It.) Squash, pumpkin; *zucchini* literally means little squashes.

zùcchero (It.) Sugar.

zuccotto (It.) A dome-shaped dessert of cake moistened with liqueur and filled with sweetened whipped cream, chocolate, and nuts; originally from Florence, it supposedly resembles the cupola of the *Duomo.*

Zucker (Ger.) Sugar; *Zuckerrübe* means sugar beet.

Zunge (Ger.) Tongue.

zuppa (It.) Soup.

zuppa inglese (It.) Literally "English soup," this is a rich dessert of rum-soaked sponge cake layered with custard and cream—a kind of trifle.

Zwetschge (Aus.) Damson plum; see also **Powidl.**

zwieback   Bread slices baked again (in German, literally "twice baked," like a **biscuit**); rusks.

Zwiebel   (Ger.)   Onion; *Zwiebelkuche* is an onion tart from Hesse, made with bacon and cream, perhaps flavored with caraway seeds—not unlike a quiche lorraine; *Zwiebelgrün* is a scallion.

Selected
Bibliography

Battistotti, Bruno; Bottazzi, Vittorio; Piccinardi, Antonio; and Volpato, Giancarlo. *Cheese: A Guide to the World of Cheese and Cheesemaking.* New York: Facts on File, 1984.

Bianchini, F., and Corbetta, F. *The Complete Book of Fruits and Vegetables.* New York: Crown Publishers Inc., 1976.

Bickel, Walter, ed. *Hering's Dictionary of Classical and Modern Cookery.* London, Dublin, and Coulsdon: Virtue, 1981.

Brennan, Georgeanne; Cronin, Isaac; and Glenn, Charlotte. *The New American Vegetable Cookbook.* Berkeley: Aris Books, 1985.

Bugialli, Giuliano. *Giuliano Bugialli's Classic Techniques of Italian Cooking.* New York: Simon and Schuster, 1982.

Casas, Penelope. *The Foods & Wines of Spain.* New York: Alfred A. Knopf, 1982.

Claiborne, Craig. *Craig Claiborne's The New York Times Food Encyclopedia.* New York: Times Books, 1985.

Conran, Terence, and Conran, Caroline. *The Cook Book.* New York: Crown Publishers Inc., 1980.

Coyle, L. Patrick. *The World Encyclopedia of Food.* New York: Facts on File, 1982.

Crewe, Quentin. *The International Pocket Food Book.* London: Mitchell Beazley, 1980.

Davidson, Alan. *Mediterranean Seafood.* rev. ed. Harmondsworth, England: Penguin Books, 1981.

———. *North Atlantic Seafood.* New York: Viking Penguin Inc., 1980.

Dowell, Philip, and Bailey, Adrian. *Cooks' Ingredients.* New York: William Morrow, 1980.

Emery, William H. *The Flavor of Spain.* Boston: CBI Publishing, 1983.

Evans, Travers Moncure, and Greene, David. *The Meat Book.* New York: Charles Scribner's Sons, 1973.

FitzGibbon, Theodora. *The Food of the Western World.* New York: Quadrangle, 1976.

Hazan, Marcella. *The Classic Italian Cook Book.* New York: Alfred A. Knopf, 1976.

———. *More Classic Italian Cooking.* New York: Alfred A. Knopf, 1978.

Jaffrey, Madhur. *World-of-the-East Vegetarian Cooking.* New York: Alfred A. Knopf, 1981.

Johnson, Hugh. *Hugh Johnson's Modern Encyclopedia of Wine.* New York: Simon and Schuster, 1983.

Jones, Evan. *American Food: The Gastronomic Story.* 2d ed. New York: Random House, 1981.

Kennedy, Diana. *The Cuisines of Mexico.* New York: Harper & Row, 1972.

Mariani, John F. *The Dictionary of American Food & Drink.* New Haven and New York: Ticknor & Fields, 1983.

Marks, Copeland, and Soeharjo, Mintari. *The Indonesian Kitchen.* New York: Atheneum Publishers, 1984.

McCawley, James D. *The Eater's Guide to Chinese Characters.* Chicago: University of Chicago Press, 1984.

McClane, A. J. *The Encyclopedia of Fish Cookery.* New York: Holt, Rinehart and Winston, 1977.

McGee, Harold. *On Food and Cooking: The Science and Lore of the Kitchen.* New York: Charles Scribner's Sons, 1984.

Montagné, Prosper. *The New Larousse Gastronomique: The Encyclopedia of Food, Wine & Cookery.* Edited by Charlotte Turgeon. New York: Crown, 1977.

Ngô, Bach, and Zimmerman, Gloria. *The Classic Cuisine of Vietnam.* Woodbury, New York: Barron's, 1979.

Ortiz, Elisabeth Lambert. *The Book of Latin American Cooking.* New York: Alfred A. Knopf, 1979.

Roden, Claudia. *A Book of Middle Eastern Food.* New York: Alfred A. Knopf, 1972.

Root, Waverly. *Food.* New York: Simon and Schuster, 1980.

Sahni, Julie. *Classic Indian Cooking.* New York: William Morrow & Co. Inc., 1980.

Saulnier, Louis. *Le Répertoire de La Cuisine.* Woodbury, New York: Barron's, 1976.

Schmitz, Puangkram C., and Worman, Michael J. *Practical Thai Cooking.* Tokyo, New York, and San Francisco: Kodansha International, 1985.

Schoonmaker, Frank. *Encyclopedia of Wine.* Edited by Hugh Johnson. London and Edinburgh: Thomas Nelson, n.d. [c. 1970].

Sharman, Fay, and Boehm, Klaus. *The Taste of France: A Dictionary of French Food & Wine.* Boston: Houghton Mifflin Co., 1982.

Simon, André L. *A Concise Encyclopedia of Gastronomy.* Woodstock, New York: Overlook Press, 1981.

———, and Howe, Robin. *Dictionary of Gastronomy.* 2d ed. Woodstock, New York: Overlook Press, 1979.

Simonds, Nina. *Classic Chinese Cuisine.* Boston: Houghton Mifflin Co., 1982.

Tropp, Barbara. *The Modern Art of Chinese Cooking.* New York: William Morrow, 1982.

Tsuji, Shizuo. *Japanese Cooking: A Simple Art.* Tokyo, New York, and San Francisco: Kodansha International, 1980.

von Welanetz, Diana, and von Welanetz, Paul. *The Von Welanetz Guide to Ethnic Ingredients.* Los Angeles: J.P. Tarcher, 1982.

Wheaton, Barbara Ketcham. *Savoring the Past: The French Kitchen and Table from 1300 to 1789.* Philadelphia: University of Pennsylvania Press, 1983.